Black Families
at the Crossroads

Robert Staples
Leanor Boulin Johnson

Black Families
at the Crossroads

Challenges and Prospects

Jossey-Bass Publishers · San Francisco

For sales outside the United States, contact Maxwell Macmillan
International Publishing Group, 866 Third Avenue, New York,
New York 10022.

Manufactured in the United States of America

The paper used in this book is acid-free and meets the
State of California requirements for recycled paper
(50 percent recycled waste, including 10 percent
postconsumer waste), which are the strictest guidelines
for recycled paper currently in use in the United States.

Library of Congress Cataloging-in-Publication Data

Staples, Robert.
    Black families at the crossroads : challenges and prospects /
Robert Staples, Leanor Boulin Johnson.
        p.   cm.—(The Jossey-Bass social and behavioral science
series)
    Includes bibliographical references and index.
    ISBN 1-55542-486-4
    1. Afro-American families.   I. Johnson, Leanor Boulin, date.
II. Title.   III. Series.
E185.86.S698   1993
306.85′08996073—dc20
                                                                92-19935
                                                                CIP

FIRST EDITION
HB Printing   10 9 8 7 6 5 4 3 2 1   *Code 9286*

The Jossey-Bass
Social and Behavioral Science Series

To my mentors,
Peter Geiser, Henry Pitchford,
and Paul Rosenblatt
—Robert Staples

To the memory of my parents,
Hebert Fitzgerald Constantine Boulin
and Linda Louise Rashford Boulin,
who for forty years demonstrated
the glory and warmth of marital love.
—Leanor Boulin Johnson

Contents

Preface   xi

Acknowledgments   xvii

The Authors   xix

1. History as Fact and Fiction   1

2. Studying Black Families   22

3. Work and Money: The Struggle   47

4. Patterns of Sexual Intimacy   72

5. Singlehood and Partner Selection   94

6. Gender Roles and Male Sexism   121

7. Marital Patterns and Interactions   139

8. The Challenges of Parenting   170

9. Kinship and Community Support   194

10. Social Change, Problems, and Prospects   221

     References   243

     Selected Readings   277

     Index   285

Preface

This collaboration grew out of our awareness that there is no central source of information on the Afro-American family. Anthologies on Black families lack the systematic analysis and consistency of an authored book. Other books are too specialized in the topics discussed or neglect the institutional role of Afro-American families. We both have the advantage of having been specifically trained in the sociology of the family and have taught a variety of classes on the family at different universities. Together, we combine more than fifty years of teaching about and studying Black American families, our primary specialization being in family sociology. Because we had collaborated on a number of projects over the years, belonged to the same professional organizations, and shared a similar perspective on the Afro-American family, our collaboration on this project seemed natural.

No other institution in American life has been subjected to the intense scrutiny that the Black family has. From its beginning on the American continent, where its structure and function have been shaped by the institution of slavery, to the current era—in which cultural, political, and economic changes have left an indelible mark on its structure—the Black family has had to confront the vicissitudes of life in the United States. Given the remarkable changes the Black family has undergone, it is surprising that no macrosociological analysis has been conducted to depict its dynamics in relation to the social forces against which it has struggled. Not since the pioneering work of E. Franklin Frazier, whose book *The Negro Family in the United States* (1939) traced the evolution of Black families, has there been a work that viewed this institution in all its dimensions.

Whereas there has been a proliferation of books and articles on aspects of Black family life, that literature has generally focused on limited segments of the Black population and has therefore sponsored a rather narrow perspective of the family as an institution. Few of the books, for instance, have systematically covered such topics as sexuality, marital patterns and interaction, singlehood, the female-headed household, and family life among the aged. Although those topics have been addressed separately, no attempt has been made to discuss them as part of a unified treatment of the Black family.

In particular, there is a need to describe and interpret the Black family form as it is unfolding in contemporary America. Due to social and cultural changes, the salient aspects of Black family life that require examination are dating and sexuality, marriage and divorce, singlehood, the female-headed household, and the extended family. The statistical data tell us that the majority of Black children are born out of wedlock, many of them to teenage mothers. Yet there are few data on patterns of dating and sexual norms that could help to explain the prevalence of such behavior. Census data inform us that a majority of adult Black women are not married. We need to know the particular set of sociocultural forces that are responsible for these unprecedented marital patterns among the majority of Black Americans, including the developments occurring in Black marriages that cause two out of three to end in divorce.

A significant trend has been the rise of Black female-headed households. Single-parent families constitute a majority of Black families. Most Black children live in such households. Consequently, the nuclear family model, especially for the lower-income groups, is no longer the dominant family type among Afro-Americans. Hence, we have examined the extended family system to ascertain its role in the rearing of children, economic assistance, emotional nurturance of family members, and so on.

The primary purpose of this book is to serve as a basic text on the Black family as an institution. To facilitate an understanding of the Black American family, the book presents an analysis of the various sociocultural forces that shape both the structure and the functions of the family as well as the way the family has experienced changes. We also analyze the larger forces outside the Black community, such as assimilation and acculturation, unemployment and underemployment, the role of government and public policy, and the imbalance in the gender ratio. Since Blacks do not comprise a monolithic group, we have attempted to consider class and gender variations in family life-styles. Moreover, this book places these various themes and orientations within Black family life in a theoretical perspective that facilitates a better understanding of the family itself. That theoretical perspective is a political economy model that assumes that the contemporary Black family structure is a function of political and economic forces that have shaped its existence for several centuries.

A primary method in writing this book has been the interpretation and synthesis of existing research on Black family life. Since 1970, more than 1,000 articles and 100 books have been published on some aspect of the Black family experience. To provide a foundation for investigating Black families in more recent periods, we have examined literature prior to 1970. We have also relied on census and survey data, integrating them into our portrait of Black families. Finally, in areas where the literature is sparse or nonexistent, we have used our own research and writings over the past twenty years selectively.

Audience

While the book holds to the highest standards of scholarship in terms of the interpretation of data and research, it is written in a style accessible to a wide readership. Its target audience is made up of faculty, students, policy makers, and anyone who works with Black families. We have tried to meet the needs both of people who have no knowledge of the Black family and of professionals working with Black families who require a reference source on the special issues and perspectives of this group. Most important, we hope that this book can be used as a teaching tool in colleges and universities throughout the world.

Presently, there is no book available that presents a view of the Black family as an institution and that surveys the significant changes that have affected it. The primary importance of such a study is the fact that it incorporates in one work the most significant information about America's largest racial minority. Because changes in the Black family are often a barometer of future trends in the larger society, a study of the Black family has implications for the direction of the American family. The book will be a valuable resource for scholars of the family and social institutions, can be used as a basic text in courses on the Black family, and will be adoptable as a supplementary text in courses on the family as well as for courses in the helping professions, sociology, anthropology, human development, psychology, ethnic studies, and home economics.

Overview of the Contents

Chapter One is an examination of classic historical theories that claim that the institution of slavery destroyed the basis of Black family life and of neohistorical theories that assert that the family structure of the African slaves was largely untouched by the slave owners. The chapter also looks at the postslavery existence of Black families; for example, it discusses the formation of values related to family life in the antebellum South.

In Chapter Two, we review the theories concerning the nature of Afro-American family life-styles, beginning with the ground-breaking study of W.E.B. Du Bois, continuing with the classic work of E. Franklin Frazier, and including the theories of Daniel Patrick Moynihan, Jessie Bernard, Lee Rainwater, and others. Each theory is placed in a historical context and evaluated for its strengths and weaknesses in enhancing our understanding of the Black family.

Chapter Three explores the impact of economic forces on the structure and stability of the Black family. It delineates the lack of fit between the skills of Blacks and the high-technology economy, as well as the role of gender in the economics of Black family life. Some statistical data are used to depict marital strain, stress, and stability as a function of the occupational and income levels of husbands and wives. We show the contribution of economic success to marital happiness and discuss the stratification of the Black community that has arisen over the last thirty years.

Chapter Four is an analysis of the bonding process among young Black men and women. We first provide historical background, focusing on the impact of slavery. Then we examine how dating evolves into sexual behavior at very young ages and the factors that facilitate young people's entry into or avoidance of premarital sexual behavior. We discuss how sex is defined by males and females, and the convergence and divergence of attitudes toward sexuality along gender and class lines. Finally, we review current research on Black sexual values, customs, and practices, within and outside marriage.

In Chapter Five, we examine how Blacks enter the world of singles and the life-styles they lead as unmarrieds in a society that places a strong emphasis on marriage and the family. A typology of singles is developed as they exist in the Black community. The coping styles of singles are examined as they confront the need to develop social supports. This chapter contains a demographic review of singles, their marriage chances, and the norms of mate selection.

Chapter Six provides an assessment of gender roles, with particular attention to male dominance in the Black family and community. We describe how male and female roles evolved in Afro-American culture in relation to its unique history and circumstances. We also review trend data to assess the gender gap in education, income, and occupational levels. Finally, we offer an analysis of the interaction between race and gender, focusing on the problem of sexism in the Black community.

Chapter Seven examines the unique problems encountered in the conjugal relationships of Black Americans. We focus on the definition of husband and wife roles, power relationships, and the sources of stress in Black marriages. The chapter contains a review of the reasons for marital dissolution and covers the demography of divorced Blacks and the stable marrieds. Also, we discuss the relationship of class and gender to marriage, divorce, and remarriage rates.

An assessment of how children are born and reared in the Black community is the focus of Chapter Eight. We discuss how the decision, if consciously done, is made to bear children and the limits imposed on the size of families. We ask who constitutes the primary socializing agent for Black children and what the role of Black fathers is. We discuss the consequences, for childrearing, of childbirth to teenage mothers and the mother's multiple roles as mother, wife, and worker. We also explore how children fare in households with only a single parent.

In Chapter Nine, we analyze the roles older generations and members of the extended kinship network play in the family. The question of how these family members supplement the primary roles of father and mother is addressed. We explore how they represent a positive force in the family constellation. We examine the role of the Black church as a source of family support.

Our final chapter is a summary of the sociocultural variables affecting the Black family, such as racism, government policies, political factors, and economic forces. The problems and prospects are examined, and best- and worst-case scenarios are offered for the future of the Black family.

September 1992   Robert Staples
                                          San Francisco, California

                                          Leanor Boulin Johnson
                                          Phoenix, Arizona

Acknowledgments

Professionally, I am indebted to Patricia Bell-Scott of the University of Georgia, Robert Hall of Northeastern University, Erma Lawson of the University of Kentucky, and Patricia Wilson of Arizona State University, who read and critiqued the first draft of our manuscript. Also, I am grateful to Paul Glick of Arizona State University and anonymous reviewers, who provided feedback on some of the chapters. I wish to thank the support staff in our departments—Kathleen McClung, Sally Maeth, and Elizabeth Sherman—for typing, editing, and bibliographical services. I also wish to acknowledge the support of the Arizona State University Department of Family Studies and the Graduate Program in Sociology at the University of California, San Francisco, which approved phone calls, faxing, and express mail during a period of severe fiscal cutbacks. Without these basic services, a joint effort would have moved at a much slower pace. In our collaborative effort, Leanor Boulin Johnson and I thank each other for mutual support and trust throughout the challenging process of putting this book together. While we are grateful to the people just mentioned for their help, the final responsibility for the book rests with us.

—*R. S.*

I wish to thank the significant individuals who have touched my life. In my tender years, I was endowed with an abundance of love, support, and spirituality. For this rich inheritance, I give thanks to my circle of childhood family: Linda and Herbert Boulin (my parents), Yvonne Maudlin Washington and Homer Linton Boulin (my siblings), uncles, aunts, cousins, adopted kin, and my Black church community. Anyone who has tried to balance family life with obtaining an academic degree or employment knows the value of a supportive spouse. Thank you, Bill, for your steadfast confidence in my ability and the sacrifices you made to support my professional goals. Your own achievements and dedication as a physician and parent continue to inspire me to maintain the highest professional and family integrity. Even spouses supporting each other cannot always meet the demands of work and family. Thus, I am deeply grateful to my mother-in-law, Margaret B. Duncan, who on countless occasions stepped in so that my sons could attend high school band practice or football games, religious services, and club meetings. Finally, I thank my sons, Linton and Donovan, and my nephews Khari, Jabari, Hakeem, Shomari, Xavier, and Valamar, who do all the wonderful things they do to enrich my life and who provide me with challenging pragmatic experiences in family studies.

—L.B.J.

The Authors

Robert Staples is professor in the graduate program in sociology, University of California, San Francisco. He received his B.A. and M.A. degrees in sociology from California State University, Northridge, and San Jose State University, respectively, and his Ph.D. degree from the University of Minnesota. He has been invited to be a visiting fellow at the Australian Institute of Family Studies on three different occasions and was a visiting fellow at the University of Warwick in Coventry, England, in 1989–90. His current research focuses on families of color in White settler nations.

Among the awards Staples has received for distinguished achievement have been commendations from the National Council on Family Relations, Howard University, and the University of Zulia in Maracaibo, Venezuela. He has written on many aspects of the Afro-American family and has published more than 10 books and 200 articles on race relations and the sociology of the Black family. His professional service has included membership on the editorial boards of *Journal of Marriage and the Family, Western Journal of Black Studies,* and *Black Scholar.*

Leanor Boulin Johnson is associate professor of family studies at Arizona State University. She received her B.S. degree in social services from East Tennessee State University, and her

M.S. and Ph.D. degrees in sociology from Purdue University. Boulin Johnson's main research activities have been in Black family studies, cross-cultural sexuality, and work-family stress. She has received several federal, private, and university grants to study work-family stress among Black and White police officers. In addition, she has been associate editor of the journal *Family Relations* and reviewer for several journals, and has published numerous journal articles and book chapters. Her 1991 testimony before Congress on work-family issues provided an empirical base for a law enforcement family support act amendment to the 1991 congressional crime bill.

Her consulting experience includes evaluating federal grant proposals for the National Institute of Mental Health (from 1978 to 1981) and developing and conducting a sexual harassment study of over 20,000 federal workers for the Merit Systems Protection Board (in 1983). She served as director of the National Council on Family Relations from 1983 to 1985. Another consulting assignment was chairing the review panel for the National Research Council's Ford Foundation Post-doctoral and Dissertation Fellowships for Minorities (in 1991). Also in 1991, she received the Marie Peters Award for excellence in the area of ethnic minority families from the National Council on Family Relations.

Black Families
at the Crossroads

1

History as
Fact and Fiction

As an institution, the Black family continues to be a subject of intense and controversial public concern. This interest is generated, in part, by the lack of consensus on what its form and function should be. The controversy is heightened by the way scholars have depicted the Black family in the past and by an ongoing debate over how the family history of Blacks relates to their current situation. Before examining developments in earlier periods, it is necessary to place some parameters around our historical review. The areas of interest are the precolonial era in sub-Saharan Africa, slavery in general, and the various views on the impact of slavery on Black family life.

The Preslavery Period

There are several historical periods of interest in tracing the background of Black family life in the United States. One era is the precolonial one on the African continent, where the Black American population originated. The basis of African family life was the kinship group, which was bound together by blood ties and the common interest of corporate functions. Within each village, there were elaborate legal codes and court systems that regulated the marital and family behavior of individual members. The philosophical basis of the family was

1

one of humanitarianism, mutual aid, and community participation. Although no two tribes in Africa were the same, the
continent was generally humane in its treatment of the individual and the creation of meaningful roles for each person
(Kayongo-Male and Onyango, 1984).

In African communities, marriage was not just a matter
between individuals, but was the concern of all family members. A woman, for instance, was not just a man's wife, but
"the wife of the family." As a result of this community control
of marriages, the dissolution of a marriage was a severe action
and used only as a last resort. Most marriages involved the
payment of a bride-price by the husband's family to compensate her family for the loss of her services and to guarantee
good treatment. This was not the purchase of a woman who
became her husband's property. After marriage, a woman
remained a member of her own family, since they retained a
sincere interest in her well-being (Sudarkasa, 1981).

Regardless of the meaningful role of women in precolonial Africa, the authority pattern in the family was patriarchal. This male control in the family was based not so much
on benign dominance, but on the reverence attached to his
role as the protector and provider for the family. His role was
to perform the heavy manual labor and to make the decisions
for the family. Only if he successfully carried out these roles
would respect and admiration be accorded him. On certain
days, the wife and children would bestow as much respect on
him as subjects would a king. If it was a fete day, his sons-in-
law and daughters would be there to present him with some
small gifts. They would pay him reverence, bring him a pipe,
and then go into another room, where they all ate together
with their mother (Frazier, 1939).

Children in African societies were considered symbols
of the continuity of life. During their formative years, they
enjoyed a carefree life. Until they reached the age of nine or
ten, they had no responsibilities. Afterward, they began to
learn their role requirements and responsibilities to the tribe.
The boys would build small huts and hunt fierce game. Girls
played house and cared for their "babies" (often a younger

sister). When they reached the age of fifteen, they were considered adults and would soon begin families of their own (Sudarkasa, 1981). The structure and function of the Black family was to radically change under the system of slavery. What did not change, however, was the importance of the family to African peoples in the New World. While the nature of marriage and family patterns was no longer under the control of the kinship group, the family nevertheless managed to sustain individuals in the face of the many destructive forces they encountered in American society.

The Causes and Nature of North American Slavery

Originally, Blacks entered the New World as indentured servants, a status that many Whites shared. Indentured servants were people who had their passage paid to this new continent and were contractually obligated to work for the people who paid for their trip for a certain period of time. Once their debts were paid, the indentured servants were free to pursue their own interests. According to historians of this period, race played a significant, but not central, role in the social relations between White and Black indentured servants. They worked together as equals and intermarriage between the two racial groups was even tolerated at this time (J. H. Franklin, 1987).

The development of tobacco and cotton created the need for a large-scale labor force to cultivate these products, preferably an inexpensive work force. The idea of a captive labor force was not new, having existed in earlier societies such as the Greek and Egyptian civilizations. It was simply an economic matter. Slavery, despite the problems it posed in terms of regulating human labor in a coercive relationship, was the most profitable source of labor available. There was little concern, in the beginning of the slave system, for the racial composition of the enslaved group. The slaveholders initially tried Whites and Native Americans. However, there were certain difficulties surrounding the use of these two groups. Whites, being part of the same racial group, easily escaped and avoided detection by assimilating into the nonslave society. Also, they disappeared into the frontiers of the virgin Western territory, where their recovery was improbable. Native Americans were soon found unsuitable for this type of labor, although thousands were killed in the attempt to enslave them (Patterson, 1982).

Before the massive depopulation of Africa, its countries had a flourishing civilization. Most of the slaves were taken from the west coast of Africa, where they had their own languages, mores, and folkways for regulating the behavior of their members, communication systems, and an extensive network of trade relations throughout the African continent. These civilizations drew on a long and rich cultural heritage that existed in Africa (Davidson, 1959). After Africans were uprooted and brought to the American continent, the practices of the slavemasters served to destroy the unity of their African culture. Frazier (1949, p. 65) describes this process of deculturization as follows: "The manner in which men and women were indiscriminately packed in slave ships . . . tended to destroy social bonds and tribal distinctions. The process of 'breaking' the Negroes into the slave system in the West Indies, where they often landed before shipment to the colonies and the United States, tended to efface the memories of their traditional culture. In the colonies, and later in the Southern United States, the slaves were widely scattered on comparatively small plantations where there was little opportunity to reknit social bonds or regenerate the African culture."

While slavery was not new to humankind or endemic to the United States, the enslavement of Africans and their brutal transportation to this country marked a new chapter in the history of man's inhumanity to man. Previous slave systems were not characterized by distinctions of race (Snowden, 1970). As Brown (1949, p. 34) says of the slave system in Greece, "The slave populations were enormous, but the slave and the master in Greece were commonly of the same race and there was no occasion to associate any given physical type with the slave status."

Similarly, in Rome, slaves were not differentiated from

free men in their external appearance. Authorities on the subject have noted that any citizen might conceivably become a slave; almost any slave might become a citizen (Snowden, 1970). The blocked mobility of slaves was also peculiar to the United States. In Latin America, for instance, slaves lost their freedom but retained the right to regain it. In the United States, Blacks were consigned to a slave status from birth to grave (Elkins, 1968). The American slave system abrogated all rights the Africans had as human beings. Slaveholders could not be punished for the way they treated their slaves; families were broken up by the sale of one of their members; there was no legal marriage for slaves; the children of a slave mother were automatically slaves; and the status of slave was a position from which no mobility was permitted (Patterson, 1982).

The Slave Family

Slavery had its greatest impact on the family life of the Africans brought to the United States. Most of the slaves who came in the beginning were males. The Black female population was not equal to the number of males until 1830. As a result, the frequency of sexual relations between Black slaves and indentured White women was fairly high. Some of these interracial relationships were more than casual contacts and ended in marriage. The intermarriage rate between male slaves and free White women increased to the extent that laws against them were passed as a prohibitive measure. Before the alarm over the rate of intermarriages, male slaves were encouraged to marry White women, since the children from such unions were also slaves, thereby increasing the property of the slavemaster (Stember, 1976).

In attempting to get an accurate description of the family life of slaves, one has to sift through a conflicting array of opinions on the subject. Reliable empirical facts are few, and speculation has been rampant in the absence of data. Certain aspects of the slaves' family life are undisputed. Slaves were not allowed to enter into binding contractual relationships. Since marriage is basically a legal relationship that imposes

obligations on both parties and exacts penalties for their violation, there was no legal basis to any marriage between two
individuals in bondage. Slave marriages were regulated at the
discretion of the slavemaster. As a result, some marriages were
initiated by slaveowners and just as easily dissolved (J. H.
Franklin, 1988).

Hence, there were numerous cases where the slave
owner ordered slave women to marry men of his own choosing after they reached puberty. The slave owners preferred a
marriage between slaves on the same plantation, since the
primary reason for slave unions was the breeding of children
who would become future slaves. Children born to a slave
woman on a different plantation were looked on by the slaveholder as wasting his man's seed. Yet many slaves who were
allowed to get married preferred women from a neighboring
plantation. This allowed them to avoid witnessing the many
assaults on slave women that occurred. Sometimes the matter
was resolved by the sale of one of the parties to the other
owner (Blassingame, 1972).

Historians are divided on the question of how many
slave families were involuntarily separated from each other
by their owners. Despite the slaveholders' commitment to
maintaining the slave families intact, the intervening events
of a slaveholder's death, his bankruptcy, or his lack of capital
made the forcible sale of some slaves' spouse or child inevitable. In instances where the slavemaster was indifferent to the
fate of slave families, he would still keep them together simply to enforce plantation discipline. A married slave who was
concerned about his wife and children, it was believed, was
less inclined to rebel or escape than a "single" slave. Whatever
their reasoning, the few available records show that slave
owners did not separate a majority of the slave couples (Blassingame, 1972; Fogel and Engerman, 1974).

This does not mean that the slave family had a great
deal of stability. While there are examples of some slave families living together for forty years or more, the majority of
slave unions were dissolved by personal choice, death, or the
sale of one partner by the master. Although individual fami-

lies may not have remained together for long periods of time, the institution of the family was an important asset in the perilous era of slavery. Despite the prevalent theories about the destruction of the family under slavery, it was one of the most important survival mechanisms for African people held in bondage (Blassingame, 1972). In their state of involuntary servitude, the slaves began to form a new sense of family. Whereas in African society, the family was based on the system of kinship within the tribe, under slavery it was in the community of slaves that individuals found their identity. Tribal affiliation was reorganized to encompass those individuals bound together by the commonality of their Blackness and their enslavement. In this context, many of the traditional functions of the family were carried out and the former philosophical principle of survival of the tribe held fast (Nobles and Goddard, 1986).

In the slave quarters, Black families did exist as functioning institutions and as models for others. The slave narratives provide us with some indication of the importance of family relations under slavery. In the family, slaves received affection, companionship, love, and empathy with their suffering under this brutal system. Through the family, they learned how to avoid punishment, to cooperate with their fellow slaves, and to retain some semblance of self-esteem. The socialization of slave children was another important function for the slave parents. Parents could cushion the shock of bondage for their children, inculcate in them values different from those the masters attempted to transmit, and represent another frame of reference for their self-esteem besides the master (J. H. Franklin, 1988).

Much has been written about the elimination of the male's traditional functions under the slave system. It is true that he was often relegated to working in the fields and siring children, rather than providing economic maintenance or physical protection for his family. Yet the father's role was not as insignificant as presumed. Ex-slaves often spoke of their affection for their fathers and the pain of separation. Although they could not perform many of the functions traditionally assigned to fathers, there were other ways they could acquire respect from their families. Where possible, they could add to the family's meager rations of food by hunting and fishing. Or they could gain the approval of their families and fellow bondsmen by making furniture for the cabin or building partitions between cabins that contained more than one family (Blassingame, 1972).

It was the male slave's inability to protect his wife from the physical and sexual abuse of the master that most pained him. Yet, as a matter of survival, few tried, since the consequences were often fatal. But it is significant that tales of their intervention occur frequently in the slave narratives. There is one story of a slave who could no longer tolerate the humiliation of his wife's sexual abuse by the master before his eyes. He choked him to death with the knowledge that it meant his death. He said he knew it was death, but it was death anyhow, so he just killed him (Absug, 1971, p. 29).

Slave children learned many valuable lessons from their parents. Some taught them submission as a way of avoiding suffering and death. However, they were not taught categorical obedience. Rather, they were frequently instructed to fight the master when their relatives were in danger. One example was W. H. Robinson's father, who told him, "I want you to die in defense of your mother" (Blassingame, 1972, p. 99). Some parents taught their children pride in their African heritage. One student related how his father often boasted of the fact that he had a pure strain of Black blood in his veins and could trace his ancestors back to the very heart of Africa (Frazier, 1939, p. 15).

The importance of the family is underlined by the numerous cases of fugitive slaves who ran away to find mates that had been sold away from them. In most cases, these couples were bound together by affection, not morality or a contractual agreement. These bonds were often very strong even when there was no legal marriage. As Nobles and Goddard (1986) have noted, the valid African marriage does not need any kind of ceremonial sanction—a bride-price or a sacred or secular ceremony—apart from the domestic consent. Yet slaves had a reverence for the legal marriage and the protection the law afforded. Bibb states that "there are no class of people in the United States who so highly appreciate the legality of marriage as those persons who have been held and treated as property" (Bibb, 1849, p. 152).

Slavery in the United States is frequently compared to the same institution in South America, where it is often considered to have been more humane. According to this view, the Spanish Slave Code and the Catholic church in Latin America provided safeguards for the slaves and their families and emphasized their worth as human beings. These two forces supposedly led to the encouragement of manumission and stable marriage among free and slave Blacks (Patterson, 1982). But this polarity of the two slave systems in North and South America does not hold up under close examination. There was considerable variation among the Latin American societies in their use and treatment of slaves. In some areas of Latin America, there was very humane treatment of slaves, and in others, brutal treatment. As for the Spanish Slave Code, it was not only unenforced, but it was never promulgated in any of the Spanish Caribbean colonies. Moreover, some of the measures encouraging marriage among the slaves in South America were designed to hold the slaves to the plantation estates with family ties (Hall, 1970).

One aspect of Black family life frequently ignored during the slave era is the free Black family. This group, which numbered about half a million, was primarily composed of the descendants of the original Black indentured servants and the mulatto offspring of slaveholders. For this minority of Black families, the assimilation and acculturation process was relatively less difficult. They imitated the White world as closely as possible. Because they had opportunities for education, owning property, and skilled occupations, their family life was quite stable. Some of them even owned slaves, although the majority of Black slaveholders were former slaves who had purchased their wives or children. It is out of this group that the Black middle class was formed in an early period (Berry and Blassingame, 1982).

After Emancipation

An indication of the importance attached to the family is provided by the numerous cases of freed slaves searching out family members from whom they had been separated during slavery. Sometimes they had been apart for as long as thirty years. The means used to reunite families ranged from placing ads in Black newspapers to the trek of one ex-slave, who walked 600 miles during a two-month stretch. Many of the slaves who had cohabited together made plans for a legal marriage with the knowledge that they no longer faced the possibility of exploitation and separation (J. H. Franklin, 1988). There has been a prevailing notion that the experience of slavery weakened the value of marriage as an institution among Afro-Americans. Yet the ex-slaves married in record numbers when they obtained this right by governmental decree. A legal marriage was a status symbol, and weddings were events of great gaiety. In a careful examination of census data and marriage licenses for the period after 1860, Gutman (1976) found that the typical household everywhere was a simple nuclear family headed by an adult male. Further evidence that Black people were successful in forming a biparental family structure are the data that show that 90 percent of all Black children were born in wedlock by the year 1917 (Bernard, 1966, p. 4).

Many students of the Reconstruction era observed the strong family orientation of the ex-slaves. One newspaper reported a Black group's petition to the state of North Carolina asking for the right "to work with the assurance of good faith and fair treatment, to educate their children, to sanctify the family relation, to reunite scattered families, and to provide for the orphan and infirm" (Absug, 1971, p. 34). Children were of special value to the freed slaves, whose memories were fresh with the history of their offspring being sold away. After slavery, the slave-born generation of freed slaves cherished their children all the more and devoted their lives to providing them with land and an education.

During the late nineteenth century, the strong role of

women emerged. Males preferred their wives to remain at home, since a working woman was considered a mark of slavery. But during a period considered the most racist of American history, Black men found it very difficult to obtain jobs and, in some instances, found work only as strikebreakers. Thus, the official organ of the African Methodist Episcopal Church exhorted Black families to teach their daughters not to avoid work, since many of them would marry men that would not make, on the average, more than 75 cents a day (Absug, 1971, p. 39). By 1880, approximately three times as many Black women as White women were in the labor force (Goldin, 1983). What was important, then, was not whether the husband or wife worked, but the family's will to survive in an era when Blacks were systematically deprived of educational and work opportunities. Despite these obstacles, Black families achieved a level of stability based on role integration. Males shared equally in the rearing of children—women participated in the defense of the family. A system where the family disintegrates due to the loss of one member would be in opposition to the traditional principles of unity that defined the African family (Krech, 1982).

This principle was to be tested during the period of the great Black migration from the rural areas of the South to the cities of the North. The rise of Black out-of-wedlock birth rates and female-headed households are concomitants of twentieth-century urban ghettos. The condition of many lower-class Black families is a function of the economic contingencies of industrial America (Litwack, 1979). Unlike the European immigrants before them, Blacks were disadvantaged by the oppressiveness of Northern segregation along racial lines. Furthermore, families in cities are more vulnerable to disruptions due to the traumatizing experiences of urbanization, the reduction of family functions, and the loss of extended family supports. Because of the higher level of racial discrimination facing Blacks in the South, they were less likely to retreat from the more vulnerable conditions of urban poverty in the North than White migrants from the South (Lemann, 1991).

In many cases, slavery was replaced by sharecropping and debt peonage for landless Blacks. Their status changed from slaves to sharecroppers; the slave barracks near the big house became dispersed wooden shacks, and money lending charged against the value of the sharecropper's share of the crop became an economic surrogate for slavery. Through constant indebtedness, the ex-slaves were as tied to the land and the landlord as they had been under slavery. The planters saw to it that there was always a debt and therefore an obligation to remain. And, if necessary, they did not hesitate to use force to discourage their tenants from escaping (J. H. Franklin, 1987). Still, sharecropping was an improvement over slavery, and there was considerably more freedom for Blacks to marry, assume custody of children, discipline them, spend more time with their spouses, and engage in family relations without the constant threat of family separation (Jones, 1985). However, J. H. Franklin (1988) claims that sharecropping and the great migration of Blacks to the urban North during World War I did not adversely affect the stability of the Black family to any significant degree. Until 1925, most Black families were intact, although extended and augmented households increased in importance.

In the transition from Africa to the American continent, there can be no doubt that African culture was not retained in any pure form. Blacks lacked the autonomy to maintain their cultural traditions under the severe pressures to take on American standards of behavior. Yet Africanisms survive in Black speech patterns, esthetics, folklore, and religion (Herskovits, 1941). These were combined with aspects of American culture. And, out of the common experiences Blacks have shared, a new culture has been forged that is uniquely Afro-American. The elements of that culture are still to be found in their family life (Foster, 1983).

The Historical Role of Black Women

Anthropologists and historians tell us that most African societies were (and still are) male dominated. One should not assume from this fact that the role of women was unimportant. The historical deeds of Black women in the preslavery period of Africa are recorded on tombs of ancient Egypt, are enumerated by Semitic writers, and are part of Greek mythology. Women formed the economic bulwark of Nigerian society. In the Balonda tribe of southern Africa, women held a position economically superior to that of men (Sudarkasa, 1981). Women played an important role in the political organization of various tribal societies in Africa, as reported in local chronicles and in the records of early travelers there. In West Africa, the ancestral home of most Afro-Americans, the women of the Ashanti tribe were reputed to have founded small states such as Mampong, Wenchi, and Juaban. Among the peoples of Niger and Chad, women reputedly founded cities, led migrations, and conquered kingdoms. There are also accounts of the courage of the female legions who fought in the armies of Monomotapa and of the privileges they enjoyed (Steady, 1981).

Some cultural continuity exists between the roles of African and Afro-American women. But while African women had the opportunity to play a central role in their society, Afro-American women had their role fashioned out of the racial subjugation they endured and the need to assume the task of Black survival.

Until the middle of the nineteenth century, most of the Black slaves were male. Originally, the slavemaster's preference was for males who could perform the heavy duties required of bondsmen. Black men were encouraged to "marry" White women in order to augment the human capital of the slave-owning class. The intermarriage rate, however, became so high that unions between Black men and White women were prohibited. After that time, there was a marked increase in the number of Black women. The end of the slave trade also led to an increased emphasis on the domestic breeding of slaves, a task for which Black women bore primary responsibility (White, 1985). In addition, black women had the responsibilities of laboring in the fields and in the slavemaster's house. This was the beginning of their dual oppression as breeding instruments and as a captive labor force. Although the Black man was formally stripped of all paternal functions except the biological one, Black women hardly fared better.

The slave woman was first a full-time worker for her owner and only incidentally a wife, mother, and homemaker. She was allowed to spend only a small fraction of her time in her quarters, she often did no cooking or sewing, and she was not allowed to nurse her children during their illnesses. If she was a field slave, she had to experience pregnancy and childbirth while performing daily hard labor in the fields. Since the children were the master's property and did not belong to the parents, the slave women frequently were breeding instruments for children who were later sold. There are reports of Black women who strongly resisted being separated from their children and having them put up for sale, even though their opposition subjected them to great physical violence from the slavemaster. Occasionally, Black women committed infanticide rather than permit their children to endure the oppression of slavery (Terborg-Penn, 1991). During this period of slavery, the Black woman's body was forcibly subjected to the carnal desires of any male who took a fancy to her, including the slavemaster, his overseer, or any male slave. If she was permitted a husband, he was not allowed to protect her. Essentially she was left defenseless against sexual onslaught by other males on the plantation. This was especially true of her relations with the white slavemaster. It appears that coercion, rather than desire, was the key element in her sexual relations with White men during that time (White, 1985).

Angela Davis (1971) has suggested that the sexual subjugation of the slave woman was the slavemaster's symbolic attempt to break her will to resist. According to Davis (1971, p. 13), "In confronting the Black woman as adversary in a sexual contest, the master would be subjecting her to the most elemental form of terrorism distinctively suited for the female: rape. Given the already terroristic texture of plantation life, it would be as potential victim of rape that the slave woman would be most unguarded. Further, she might be most conveniently manipulable if the master contrived a ransom system of sorts, forcing her to pay with her body for food, diminished severity in treatment, the safety of her children, etc." The sexual exploitation of the slave woman did not derive simply from carnal desire but from the slavemaster's design to intimidate the entire slave population. He wanted to assert his control over the entirety of the slave's being—over that of the male as well as the female slave. The rape of the slave woman brought home to the slave man his inability to protect his woman. Once his masculine role was undermined in this and other respects, he would begin to experience profound doubts about his power even to break the chains of bondage (Davis, 1983).

Consequently, the slave woman was the center of the family. The Black father, if present, had little authority. Under slavery, the Black man's function was fieldwork and service. The mother named the children and often had sole responsibility for their care and discipline. Whatever authority the mother did not have belonged to the slavemaster (White, 1985). It is this fact that led to the emergence of the notorious Black matriarchy hypothesis. A matriarchy is formally defined as a system of government ruled by women. This concept implies great advantages for women in the society. Instead of having any particular privileges under the slave system, Black women were, in reality, burdened with the dual role of laborer and mother. Hence, this is the origin of her two-pronged burden, which has been mislabeled a "matriarchy" (Collins, 1990).

The Historical Debate

Among other topics, the growing literature on Black families in this century has focused on the impact of slavery on Black families. Historical studies have both developed and corrected many misconceptions about the nature of family life among the Black slave population. As was true of other investigations of Black family life, early historians constructed their view of slave family life from preconceived assumptions and faulty methodology. A popularly held theory was that slavery destroyed the family traditions and values brought to this continent by Africans (Elkins, 1968; Frazier, 1939). There was much validity to the old historical research that found that there was no legal basis for a marriage between slaves, that slave families could be and were disrupted by the sale of their members, and that the exercise of normative sex and parental roles was constrained. These findings were partly built on theories of history, which were supplemented by the use of plantation records and slave owners' diaries. But the new historical research employs a more extensive and reliable analysis of slave narratives and census records as well as the traditional sources.

African survival is a controversial theory that states Blacks in the diaspora have retained many of the cultural traits they brought over from the African continent. Primarily associated with the late anthropologist Melville Herskovits (1941), it begs the question of how these traits have been maintained and in what form. The Herskovits answer was that some Africanisms—including practices such as voodoo— were retained by New World Blacks because they were practiced in secret. As to the form they took, he claims they were often disguised as a combination of cultural elements that had been integrated to form one cultural complex. This process of syncretism is expressed in Afro-American music, language, customs, food, and religion. In the case of Afro-American social organization, many characteristics regarded as European were actually African in origin. The prevalence of female-headed households, common law marriages, and respect shown to elders are but a few examples (Foster, 1983).

However, no matter how convenient it might be to believe that Afro-Americans are an African people in their cultural behavior, there is not sufficient evidence to reach such a conclusion. The retention of African features has a stronger case in some Caribbean and South American societies, for reasons that are peculiar to them. On the other hand, a group rarely is totally stripped of all its cultural heritage, especially when they live the kind of segregated existence of

American Blacks. Blassingame (1972, p. 18) provides us with a good evaluative yardstick for assessing Africanisms in Afro-American culture with his statement that "whenever the elements of Black culture are more closely similar to African than European traits, we can be reasonably certain that we have identified African survivals."

For years, the works of Frazier (1939) and Elkins (1968) were accepted as the definitive history of Black families and posited as a causal explanation of their contemporary condition. Applying traditional historical methods and using plantation records and the testimony of slave owners, both men reached the conclusion that the culture of the slaves was decimated and, in particular, that the family was destroyed under slavery. The first historian to challenge that thesis was Blassingame (1972), whose use of slave narratives indicated that in the slave quarters, Black families did exist as functioning institutions and role models for others. Moreover, strong family ties persisted in face of the frequent breakups deriving from the slave trade. To further counter the Frazier/Elkins thesis, Fogel and Engerman (1974) used elaborate quantitative methods to document that slave owners did not separate a majority of the slave families. Their contention, also controversial, was that the capitalistic efficiency of the slave system meant it was more practical to keep slave families intact.

Continuing in the vein of revisionist historical research, Genovese (1974) used a mix of slaveholders' papers and slave testimony. He concluded that Black culture, through compromise and negotiation between slaves and slave owners, did flourish during the era of slavery. Within that cultural framework, there were a variety of socially approved and sanctioned relationships between slave men and women. The alleged female matriarchy that was extant during that era is described by Genovese as a closer approximation to a healthy gender equality than was possible for Whites. Finally, it was the landmark study by Gutman (1976) that put to rest one of the most common and enduring myths about Black families. Using census data for a number of cities between 1880 and 1925, he found that the majority of Blacks of all social classes

were lodged in nuclear families. Through the use of plantation birth records and marriage applications, he concluded
that the biparental household was the dominant form during
slavery. More important than Gutman's compelling evidence
that slavery did not destroy the Black family was his contention that this family form evolved from family and kinship
patterns that emerged under slavery, thus giving credence to
the notion of Black culture surviving slavery.

Social historians and historical demographers have
also made contributions to our understanding of Black family history. Furstenberg, Hershberg, and Modell (1975) investigated the origin of the female-headed Black family and its
relationship to the urban experience. Basing their analysis
on samples from the decennial federal population manuscript schedules for the period from 1850 to 1880, they found
that Blacks were only slightly less likely to reside in nuclear
households than native Whites and immigrants to Philadelphia. While these historical works have successfully challenged the Moynihan (1965) view that slavery created the
conditions for Black family disorganization, the prevalence
of marital breakups at the hands of slave owners means that
many marriages were not stable. And even the use of slave
accounts does not eliminate bias in slave history. Many of
the slave narratives were edited by Northern abolitionists,
and they constitute the reports of highly literate slaves. This
raises questions about ideology and its role in the conceptualization of Black family organization.

The role of ideology is not unique to the field of family
history. Under the rubric of the sociology of knowledge, it
has been asserted that the social location of individuals within
a given society will influence the knowledge they possess
(Mannheim, 1936). Since the study of Black families has been
dominated by White middle-class males, a debate centering
around the insider-outsider thesis has arisen (Merton, 1972;
Staples and Mirande, 1980). One side contends that Blacks
possess a special capacity to understand the behavior of their
group, while the other side contends that the use of objective
scientific methods nullifies the racial membership of the inves-

tigator as a significant factor. Those holding the latter view often choose to conceptualize this whole issue as a conflict between ideology and science (Zollar, 1986).

Other questions concern the division of historical researchers according to methodology. Many of the Black researchers have used the essay and slave narratives as their main tool in understanding slave families. In part, this is due to a need for a broader understanding of the behavioral processes that constitute the historical background of American Blacks. Since White males have dominated the historical studies of slave families, they have often dismissed their Black counterparts with the charge of being polemicists who substituted speculation and ideology for objective data. This question of objectivity versus ideology would be beyond cavil were it not for the fact that Black families, for the longest time, were treated pejoratively in the historical literature.

As of the 1990s, there ceased to be a clear-cut racial division in the study of some aspects of Black history. Many of the corrective historical studies were undertaken by White historians, such as Gutman (1976) and Genovese (1974). However, with the exception of the work of the White anthropologist Herskovits (1941), their research did not change until America's racial climate changed. This fact led Chancellor Williams (quoted in Toure, 1991) to assert, "There are two widely different schools of scholarship. Members of the orthodox majority develop their work faithfully in line with the authorities in the field, relying on them as sources of final truth. . . . The other school dares to challenge much of this authoritarian scholarship by subjecting the masters to critical analysis, raising all kinds of questions . . . and even inquiring about some fundamental presuppositions which underlie and color so much of their work" (p. E-1).

The fact must be accepted that the Black family cannot be explained by the use of normative historical methods. For the most part, history has been a traditionalist science operating with the acceptance of the status quo models. What this means is that the traditional approach to the study of Black family life has been to define the history of Afro-American family behavior on the basis of standards set by the White community—not by the White community in general, but by White middle-class people in particular. Rather than using a more objective approach and accepting the fact that Black families are different and that one must understand the way they function and their values and standards—other values and standards—White norms have been imposed on the historical study of Black family life. The result has been that the Black family continues to be defined as a pathological unit whose unique way of functioning sustains the conditions of its oppression.

However, there is no definitive evidence of a racial polarization of historical research on the Black family. The purveyors of the pathology view have belonged to both racial groups, just as the defenders of the Black family have. The difference most likely arises from adherence to a class ideology and values rather than a value-free approach to the study of Black family history. A problem remains that much of what we know is a mere oversimplification of popular stereotypes about Black family life, which serve to inculcate in the public mind a host of useless and invalidated generalizations—and there is much that we need to know that has not yet been explored.

Summary

Sorting out the validity of different historical theories and research on the evolution of Afro-American families is a daunting task. Just as historians are challenged by the task of determining the nature of historical events, it is difficult for us to evaluate the validity of their interpretation. What has been learned is that slavery radically altered the family system known to Africans before their forced transplantation to the Americas. However much they may have attempted to maintain their family organization under slavery, the vicissitudes of bondage made an indelible mark on the type of family life they were allowed to have. That slavery made its mark on Afro-American families is unquestionable. Whether the experience of maintaining family life over a period of 300 years in bondage left much of a legacy remains a question to be answered.

The classic historical theories that slavery created the basis for a deinstitutionalization of marriage and an inversion of gender roles in the family seem to have been successfully challenged by the neohistorical theories of Blassingame (1972), Genovese (1974), and Gutman (1976). Their research has the advantage of letting slaves speak in their own voices and of utilizing census data and government records that more effectively document marriage and out-of-wedlock birth rates. The fact that 75 percent of Black families were intact up to 1925 serves as a strong antidote to the historical generalization that the institutional role of marriage was destroyed under slavery. If one accepts the hypothesis that slavery created the conditions for a Black matriarchy, more current research on power relationships within Afro-American families provides strong evidence to the contrary.

Finally, we must examine how history illuminates the role of class and race in influencing Black family patterns. Traditionally, historians have posited race as the dominant variable, because certain historical experiences (that is, slavery, Jim Crow) were unique to Afro-Americans and were thought to have created a pathological culture and personality in Black communities. Yet slavery was first and foremost an economic system. Black slavery occurred in the Americas because it was the cheapest and "best" economic system from a certain standpoint (Patterson, 1982). It acquired its racial characteristic in its latter stages to serve economic ends. Given the social class traits that differentiate intact and broken Afro-American families in the latter part of the twentieth century, it seems apparent that current economic conditions supersede historical events as the main factor in Black family disorganization.

2

Studying
Black Families

For many years, the Black family has been the focus of research studies by sociologists, psychologists, and educators. Yet there is no comprehensive theory that fully explains its nature and structure. In a limited sense, various disciplines have attempted to relate their theoretical framework to the study of this institution. But at this point, no family sociologist has integrated the separate theories into a general theory of the Black family (Engram, 1982). One reason for the paucity of theories specifically concerning the Black family has been the lack of theories on the family in general. According to some scholars, no such theory is needed; the family can be studied by the theories already available. Goode (1959, p. 180) has observed that "there remains a widespread feeling among younger theorists that the structure and workings of the family do not explain the rest of the social structure. The family is said to be made up of dependent, not independent, variables—i.e., it is thought possible to explain the family by other institutions but not other institutions by the family." (Goode (1959, p. 180) further asserts that "no theorists have been able to state, let alone prove, any set of systematic propositions about the relations between the family and other institutions, no matter which is independent."

One of the most important concerns of family sociologists has been theory building in the area of marriage and the family (Booth, 1991). The general consensus is that systematic theory building is a major need in family study. Hill and Hansen (1960) note that most past research was sophisticated in method but needed to grow in theoretical relevance. Empirical studies should be theory oriented to help structure the research design and to avoid erroneous ex post facto interpretations of research findings. In an important article on the development of family theory, Reuben Hill (1966) cites three goals for developing a theory of the family: (1) establishing an all-purpose family framework that can be used by the members of the various disciplines working in family study; (2) building interpretive bridges linking each of the conceptual frameworks and enabling theories developed in one framework to be translated into the concepts and language of other frameworks; and (3) creating a way of moving from descriptive taxonomic frameworks to explanatory models for the mutual enrichment of each.

Looking through the sociological literature, it is difficult to find a consensus on the definition of theory. It is sometimes viewed in terms of the classic works of the famous sociologists of the past or as a commentary on sociological writing from a historical perspective (Zetterberg, 1965). As the discipline of sociology becomes more oriented toward theory, more precise definitions must be used. In a theory, one should be able to develop more abstract propositions from which empirical generalizations can be derived. To test a theory, propositions—or interrelationships of individual concepts—should conform to data, and several propositions in conjunction with each other should account for the outcome of a given situation. In other words, observed events will conform to known propositions as an indirect test of the theory (Zetterberg, 1965).

Probably none of the frameworks used to study families can meet the most stringent definitions of a theory. Several decades ago, Hill and Hansen (1960) referred to the main approaches in the family field as conceptual models. They are not systematic theories of the family but contain concepts that alert family researchers to what is important for them to pay attention to when studying family relationships. Hill and

Hansen identified five conceptual models as particularly
appropriate to the study of the family: institutional, interac-
tional, structural-functional, situational, and family development. Two additional models emerged in the 1970s as major
approaches to the family: the exchange and conflict models
(Nye and Berardo, 1981).

Reviewing the studies of Black families over a hundred-
year time span reveals that most have been atheoretical. While
the frameworks just mentioned have occasionally been used
in research on Afro-American families, other conceptual models not normally associated with mainstream family research
have more frequently been applied. While we will critique
the Black family frameworks, it should be noted that we are
in agreement with Engram (1982, p. 7), who notes that "most
of the frameworks so examined were conceptualized in
response to the empirical stimuli of western and mainstream
families. Often the analysis of ethnic and lower-class families
within the context of these frameworks has, therefore,
required truncation or stretching of data to fit the theoretical
realities posed by them."

Conceptual Models for Studying Black Family Life

In this section, we review some of the most relevant conceptual models that contain elements that can be used to understand the structure and dynamics of Black family life. Some
of these models may not have found wide application in
Black family research. But we believe that they are relevant to
the understanding of Black families in the United States.
While we realize that these are conceptual models, not theories, we will use the two terms interchangeably, as they are
used in much of the family literature (Dilworth-Anderson,
Johnson, and Burton, 1992; Davis, 1990).

The Afrocentric Model

If we applied this model to the study of Black life in America,
our focus would be on the continuities in African cultural

strands among the Afro-American population. Afrocentricity sees all people of African descent as having a common history, experience, and culture. Hence, Afro-Americans are considered dislocated Africans. The structure of African culture remains the same, although the form may have changed through the adaptations imposed on Black Americans. A basic assumption is that a culture group never completely loses its cultural heritage; it simply evolves into another form (Asante, 1987; Nobles, 1988). A virtue of this model is its focus on the comparative study of African and Afro-American cultures. It provides an important link to the past and serves as the foundation for any analysis of Black cultural values and patterns. Some significant work has already been done in the area of music, speech, and family patterns. However, much historical research is needed to determine the origin of African cultural traits, the means of transmitting them among Africans in another country, and the forms they exist in among contemporary Afro-Americans (Sudarkasa, 1988).

Cultural variations can be determined by studying the different forms of family behavior found among peoples of African descent. This refers not only to the variations that exist within the African continent (for example, matrilineal and patrilineal systems), but the different types of African family forms in other parts of the world. For instance, in the United States, one might compare Muslim and Christian families, working- and middle-class families, rural and urban families, and so on (Nobles and Goddard, 1986). The significance of the Afrocentric approach is that it liberates the study of Afro-American families from the domination of White referents in the study of Black life. A comparison of Blacks and Whites in America is useful for illustrating the effects of racial inequality. But others believe that if a meaningful analysis of Black cultural forms is what we are about, the focus must be on those cultural traditions that are maintained in the nature and function of institutions such as the family (Harvey, 1985).

Though the Afrocentric perspective is valuable for understanding the family traditions that remained intact or were modified in the diaspora, the political and economic forces that the Afro-American family encountered that influenced its character also need to be understood. Afrocentricity as a conceptual model has concentrated more on cultural forms than on the effect of a society's political economy. Moreover, historical and anthropological methodologies have to be refined and strengthened so that contemporary Afro-American families can be understood in light of historical and cross-cultural facts (Staples and Mirande, 1980). Proponents of this school of thought acknowledge that they have to develop a literature and data base (Coughlin, 1987).

Black Feminist Theory

The burgeoning of the women's liberation movement has given rise to a number of books on Black women. In earlier years, they tended to be nonempirical works that focused on the role of Black women in their community and the larger society (Cade, 1970; Rodgers-Rose, 1980; Staples, 1973; Noble, 1978). Among the better books was Ladner's study (1971) of Black teenage females growing up in a low-income community. Through the use of systematic open-ended interviews, participatory observation, and her own experiences, she explored how these young women coped with the forces of poverty and maintained a sense of positive identity. Many of the early books on Black women emphasized that they were strong because of the need to face adverse forces in the society but were not overbearing matriarchs. At the end of the 1970s, a young Black feminist broke ranks with her more conciliatory sisters and issued a broadside attack on male chauvinism in the Black community (Wallace, 1979). Her book was a harbinger of the 1990s, and later literature on Black gender roles has reflected a feminist ideology.

Feminist theory in the Black community arose later than in the White community, has different concerns, and has dealt with separate issues or given them a different priority. While White feminists have protested against White male domination of this society's values, Black women have found themselves the victims of Black men's powerlessness. Many

White feminists reject conventional family structures and roles, whereas Black women have rarely had access to those structures and roles. Some White feminists advocate single-hood, careerism, alternative life-styles, and childlessness (Komarovsky, 1988; Thorne and Yalom, 1982). Most Black feminists have wanted to promote the goals of racial equality, the care and nurturing of children, and the strengthening of the Black family system (Joseph and Lewis, 1981). A major impetus for Black feminism was Black women's feeling of exclusion from Black movements and institutions because of male chauvinism, as well as alienation from the mainstream women's movements because of the problems caused by racial tensions (Collins, 1990).

For the Black community, the 1980s might be termed the decade of women. In that decade, most of the few Black gains in the areas of education, occupations, income, health, and literature were achieved by women, while Black men lost ground (Staples, 1991a). Still, despite narrowing the gap between themselves and Black men, Afro-American women still occupy the bottom of the socioeconomic ladder in comparison to other gender/race groupings. Not only are they the poorest of all gender/race groups, but they are increasingly forced to fend for themselves, since only 30 percent of adult Black females were married and living with a spouse in 1991 (Bureau of the Census, 1992). One consequence of the decline in Black marriage rates has been a more strident attack on sexism in the Black community (Hooks, 1981).

The volume of works on and by Black women has contributed to our understanding of Black family life. As more and more Black women have concentrated on their gender identity, a rich literature has evolved (Bell-Scott and others, 1991; Hull, Scott, and Smith, 1982). However, it is limited as a holistic theoretical framework for understanding Afro-American families. While the family is often the center of gender domination, violence, and sexual problems, that is not all it is about. By focusing on women's roles, including childrearing, Black feminists neglect an entire half of the family formation. Even when men are absent as husbands and fathers, they have an involvement with women as boyfriends, sons, and brothers. And everything about the roles they play in the family is not necessarily negative. Thus, Black feminist studies need to be supplemented by Black family studies.

The Culture of Poverty

A slight variant of the cultural deprivation theory, this theory assumes that Black culture is a pathological version of the general American culture. Black culture is characterized as a response to poverty that results in specific traits, such as female dominance, desire for immediate gratification, fatalism, and disorganization (Demos, 1990). This theoretical approach often focuses on Black family organization and the values springing from the family environment as the major source of these negative traits. The studies of Rainwater (1970) and Moynihan (1965) in particular charge the Black family with being a major cause of racial inequality in American society.

The basis of the model is that poverty breeds poverty— that is, that the conditions imposed on the poor account for the pathological cultural forms that keep them in impoverished circumstances. Poverty, then, becomes something transmitted from generation to generation, because the values poor people possess are a deterrent to achieving upward mobility in the social structure. Among the criticisms of this approach are that many of the features associated with the culture of poverty—unemployment, substandard incomes, congested living conditions—are merely definitions of poverty itself, not of a distinct culture. In essence, this theory is simply an attempt to shift the responsibility for the conditions of racial and class inequality onto the victims themselves. It is an effort to rationalize why some Americans fail to achieve the culturally prescribed goals of the society (Valentine, 1968).

Exchange Theory

This theory focuses on the reinforcement patterns and the idea of rewards and costs that prompt people to behave in a particular manner or engage in a certain pattern of interaction (Blau, 1964; Homans, 1961). Essentially, the theory argues that people will continue to do what they have found rewarding in the past. We believe that this perspective, plus the individual's history of rewards and costs, assists in understanding contemporary marriage and family patterns. Our basic premise is that there is a relationship between family structures and ideas of reinforcement, rewards, and costs as these relate to exchange values among those engaged in family interaction.

When we speak of family life, we should note that the general pattern consists of a one-to-one relationship between a male and a female. This male-female bond is very important to the majority of Blacks, especially women. The fact that a majority of Black Americans are not married and living in traditional nuclear family units does not necessarily imply a devaluation of marriage qua institution; it is often a function of limited opportunities to find acceptable individuals in an increasingly restricted and small pool of potential partners who can successfully fulfill the normatively prescribed familial roles. While many Blacks fail to marry, the history of those who do marry indicates that only a minority survive a lifetime with the same spouse. Exchange theory suggests that a person will not want to remain in a relationship where the rewards provided seem relatively meager compared to what the person knows or perceives about other relationships. Based on that assumption, we might surmise that many Blacks may prefer to remain single because the perceived outcome, based on their own experience or on the experience of friends and relatives, might suggest that the costs and risks far outweigh the rewards (Thibaut and Kelley, 1959). This cost-benefit analysis is mediated by the sociocultural and economic conditions that adversely affect the Black male population and thus help to give rise to dissonance between Black family ideology and actual family arrangement (Jewell, 1988).

While exchange theory indicates that individuals use a cost-benefit analysis to determine their actions and relationships, the idea of exchange is actually a system of mutual expectations in a relationship or marriage (Hatfield and Walster, 1981). Men and women like to think they get what they deserve in a relationship. The most common exchange in patriarchal societies is that of female sexual access for a male's socioeconomic status. This sort of transaction has been undermined by the sexual revolution and female economic independence. Exchange theory seems most applicable to dating situations and bad marriages, since it is unlikely that most family relationships are ordered in such a calculated and rational manner. Although exchange theory has been used by students of the Black family (Jewell, 1988; Staples, 1981), it is limited in its application to this institution. Unless they are members of the middle class, Black men and women do not have extensive resources to exchange.

Historical Materialism

This school of thought—which views the family as a product of economic forces—is primarily attributed to the socialist theoretician Karl Marx (1936). According to Marx, the functions of the family are determined by class relationships. In capitalist societies, women and children are mere appendages of machines, to be used as a reserve labor supply in cases of economic expansion. Marx believed that the capitalist economic order makes family life almost impossible for the working class, since women are forced to work and their employment ipso facto destroys the family. His collaborator, Engels (1950), asserted that the working man is dependent on the family and that the result is a continual succession of family troubles. These include domestic quarrels, neglect of domestic duties, and increases in juvenile delinquency and child mortality.

Historical materialism's emphasis on political and economic influences in shaping family life has considerable significance for understanding variations among Black families of the diaspora. There are indications, for instance, that the female-centered family is primarily related to wage-labor systems that require the mobility of the male labor force, which produces an imbalance in the gender ratio (Davis, 1989). In North America, the political system may have produced the same results (Davis and Davis, 1986; Staples, 1985). This model is also useful for understanding the oppression of women, family conflict, and other forces that act on the family. A good combination of Afrocentric elements and insights from historical materialism would be a syncretic model that illustrates how economic forces act on family relations and how these forces are counteracted by cultural adaptations to each event. Moreover, one might analyze families of the diaspora by examining the economic forces that characterized various eras and the modification of family forms in response to those vagaries. However, the economic base is not the only causal factor in the historical movement and transformation of Black families. Other elements of a given society also influence the quality of a group's family life. Using only economic factors does not sufficiently distinguish the Black family from poor White families. Racial factors must be integrated into any study of Black families (Robinson, 1983).

Internal Colonialism

This conceptual model contains some of the essential elements of historical materialism but focuses on the use of racism for the purposes of political and economic exploitation. A colonial system is typified by the differentiation of racial groups into superordinate and subordinate categories, with the racially subordinate group being denied equal participation in society and the dominant group accorded special privileges at its expense (Blauner, 1972). Central to the understanding of Afro-American family life are the concepts of *racial privilege* and *cultural domination*. As Blauner (1972) has noted, internal colonialism is distinguished from capitalism by its use of culture as an instrument of domination. In the case of Afro-American families, the Anglo-Saxon family pattern was imposed on them while attempts were made to destroy the African family system. A good example is the vitiation of the parents' rights in their children under the system of slavery. The husband's domestic rights in his wife were also eliminated, since they were abrogated by the slavemaster. The continuation of White cultural domination is seen in the negative labeling of Black families who do not conform to Anglo-Saxon family norms. Furthermore, the conditions necessary for approximating the middle-class family model are denied many Black Americans, since the economic needs of the higher classes take precedence over Black family requisites.

Among the special privileges accorded White American males was, historically, sexual access to Black females, while Black males were denied similar contact with White females. Black females were used sexually to maintain the sexual "purity" of White females while existing themselves beyond the pale of consideration for marriage. The barriers to interracial marriage maintained the special privileges of the dominant racial group. As King (1973, p. 17) has observed, "Marriage between members of the ruling class and those whom they oppress inevitably undermines the rationale for the basis of oppression." The social taboos on interracial marriage prevent challenge to the superior position assigned to Whites in other ways. A low frequency of racial intermarriage makes Black accumulation of wealth through inheritance from a White improbable. It also prohibits Blacks from obtaining jobs through social contacts and kin connections and prevents Blacks from obtaining a familiarity with the social world of Whites, which is necessary for obtaining certain jobs and otherwise advancing in a White-dominated society (Spickard, 1989). Even when interracial marriages are permitted on a limited basis, they reflect the colonial relationships extant in the United States. Since the dominant culture assigns positive values to beauty and personality traits possessed primarily by White females, they become more desirable marriage partners to some Black males. Because of the differences in the social status of Black males (low) and White females (high), a large proportion of interracial marriages involve Black males in fairly high economic brackets. The theory is that the woman is exchanging her higher social status for the man's higher economic status (Murstein, Merighi, and Malloy, 1989; Tucker and Mitchell-Kernan, 1990).

The internal colonialism model may explain other aspects of Black family behavior not adequately captured by the pathological approach to studying Afro-American family patterns. By employing this framework, we might better understand Black family violence, the middle-class Black family's contradictions, and how the strengths of Black families have been defined by the nature of racism. This approach, however, needs to become more theoretically sophisticated, lest it be applied mechanically to the American experience and specifically to Afro-American family life (Staples, 1987). A further limitation of this model is its emphasis on the negative and oppressive aspects of Afro-American life. It needs to be combined with the Afrocentric perspective to shed light on the continuity of cultural strands as well as the imposition of Anglo-Saxon cultural forms that threaten to destroy the African cultural heritage.

Stages of Black Family Studies

For a hundred years, the Black family has been the subject of scientific investigation. This study has had a variety of purposes, methodologies, and conclusions (Davis, 1990; Demos, 1990). Concomitant with these have been the prevailing state of race relations and other circumstances of the Black population. This observation is congruent with Mannheim's thesis (1936) that ideas are a function of environment, that the nature of a society influences the kind of knowledge that individuals are exposed to depending on their location in a certain niche within the social structure. This obviously raises the question of what type of Black family really exists in the United States. Probably there is no monolithic Black family grouping that we can use as a model, since there are numerous differences in family organization and functioning within the Black community. These variations exist by class, along religious and regional lines, and so on. However, there are similar conditions that all Black families encounter; adaptations to those circumstances will produce similarities in their family life-styles.

Another problem is that the study of Afro-American families has always used the White middle-class family as a referent. Black families will always be perceived negatively according to this yardstick, among other reasons because the White middle-class family is only an analytical construct, an ideal type that no longer fits the majority of White families in this country. Only 26 percent of American households consisted of a married couple with children under age eighteen in 1990 (Bureau of the Census, 1991c).

Poverty-Acculturation

The original studies of Black family life (Du Bois, 1908; Frazier, 1932a, 1932b, 1939) focused on the economic conditions of the Black population that allegedly brought about their family "disorganization." It is important to note that these studies were undertaken at a time when urbanization was having its most devastating effect on the Black community. In particular, Du Bois (1908) wrote his classic work *The Negro American Family* at a time when the massive migration of Black folk from an agrarian setting to the city was taking place. Hence, it is not surprising that he found much higher rates of out-of-wedlock births and female-headed households than in the past century, when free Black families lived in the rural South. He was not studying a stable group of Blacks but one that was being uprooted from its folk culture and forced to the cities, where it became part of the landless, urban proletariat.

But much of Black family organization reflected a continuation of African values relating to family life. Because Du Bois, Frazier, and others believed that the solution to Black poverty was the integration of Blacks into the White world, they stressed that Black family norms must come into conformity with White middle-class family behavior. At the same time, they gave recognition to the African past, although in different ways, and noted the variety of Black family types that existed. Moreover, they believed that the disorganization of Black families was a result of slavery, racism, and poverty. Family disorganization was not cited as a major cause of Black poverty and oppression by Black scholars during that period (Engram, 1982; Davis, 1990).

The Pathologists

The pathologists' approach is primarily identified with Daniel Patrick Moynihan's report (1965) on the Negro family, which contained the thesis that weaknesses in the Black family are at the heart of the deterioration of the Black community. While using many of the same indices of family disorganization as the poverty-acculturation approach, Moynihan's approach is distinguished by at least three other factors: (1) it occurred in a different era and had significant import for the formulation of public policy; (2) most of the scholars using this model were White; and (3) in effect, it placed the blame for racial inequality on the Black family, specifically on Black women.

Moynihan and his followers (Aldous, 1969; Bernard, 1966; Rainwater, 1970) initiated the study of the Black family as a pathological form of social organization at precisely the time when Blacks were beginning to indict institutional racism as the cause of their lower status. The civil rights movement was entering a militant phase when the government-subsidized Moynihan study made public the assertion that weaknesses in the Black family, such as out-of-wedlock births, female-headed households, and welfare dependency, were responsible for poverty, educational failures, and lack of employment in the Black population. His efforts put Blacks on the defensive and diverted their energy into responding to his charges (Rainwater and Yancey, 1967). In the mid 1960s, the Moynihan thesis was taken up by a number of behavioral scientists who found it very easy to get funds for studies concentrating on the identification of Black family dysfunctions. During this period, one found the strange situation of the majority of White family research being based on middle-class families and almost all of the studies of Black families dealing with the lower 25 percent of the Black class strata (Demos, 1990).

The Reactive Period

Lasting roughly from 1966 to 1971, the behavioral scientists during the reactive period included both Blacks and Whites. Basically, this group argued that Black families were much like White families except for their impoverished status and history of slavery. Although there were exceptions, most agreed that permissive sex, out-of-wedlock children, and female-headed households were undesirable and that improved economic conditions would reduce the prevalence of these phenomena among Black families. In some cases, investigators denied any significant distinctions between Black and White families. If one considered social-class differences, Black families were much the same as White families. Even upper lower-class Black families were found to have the same value system as White families (Scanzoni, 1978; Liebow, 1966; Willie, 1970).

While the research and theory during this period portrayed the Black family as victim rather than criminal, it still gave no positive value to the unique traits of Black family structure. For the most part, it apologized for the political-economic system that had imposed these "undesirable" family characteristics on Afro-Americans. It was rare for any members of this group to call into question the value of the dominant group's form of family organization. To have done so would have undermined the dominance of the Anglo-Saxon values, which had prevailed since the first White settlement on these shores. However, as the White youth of America began to reject traditional family life-styles, their emerging forms of marriage and the family approximated those of Black families. Hence, what had been negatively labeled when associated with Blacks had to be validated when it became part of the White cultural system.

What was known as the notorious matriarchy among

Blacks is now regarded as female-centered families in the White community. The common law marriages (or shacking up) that existed among Blacks have been redefined and re-evaluated as heterosexual cohabitation for Whites. In the past, Black involvement in premarital sexual relations was seen as immoral and licentious. Today, it is interpreted as part of the sexual freedom movement and has become an annual $10 billion dollar industry. All of these changes may be perceived as part of a social system that denies any value to a racial minority's value system unless or until it becomes a part of the dominant group's cultural context (Skolnick, 1992).

Black Nationalist Family Studies

Research from a Black nationalist perspective not only considers Black families nonpathological but delineates their strengths as well. The first significant work was that of Andrew Billingsley (1968) in the era of Black power movements. Billingsley's work was a combination of the reactive and nationalist orientations. He challenged the Moynihan report for its depiction of the Black family as pathological but continued to accept many normative values of White middle-class family life. Billingsley was, however, one of the first scholars to perceive the Black family as viable and to indict the political and economic system for its neglect of Black families. His initial study has been elaborated on and extended by a number of other Black scholars. In the post-Billingsley (1968) period, the more significant works on Black families were produced by young Black scholars. A large number of articles and books were devoted to the strengths of Black women (Cade, 1970; Ladner, 1971; Staples, 1973). In general, these studies focused on the severe conditions that Black women encountered and their courage and strength in overcoming those obstacles. Another landmark study was by Robert Hill (1972). Hill was the first scholar to systematically define and examine the strengths of the Black family. Furthermore, he used quantitative data to support his propositions about the positive values in the Afro-American family life.

At the end of the 1960s, controversy was still raging over the Moynihan report (1965). Moynihan's assertion that "at the root of the deterioration of Black society was the deterioration of the Black family" (p. 5) stimulated extensive theory formation and research on the Black family. Over 100 books and 1,000 articles related to the Black family were published between 1970 and 1990. That twenty-year period produced ten times more Black family literature than the entire hundred years before. Moreover, it was a qualitatively different genre. In the early stages, it was primarily a response to the triumvirate of Frazier (1939), Moynihan (1965), and Rainwater (1970), who had uniformly depicted the lower-class Black family as pathological. Subsequently, researchers began to produce studies of the Black family as an autonomous unit.

The Neoconservative Era

Two decades after the Moynihan report, there was a basic transformation in ideology and research on the Black family. Prior to the seventies, the common wisdom was that Black families, in comparison to White middle-class families, were dysfunctional units that could not carry out the normative functions ascribed to that institution. In the following decades, the research emphasis shifted to the investigation of stable Black families and their conformity to middle-class family norms. However, it was in those same decades that the economic losses of Blacks were translated into greater family instability for many of them, again raising the question of the relationship between Black family stability and changes in the larger society. Based on the latest census data (Bureau of the Census, 1990), there was a dramatic increase in teenage pregnancies, out-of-wedlock births, single-parent households, and marital dissolution among Blacks of all social classes. While these trends parallel developments in White families during the same period, they inspired a change in theory and research on the Black family.

The neoconservative mood of the 1980s gave rise to a greater visibility of books on the Black family that could be embraced by political conservatives. Among those books were the works by Jewell (1988) and Wilson (1987). While both authors appear to disclaim the label of neoconservatives for themselves, their theories of Black family problems lend themselves to the conservative side of the political spectrum. For example, Wilson simply repeats the Moynihan line about the social pathology of inner-city Black families. His call for the deemphasis of race-specific policies will be used to undercut support for affirmative action and a host of social welfare measures. Jewell's book (1988) advances the thesis that liberal social programs played a major role in the decline of biparental Black families over a twenty-year period. Her alternatives to these welfare measures are a combination of self-help measures through the use of kinship networks and institutions in the Black community.

Along with the expansion of Black family research came the development of new theoretical constructs. Allen (1978) has identified three ideological perspectives or value orientations in Black family studies: cultural deviant, cultural equivalent, and cultural variant. The *cultural deviant* approach views Black families as pathological. The *cultural equivalent* perspective confers a legitimacy on Black families as long as their family life-style conforms to middle-class family norms. The *cultural variant* orientation depicts Black families as different but functional family forms. In an analysis of the treatment of Black families in the research literature between 1965 and 1978, Johnson (1988) discovered that the literature shifted dramatically from a cultural deviant to a cultural equivalent perspective in the 1970s. The cultural variant perspective, which views the Black family as a culturally unique, legitimate unit, continues to be underrepresented in mainstream journals. In fact, predominantly Black journals and the special issue of the *Journal of Marriage and the Family* on Black families (Peters, 1978) accounted for 74 percent of the articles published using a cultural variant perspective in the 1970s.

Major Scholars of the Black Family

It is generally accepted that the precursor of sociological research and theories on the Black family was the late Black sociologist E. Franklin Frazier. He began investigating the Black family in the 1920s, and his works are still considered the classic studies of Black family life in America (Frazier, 1932a, 1932b, 1939). As a sociologist, Frazier was primarily interested in race relations as a social process, and he sought to explain that process through the study of the Black family. Through his training in the University of Chicago's social ecology school, Frazier came to believe that race relations proceeded through different stages of development, with the final stage being assimilation. Since it is through the family that the culture of a group is transmitted, Frazier chose this group as the object of his sociological study. Using the natural history approach to the study of Black family life, he explained the present condition of this group as the culmination of an evolutionary process, its structure strongly affected by the vestiges of slavery, racism, and economic exploitation. Slavery virtually destroyed the cultural moorings of Blacks and prevented any perpetuation of African kinship and family relations. Consequently, the Black family developed variegated forms according to the different situations it encountered (Frazier, 1939).

Variations in sex and marital practices, according to Frazier, grew out of the social heritage of slavery, and what slavery began, the pattern of racism and economic deprivation continued to impose on the family life of Afro-Americans. The variations that he spoke of included the following: (1) the matriarchal character of the Black family, whereby Black males became marginal and ineffective figures in the family constellation; (2) the instability of marital life, because the lack of a legal basis for marriage during the period of slavery meant that marriage never acquired the position of a strong institution in Black life and casual sex relations were the norm; and (3) the destruction, through the process of urbanization, of the stability of family life that had existed among

Black peasant folk in an agrarian society (Frazier, 1939). Most of Frazier's studies were limited to pre–World War II Black family life. His research method was the use of case studies and documents whose content he analyzed and from which he attempted to deduce a pattern of Black family life.

The next large-scale "theory" of the Black family was developed by Moynihan (1965) and pertained to Black family life that existed in the 1960s; it was based largely on census data. Moynihan developed the thesis that "at the heart of the deterioration of the fabric of Negro society is the deterioration of the Negro family" (p. 5). He attempted to document his major proposition by citing statistics on the diminishing rate of Black marriages, the higher rate of Black out-of-wedlock births, the prevalence of female-headed households in the Black community, and the shocking increase in welfare dependency caused by the deterioration of the Black family.

This study of the Black family, commonly referred to as the Moynihan report, generated a largely critical response. The reasons are obvious. In effect, Moynihan made a generalized indictment of all Black families. And, although he cited the antecedents of slavery and high unemployment as important variables historically, he shifted the burden of Black deprivation onto the Black family rather than indicting the American social structure (Rainwater and Yancey, 1967). The Moynihan report assumed a greater importance than other studies on the Black family for several reasons. As an official government publication, it implied a shift in the government's position on dealing with the effects of racism and economic deprivation on the Black community. The conclusion drawn by most people was that whatever his solution, it would focus on strengthening the Black family rather than dealing with the more relevant problems of racial segregation and discrimination.

It is reasonable to assume that if Frazier had written in a later period, he would probably have taken Black nationalist tendencies and their impact on Black family structure into account. Unlike Moynihan, he would undoubtedly not have placed the blame for the Black condition on family structure.

But Frazier's and Moynihan's studies share certain commonalities. Both deal with the Black family in a structural manner. That is, they examine its form and the arrangement of roles within the family constellation rather than the behavior that transpires within the structure (Platt, 1987). Only in the post-Moynihan study by Lee Rainwater (1970) are the dynamic processes that take place critically examined.

Just as Moynihan attempts to quantify Frazier's suppositions about the Black family, Rainwater tries to expand on, and analyze in depth, the Black family's role in the "tangle of pathology" that pervades the Black community. The Rainwater thesis is essentially the same as Moynihan's: that Black family disorganization evolved out of a history of enslavement and racial discrimination and that as a result, Black family life itself has become a major factor in sustaining and perpetuating the poor conditions under which Black Americans are forced to live. Or, as Rainwater (1966, p. 258) states the problem, "The victimization process as it operates in families prepares and toughens its members to function in the ghetto world, at the same time that it seriously interferes with their ability to operate in any other world." There are some, albeit minor, distinctions between the Moynihan and Rainwater investigations of Black family life. Unlike Moynihan, Rainwater confines his analysis to lower-income Black families and does not generalize his findings of massive family disorganization to the entire Black population. But he does note that other literature on Black family life suggests that his findings are not applicable only to his sample of 10,000 people in the Pruitt-Igoe housing projects in St. Louis.

The work of Jessie Bernard (1966) reflects a typical middle-class bias in studying Black family life. Bernard ignores income levels as determinant variables in the explanation of Black family life and formulates the concept of two "cultural strands" to shed light on Black family patterns. These relate to the degree of acculturation—that is, to the extent to which individuals have internalized the moral norms of Western society as these exist in the United States. One strand is labeled the *acculturated;* in this case, Western norms become an intrinsic part of people's personality. This is generally considered the "respectable" strand. The other strand is known as the *externally adapted*. Among this group, the norms relating to marriage and the family are only superficially adhered to; they are not a matter of internal conviction. This group learns to use and manipulate White culture rather than taking over its norms (Bernard, 1966).

A somewhat similar middle-class bias occurs in Billingsley's work (1968), but unlike Bernard, he concentrates heavily on economic forces influencing the pattern of Black family life. Billingsley views many manifestations of the Black family as a result of the overrepresentation of Black families in the poverty category. The Billingsley position differs from that of Moynihan and Rainwater in that he sees the Black family as a strong and resilient institution, both in a historical and a contemporary sense. However, Billingsley uses middle-class models and norms to support his position. Instead of stressing the fact that Black marital and family behaviors represent positive functions and values in the social organization of the Black community, he accepts the negative view of the Black family and responds that this negative situation is a predictable response to repressive forces in American society. For example, he devotes an entire chapter to successful upper-class Black families rather than outlining the positive values in much of working-class family life (Billingsley, 1968).

Even more disappointing is Billingsley's structural study of the Black family. Like previous authors, he confines himself to describing the family structure and the arrangement of roles in the family constellation. He does not explore the interior of the Black family and examine some of the sociodynamic processes that contribute to its character. His view is mostly that of the middle-class sociologist who accepts middle-class norms, concludes that most Black families share middle-class value orientations, and prescribes action to eliminate poverty to bring disadvantaged Black families into conformity with the model middle-class family.

But despite its weaknesses, Billingsley's work represents an advance over previous research and theory on the Black

family. At least he recognizes that the Black family constitutes
a unit of considerable variety and complexity, that many of
its constituent features are a misunderstood source of strength
in the Black community, and that some of its characteristics
have been given invidious labels by those whose motives are
politically suspect.

On this foundation, others have tried to develop a sociology of the Black family. In the post–Billingsley era, most of
the theorists have responded to the Moynihan thesis about
the instability of Black families. Additionally, they have
attempted to delineate the structure and function of Black
families. The goals may have been similar, but the perspectives, again, have fallen into one of Allen's typologies (1978).
Studies by Heiss (1975), Scanzoni (1978), and Willie (1988)
would belong in the cultural equivalent category. Both Heiss
and Scanzoni use quantitative analysis to illustrate that Black
families are stable, egalitarian, and functional units. They
make this judgment on the basis of how well these families
meet the Anglo-Saxon middle-class ideal. Willie uses qualitative analysis and examines a variety of Black families. Poor
Black families are still depicted as less-than-healthy units.
Hill's study (1972) of the strengths of Black families occupies
a middle ground. Through the use of census data, he demon-
strates that Black families, like White families, adhere to such
sacrosanct American values as strong work, achievement, and
religious orientations. He also stresses the more unique traits
of strong kinship bonds and role flexibility in the Black family, although he does not link them to an autonomous cultural system.

Reflecting the conservative political ideology of the
period, many books and articles appearing in the 1980s
argued that liberal welfare and social policies had created a
welfare-dependent class that was destroying the Black family.
One of those books was by K. Sue Jewell (1988). She contends
that these social policies not only failed to bring about the
significant Black progress expected in the civil rights era, but
they destroyed the mutual aid and support networks of Black
American families.

Her methodology consists mostly of examining the literature on Black families and social policies and drawing her own conclusions about the status of Black families and the effectiveness of social policies. Although she claims a nonpartisan approach, most of her criticism is reserved for the "liberal" social policies of the 1960s and 1970s. This thesis has several serious flaws that render it less than useful to policy makers and students of the Black American family. One is her central assumption that social policies played a major role in the decline of the two-parent families among Black Americans. Her main support for this thesis is that the decline of the biparental black families happened during the twenty-year period when these social policies were created or were in effect. Other students of Black family destabilization have been more inclined to attribute those changes in family structure—for both Blacks and Whites—largely to the shift of American jobs overseas, the change from industrial jobs to service and high-technology occupations, and the redistribution of wealth from the poor to the wealthy in the 1980s.

The work of Wilson (1987) has assumed the dominant position in Black family studies once occupied by the Moynihan report (1965) and, in some circles, is almost as controversial. Wilson's book *The Truly Disadvantaged: The Inner City, the Underclass, and Public Policy* is not a study of the Black family but of the lower-income Black population in general. Only one chapter in the book directly concerns the Black family, and it solely discusses the impact of economic changes on its structure. While Wilson acknowledges that the cause of Black family destabilization is the high rate of unemployment among Black males, he only sees economic forces as a contributing factor; he fails to emphasize the combination of racial and economic forces that have placed Blacks in such a high-risk position in the American economy from the outset. When he deals with noneconomic variables, it is to depict the culture of inner-city Blacks as dysfunctional in meeting the requirements of American industry. This work is a logical continuation of his earlier book, *The Declining Significance of Race: Blacks and Changing American Institutions*

(1980), in which he argues that class factors have become more important than racial forces. The appeal of that earlier work seemed to be the deemphasis on racial discrimination as a significant variable and the attendent implication that race-specific remedies were no longer necessary.

Summary

In this review of perspectives on Black family life, it is clear that few studies have had the explanatory power to enrich our understanding of this institution. This theoretical deficit exists partly because there is no theory of the family in general and also because the theories applied to this unique institution have been designed to explain nonfamily phenomena. The explanations of Black family functioning we have were all developed in some kind of political context, either positive or negative. Politics enters the study of the Black family because this social unit has not been perceived as an institution, but as a social problem. The research has focused disproportionately on lower-class Black families to address the problems of poverty, welfare dependency, and crime. These problems might best be understood by other theories regarding social structure, not by studying their consequences in the family life of Black Americans.

In summary, it can be said that in trying to understand Black family life, there remain questions to be answered and answers to be questioned. What we know from past research is that the Black family has evolved a unique structure and style to cope with the circumstances it has confronted. To build a theory of the Black family, we must ascertain the norms and values that animate the process of family interaction and determine how that process is related to the forces that have shaped it and its various expressions in American life. This is the task before us; how we can fulfill it is not clear. In this summary and analysis of theory on the Black family in the past century, one fact seems certain: we cannot develop a viable theory of the Black family that is based on the myths and stereotypes that have pervaded the research of past years.

3

Work and Money:
The Struggle

Money derived from work is a basic determinant of the way families survive, maintain self-esteem, and acquire social prestige within their communities. While work has always been a part of the Black experience, it has not always generated monetary and self-gratifying rewards. Underemployment, pay inequity, and job layoffs have resulted in dehumanizing experiences for far too many throughout history. Among Blacks in precolonial Africa, work took place within two distinct arenas—their home and their own communities. There work and money were equally yoked: one reaped what one sowed. After colonization, a third arena was added—the unpaid and paid work force of the White world. It is in this last arena that the equity between work and money broke. Within these three arenas, we chronicle the work and money nexus and its impact on Black family life.

Transition Economy: Africa, Slavery, Freedom

Since antiquity, the family has been an economic unit that most often divides its labor along gender lines. This is not to imply that "men's work" and "women's work" are biological imperatives, noninterchangeable, or never shared. Cross-cultural studies clearly show that task assignments (apart from childbearing) are primarily a function of cultural, political, and economic forces and not biology. Among the African Nambikwara, for example, infants are cared for by the fathers, and the chiefs' concubines prefer to engage in hunting rather than domestic work (Strong and DeVault, 1992). Among the Ibo tribe of the Niger Delta region, women and men toil together in planting, weeding, and harvesting, whereas the Yoruba women only help with harvest. While caution must be taken in generalizing from the diverse traditions of various African peoples, studies of contemporary West African women reveal a fairly common feature of economic independence—a pattern rooted in their early history.

In precolonial West African societies, for example, women had entrepreneurial relationships with domestic and foreign traders. As producers, processors, traders, craftswomen, distributors, and manufacturers, they parlayed their profits into larger and more profitable enterprises. Not only were women cherished as daughters, but they were an economic asset as wives and a cornerstone of the economy; thus they accrued high self-esteem and enormous influence in their communities. African wives enjoyed complete control over their goods and profits. While family authority rested with the husbands, the wives' ownership of goods remained completely separate from their husbands'. Their earnings enabled them to buy clothes and jewelry, improve the family menu, provide gifts for relatives, and in effect contribute to the family's wealth. In patrilineal societies, wives' economic independence was facilitated by the fact that children belonged to the fathers. A wife had no primary responsibility for either the rearing or economic support of the children, thus allowing her greater liberty in using her earnings to her own desires (Griffin, 1982).

With the advent of slavery, the ruthless exploitation of African-American labor began: the linkage between money, work, and self-worth was broken. The division of labor that existed prior to enslavement was replaced with a work structure of the masters' choosing. Without a legal right to acquire property or to acquire literacy skills, slaves had no relationship to the means of production that could bring them status in the slave or nonslave communities. Slaves gained few tangible physical benefits from their work in increasing the crop profits or in making White families comfortable. Self-esteem and worth primarily derived from the slaves' contribution to their own families and communities. Grannies' folk medicine usurped the White physician, who rarely took calls from the slave quarters. Despite inordinate hours of slave work, fathers and grandfathers found energy to make animal traps for catching game and to tend gardens in order to supplement their families' limited diet. They also made furniture and shoes to enhance their families' comfort and health. Ironically, even their efforts to care for themselves and their families helped maintain their masters' work force and enhance their profits (Jones, 1985; Blassingame, 1972).

Females and males were equal in the sense that neither gender wielded economic power over the other. Slaveholders did not support sentimental platitudes about the delicate constitution of female slaves. Both genders worked at a forced pace under close supervision of White men and women. Because slavemasters frequently suspected slave women of faking illness or "playing the lady" at their expense, many were brutal in forcing women into the field during pregnancy and soon after childbirth. Women at times were mandated to labor in areas generally reserved for men, such as in the muscle-power work of clearing land of trees, rolling logs, and chopping and hauling wood. However, only male slaves labored as skilled artisans or mechanics. The cost of training women for these trades was considered too high, since their work lives were frequently interrupted by childbearing and nursing.

While many historians often make distinctions between the work-load intensity of the house and field slave, there is little evidence supporting the advantages of housework. From late July to December every man, woman, and child was engaged in picking cotton. As few as 5 percent of all antebellum adult slaves served in their master's house. Of these, most lived in the slave cabin at night and rose early in the morning to perform duties in the master's house before heading for the fields. Further, housework was laborious, and juggling the demands of each member was frustrating. Meals had to be cooked and served three times a day, "flies minded" with peacock-feather brushes, and dishes washed (Jones, 1985; Jones, 1982; Griffin, 1982). An account of a son's memory of his mother's work illustrates how writers have exaggerated the elite position of the house slave: "She served as personal maid to the master's daughter, cooked for all the hands on the plantation, carded cotton, spun a daily quota of thread, wove and dyed cloth. Every Wednesday she carried the White family's laundry three-quarters of a mile to a creek, where she beat each garment with a wooden paddle. Ironing consumed the rest of her day. Like the lowliest field hand, she felt the lash if any tasks went undone" (Jones, 1982, p. 246). Because of the watchful eyes of multiple masters within the house, many slaves preferred the open field. Regardless of work location, unremitting toil without pay was the dominant characteristic of the enslaved African.

Their chains loosened by the distractions of the Civil War, nearly 400,000 slaves voluntarily or involuntarily joined the Union Army in hopes of freedom for themselves and their families. For most, it was their first promise of a cash incentive for their labors as well as the beginning of their experience with unpredictable and unequal wages. Throughout the war and into the early 1900s, Blacks resisted the Northern work ethic of yielding to employers all authority over their individual working conditions. They also resisted the Southern system, which expected the entire family—husband, wife, and children—to work in the fields (Pinderhughes, 1991; Malveaux, 1988; Jones, 1985). In an effort to control both their labor and family life, former slaves turned to sharecropping.

As sharecroppers, they cultivated and harvested all the crops on a White person's land in exchange for shelter and a share of the profits or produce. This voluntary system, however, was not benevolent. Blacks were disenfranchised and constantly struggled with the unscrupulous financial dealings of their White employers. The constant pressure of poverty meant that sharecroppers in the rural South experienced many of the situations common in contemporary inner cities. For example, female-headed households increased as men migrated from rural areas in search of temporary work in the burgeoning industrialized Southern towns. Men's mobility and the labor-intensive agrarian economy meant that there was little social condemnation of out-of-wedlock childbearing. Under these conditions, children were a genuine labor asset. Nevertheless, most families were headed by two adults who (like single parents) were often embedded in a supportive extended family (Lemann, 1991; Williams, 1990; Jones, 1985; Harris, 1976; Johnson, 1934).

Exercising the limited control they had over how family labor would be organized, sharecroppers chose to sharpen the sexual division of labor—the major obligation of wives was domestic, and husbands' responsibility was fieldwork. This was not an effort to model the White nuclear family, for as seen in Chapter Nine, the extended family was a viable structure. Rather, all efforts were being made to keep wives and daughters away from the dangerous whims of White supervisors.

Low and unpredictable wages meant that most families relied less on wages and more on family farming, fishing, and trapping to keep body and soul together. Few wives could remain home only tending children. Some wives tried to turn special talents and skills into a secure living, but the poor Black community could not support such professions as seamstresses, midwives, and schoolteachers. Further, Whites as employers were too resentful and unreliable. Whites believed that any able-bodied Black should be confined to the soil or serving as a domestic worker. To the liking of Whites, low wages paid to Black men forced most Black working women into one of the few available occupations—domestic work with White families. According to the 1890 census, almost 40 percent of all Black women were employed outside the home, the overwhelming majority in farming and the legendary domestic and washerwomen occupations. Household employment not only paid poorly, but it was irregular, part time, and seasonal—a pattern that remains even today. In some areas, domestics waited on designated streets as potential employers drove by to choose their employee for the day. The

low pay and unpredictability of such work forced Black
women into holding multiple jobs (Harrison, 1989; Jones,
1985; Malveaux, 1988).

Pushed out of the South by agricultural mechanization
as well as by the boll-weevil infestation and storms that
destroyed cotton in the early 1900s, Blacks began their great
migration North. On arrival, Black domestic workers found
themselves in head-on competition with White immigrants.
These immigrants organized to keep Black men and women
out of the most menial jobs. Consequently, the majority of
Black workers remained in agriculture. However, when European immigration was stopped during World War I, Black
workers replaced White immigrants in domestic work. As the
demands of the war economy increased and the national man-
power crises intensified, Blacks were overtly recruited from
the South to the North to work in the steel mills, auto and
railroad companies, and cotton industries. Some entered fac-
tory work over the resistance of lower-class Whites, who
wanted these higher-paying jobs for themselves. These jobs
doubled the salaries of many Blacks. From 1910 to 1920, more
than 50,000 Blacks arrived in Chicago, increasing the Black
population by 117.1 percent. Similar influxes were reported
in Pittsburgh, New York, Philadelphia, and St. Louis
(Lemann, 1991; Harrison, 1989; Wilson, 1980).

It was shortly after this period that Frazier (1939) wrote
about the disorganizing effect that slavery and urbanization
had on Black families. Occasionally the men came first, with
the idea of sending for their wives and children. Some families that were reunited later experienced the husband-father
deserting when jobs were not forthcoming, while others were
never reunited. Thus, female-headed households rose in number. Frazier further notes that marriages were kept together in
the South by the social control exercised by the church, the
lodge, and the opinions of socially close neighbors; these controls were lost in the Northern cities. The social upheaval
that resulted in loss of community support for family stability
was further compounded when the White soldiers returned
from each of the World Wars and took over their old jobs,

leaving many Black heads of households unemployed or underemployed and struggling to capture the most menial work. The Depression placed hardships on all Americans, but Blacks were hit the hardest. Black and White wives, who were more apt to get a job than their men partners, pitched in to weather the economic storm. This is not to say that women had economic superiority during this time. When men worked, regardless of race, they were more likely to work more hours per week and earn substantially more than their wives; thus as an aggregate they did better than the women. For those who could not find work, the New Deal programs developed under the Roosevelt administration helped to create jobs—reducing unemployment from seventeen to seven million (Darity and Myers, 1984; Bullock and Stallybrass, 1977; Harwood and Hodge, 1971). But even here, legislation was designed in such a way that it discriminated against some of the occupations in which Blacks were concentrated. Thus, many Black workers fell through the cracks of social programs (Jones, 1985).

Until recently, this trend of economic hardships was said to have created a fragile Black family. It is argued that no woman wants to marry or stay married to a man who lacks a job. Conversely, men without jobs and money lose not only status in the eyes of women, but faith in their ability to perform the culturally prescribed roles of husband and father. Thus, a Black man is less likely to ask for a woman's hand in marriage or stay in a marriage. Lack of job or money is the most frequently emphasized explanation for marital instability. However, the contemporary indictment of unemployment and poverty for hindering marital formation and stability is not historically justified.

Historical revisionists note that Black families have survived periods of severe hardships. Despite Frazier's concern about female-headed households emerging from slavery and the great migration, the overwhelming number of Black marriages were intact during these periods as well as up until the late 1960s. The question that begs an answer is why poverty and unemployment create family disorganization in contemporary society but built family strength in an earlier era. A response to this question is needed to fully understand the socioeconomic dynamics of present marital relationships without placing primary blame on Black families.

Some argue that under slavery, Blacks were exploited but fully employed. Because they were valued as property, the White masters assured them the minimum subsistence of meals, lodging, and clothing. For the sake of worker morale, families were generally preserved (Frederickson, 1976). Fogel and Engerman (1974) extend the nonexploitation argument by claiming that slaves were willing collaborators in a capitalist enterprise. They worked for real incentives, which included upward mobility within the slave system and protection of their families. Yet emancipation brought massive unemployment and meager wages and the marital union remained intact. This is attributed to the fact that postslavery families were often able to make ends meet by combined efforts of family members working at multiple jobs. Moreover, the farming experience of Blacks matched the demands of an agrarian work force. When the economy moved toward industrialism, Blacks found jobs as reserve labor during the two World Wars and as strikebreakers during labor disputes (Johnson, 1990).

Today, competition for the most menial jobs is keen. This situation is due to four factors—technological revolution, job relocation, immigration, and trade policies. When high technology replaced the agricultural and industrial economy, Blacks lacked the required skills to compete. This crisis intensified when jobs moved from the inner city to the suburbs. Lack of efficient transportation from the inner city to the suburbs meant that suburbanites and those most affluent captured these jobs. Moreover, within the urban Black ghetto a substantial number of the "mom-and-pop" stores that provided employment for local residents closed not only as a result of the urban riots of the 1960s, but also because of the changing nature of Black family residential patterns. As Black consumers have become less segregated, they no longer provide the captive stable consumer market on which Black retail merchants depend.

Further, Black merchants must compete against two major groups—large regional or national corporations with outlets in the ghetto and merchants of other ethnic and racial descent. Finding few job opportunities outside of the Black community, Asian, Hispanic, and Middle Eastern immigrants have replaced Black family stores, filling the new stores with their own family members. As a result, these merchants have been targeted with anger, protest, and riots from Black residents, who claim that they take from the community without giving back jobs. These groups—along with White women—have also displaced Blacks in menial service and domestic jobs in restaurants, airports, and department stores (Brock, 1991; Gibbs, 1988b). In the private sector between 1974 and 1977, White women occupied 53 percent of new jobs, White men 26 percent, and Hispanics 12 percent. Despite the fact that Asians represent only one-fifth the number of Blacks, they obtained the same number of these jobs as Blacks— 5 percent.

Mom-and-pop stores proved to be a mixed blessing for Black American urban dwellers. These stores served as a stepping-stone for many families, who used the stores' proceeds to educate their children in colleges desegregated by the civil rights movement. Rather than use their education, management, and technical experience to expand the family business, these children chose less risky occupations with higher and more predictable pay. Of those who pursued entrepreneurship, the majority developed service firms (for example, law, accounting, automobile sales). Given the reluctance of banks to lend money to businesses located in the ghetto, most of the firms are outside the reach of ghetto residents. Unfortunately, for those remaining in the lower-income urban neighborhoods, the family store stepping-stone has vanished (Brock, 1991; Jeffries and Brock, 1991; Hill, 1990; White, 1992).

Adding to this situation is the loss of jobs due to imports. Black men are disproportionately affected by imports in the auto, steel, and rubber industries, and Black women by imports in the apparel industry. During the 1970s, the "internationalization" of the American economy was established.

Japanese and Western European electronics producers and automakers, among other foreign firms, began importing to the United States. The foreign competition forced many American factories to close. As a result, in 1970 Blacks gained 229,000 jobs through exports but lost 287,000 jobs because of imports—a net loss of 58,000 jobs. Once unemployed, Blacks are twice as likely as White displaced workers to remain unemployed (Jeffries and Brock, 1991; Hill, 1990).

The unemployed often rely on welfare. Whether public assistance undermines the institution of marriage is an ongoing debate. This debate is spurred by the fact that among welfare families, marital dissolution is almost twice as high as the chances of marital formation. No doubt those states that continue to require the husband's absence as a condition of welfare receipt force marital separation. However, it is a mistake to assume that welfare itself increases marital dissolution and deters marriage formation. There is no convincing evidence that length of time on welfare, changes in welfare benefits, or number of programs from which benefits are received have any significant effects on the likelihood of marital formation or divorce (Washington, 1989; Furstenberg, Brooks-Gunn, and Morgan, 1987; Rank, 1987; Darity and Myers, 1984). The culprit is not welfare, but the economic difficulty of Black urban life—high male unemployment and the declining pool of eligible males to head families.

The lack of fit between the skills of Blacks and the present technological economy, coupled with unintended negative consequences of trade and immigration policies, has created an unprecedented job crisis for Black families. This crisis has occurred during a period when American firms were engaged in large-scale mass production of consumer goods. The capacity of American families to consume these goods emerged as and gave definition to the American dream. Of course, the ability to consume depends on adequate incomes from jobs. Because most Whites had jobs, they were able to consume these goods without seriously straining the household budget; thus, a new and higher standard of family living emerged. The high unemployment and heavy concentration of Blacks in blue-collar and low-paying occupations means that many Blacks cannot even hope to create this new lifestyle for themselves or their families. Thus, many are discouraged from marrying. For example, among both Black and non-Black men, the proportion with intact marriages rises as income increases. Not surprisingly, this income–marital status relationship is stronger for Blacks than for Whites (Jeffries and Brock, 1991; Myers, 1990; Taylor, Chatters, Tucker, and Lewis, 1990; Bureau of the Census, 1983).

Given this economic context, it is not surprising that most recent studies focusing on Black-White differences in divorce find that Blacks have higher marital separation and dissolution rates, lower remarriages (one-fourth the rate of Whites), a faster declining remarriage rate over the last two decades, and a longer period between divorce and remarriage. In fact, if divorce and separation rates are combined, the Black-White differences are even greater. The justification for combining the two is that desertion and separation are "the poor person's divorce," reflecting the difficulty those in the low-income brackets have in obtaining the money for divorce. Despite this difficulty, Blacks are more likely to separate and divorce regardless of income (or the presence of children), although the differences rapidly narrow as income increases (Hampton, 1982; Glenn and Supancic, 1984; Leslie and Grady, 1985; Bumpass, Sweet, and Martin, 1990; Bureau of the Census, 1991c).

Gender Economics

Apart from the purely economic issues, there is an important interplay between social norms and economics that weighs heavily on Black families. In American tradition, the role of wage earner is prescribed to the male, leaving housekeeping and childrearing to the female. The economic stability of the White patriarchal family is based on this division of labor— most important, on the economic dependency and general subordination of the wives. Inadequacy in these prescribed roles is likely to create individual and marital tension. In attempting to fulfill these roles, Afro-American marriages, however, have faced obstacles not encountered by most Americans. The Black male is generally assumed to be in a humiliating "double bind"; he must prove his manhood by being the primary—or ideally the sole—wage earner, but he is denied access to legitimate ways in which to fulfill this role (Cazenave, 1981). He is the last to be hired and the first to be fired. When he works, he earns on the average less than three-quarters of the income of Whites (Bureau of the Census, 1991a). Once unemployed, he is about twice as likely as White displaced workers to remain unemployed (Hill, 1990). While it is true that during the 1970 and 1980 periods of economic recession and recovery, unemployed Black women found jobs more slowly than Black men, White men, and White women, society holds males as the primary family breadwinner; a woman's unemployment is viewed less harshly. A sizable majority of young Black people, particularly females, believe that regardless of who is the better wage earner, the primary responsibility of the male is to financially provide for his family (Harrison, 1989; Heiss, 1988; Johnson, 1980). This preference for male financial leadership is perhaps even stronger in American West Indian families, who represent a growing minority within the Black community. For them, any departure from male authority directly attacks manhood and is totally intolerable (Millette, 1990).

The "double bind" tightens in the face of flashy mass media messages that stimulate in American families an insatiable appetite for material goods. Black more than White wives play the role of "chief consumptionist." Irrespective of their own financial contribution, many Black women, particularly middle-class women, expect marriage to double their material wealth (Heiss, 1988; Osmond, 1977; Scanzoni, 1978). A honeymoon on a Princess Cruise Line ship and yearly vacations thereafter, a home, fine clothing, the latest home technology, cars, campers, and so on are all part of their American Dream. In trying to fulfill this dream, credit buying is used to compensate for lower income. Almost twice as many Black as White middle-class people owe on their credit accounts.

The higher the social class, the more likely Black families will be to be in debt with a new car. In contrast, the White upper and lower middle classes have new cars in the same proportions.

Moreover, there is no evidence that Blacks have given up their fetish for "fine threads," or what Frazier in 1957 labeled the "clothing cult." Even when their income is lower and their families smaller, Black upper and lower middle-class families spend more on clothes than their White counterparts (Landry, 1987). In the wake of low income, pay disparities, desires for increased consumption, and mounting debts, the American Dream is a nightmare for many Black males. This nightmare is intensified by the four back-to-back recessions and record-level inflations of the 1970s and 1980s, which reduced the "real income" of Blacks to a greater extent than Whites—by 11.6 versus 9.4 percent (Bureau of the Census, 1991a). Not surprisingly, Blacks are half as likely as Whites to express satisfaction with their salary and more likely to complain about the cost of living (Gallup, 1980). They cannot even expect to live up to the standards of the particular class in which they find themselves. Even among the upper-middle class, Whites not only exceed the income of Blacks by nearly $2,000, but they have four times their total wealth (Landry, 1987).

Tragically, the Black male's best efforts in preparing for the job market do not necessarily assure him equal employment opportunities or the chance to live out the dream. One such example is reflected in the relationship between education and unemployment rates of Blacks and Whites (National Center for Education Statistics, 1991a; see Table 1).

With one exception, at each educational level Blacks are twice as likely as Whites to be unemployed. Further, Whites with an elementary school education have lower unemployment rates than Black high school graduates, and Blacks attaining four or more years of college have an unemployment rate similar to White high school graduates. Employment discrimination is an inescapable reality. The exclusion of Black youth from the expanding sectors of the economy

**Table 1. Unemployment Rate by Education of Persons
Sixteen Years and Over, March 1989.**

Educational levels	White race	Black race	Difference
All educational levels	4.6	11.7	–7.1
8 years or less	8.4	13.7	–5.3
1–3 years of high school	9.9	21.4	–11.5
4 years of high school	4.9	11.9	–7.0
1–3 years of college	3.2	7.4	–4.2
4 or more years of college	2.0	4.5	–2.5

Source: Adapted from National Center for Education Statistics, 1991a, p. 361.

destroys hope of racial parity in the near or distant future
(Myers, 1990; Harrison, 1989; Malveaux, 1988; Larson, 1988;
Smith, 1985; Beckett and Smith, 1981).

Moreover, Blacks learn early that even money does not
give them the sense of mastery over their life that is available
to Whites. Blacks at the same social status as Whites receive
fewer dollars and less respect, prestige, and sense of social
worth. Over the past few decades, Blacks have shifted their
measurement of family well-being. Rather than using their
distance from slavery as their benchmark, they now evaluate
how close they are to the American Dream relative to Whites.
Of particular interest to Blacks is parity in education, income,
and job status. Unfortunately, while Blacks have made absolute progress in terms of educational, occupational, and
income attainment, the more they strive, the more they
become disadvantaged relative to Whites (Bureau of the Census, 1989; Scanzoni, 1978). A review of every age and educational group since 1940 provides strong support for the fact
that Blacks are disproportionately "learning without earning." The 1989 census data (Bureau of the Census, 1991b)
illustrate this continuing disparity (see Table 2).

Hence, in order to survive and to reach the American
Dream, many Blacks have taken on alternative life-styles.
Most noteworthy are the dual-worker couples.

Table 2. Mean Income by Years
of School Completed, March 1989.

Race/gender	High school years		College years		
	Less than 4	4	1 to 3	4	5 or more
Male					
White	21,122	27,461	32,311	42,498	54,280
Black	18,914	21,310	25,935	33,060	42,289
Difference	2,208	6,151	6,376	9,438	11,991
Female					
White	13,994	18,030	21,982	27,118	33,564
Black	12,929	16,039	19,457	24,481	29,764
Difference	1,065	1,991	2,525	2,637	3,799

Source: Adapted from Bureau of the Census, 1991b, pp. 59–61.

Dual Earners

The high proportion of dual earners among Black families reflects their strong work ethic and their determination to survive in a racially hostile society. Although the majority are clustered in low-paying and unskilled jobs without fringe benefits or the protection of a union, they seldom voluntarily leave the work force. In 1984, there were 6.8 million Afro-American families, 3.5 million of which were married couple families. The majority (64 percent) of these married-couple families had working wives (Malveaux, 1988). This dual-earner tradition traces back to 1890, when Black wives were ten times more likely than White wives to be in the labor force. In 1984, when Black families earned 55.7 percent of White family income, income from the wife narrowed this gap to 82 percent. Her gap-narrowing contribution continues even today (Bureau of the Census, 1989; Harrison, 1989; Malveaux, 1988).

Furthermore, Black women contribute more to the total family income than do White working wives (40.6 versus 32.8 percent in 1990), and their relative contribution within the family is projected to increase. The percentage differential between Black male and female employment rates has declined from 27.0 in 1970 to 17.4 in 1980. It is projected to decline to 9.3 in 1995, representing a labor force participation rate of 61.2 percent of all Black females (Bureau of the Census, Racial Statistics Branch, Population Division, special requested statistics, Feb. 1992; Harrison, 1989).

The Black middle class owes its existence to the working wife. Without wives' income, middle-class Black families fall below their class's standard of living by several thousand dollars, whereas middle-class White families exceed this standard by several thousand dollars. When faced with the hypothetical question of what the impact would be if the wife lost her job, two-thirds of middle-class Blacks said it would make things difficult or create a crisis. Blacks were more likely to anticipate a serious crisis than Whites (Landry, 1987). Yet today, we know more about Black female-headed welfare families and absent nonworking husbands and fathers than we know about how the majority of married Black couples negotiate and balance their work and family lives, or how they feel about their work-family experiences.

Because Black females have been more economically independent, many developed attitudes of freedom and equality unknown to most nineteenth-century and even many twentieth-century females—attitudes that predated the modern women's liberation movement. The consequences of this independence for Black marriages are of concern. While African men consider economically independent women an asset, it is unclear whether such women are considered in the same light among Afro-Americans. Messages received from the mass media strongly indicate that Black males are threatened by the accomplishments of Black women.

Contrary to the prevailing media hype, Black working wives tend to increase the perception of their husbands' own sense of job competence and marital happiness, at least among the middle aged. Whereas White husbands' perceived job competence rises as wives' employment status drops from white collar to blue collar to unemployed, that of Black husbands is highest when wives hold white-collar jobs and lowest when wives are homemakers (Draughn, 1984). Unlike Whites, both Black males and females expect wives to enact both a "family-oriented" and a "job-oriented" role in marriage. Furthermore, Black husbands rate their wives higher than White husbands do on having the knowledge and experience to hold a job. In general, the employment status of wives has a minimal effect or no effect on the likelihood of divorce or feelings of satisfaction with marital affection, companionship, communication, and understanding. Some studies, however, show that husbands' tempers tend to be shorter in dual-job families. And if they have to perform most of the in-home chores without help, they are likely to become dissatisfied with their family life (Broman, 1991; Strong and DeVault, 1992; Taylor, Chatters, Tucker, and Lewis, 1990; Scanzoni, 1978). But these findings appear to be more related to overwork and equity issues than to the gender of the person making the financial contribution.

The weight of the evidence indicates that for Black families, the gender identity of the individual contributing may not be as predictive of satisfaction as overall family life-style, prestige, and economic status (Strong and Devault, 1992; Ball and Robbins, 1986; Scanzoni, 1978). Higher occupational status is tantamount to higher income. In the context of traditional gender-role expectations, it is assumed that a family's life-style is determined by the male head of household. Thus, when the Black wife works, she creates an illusion that the life-style they enjoy can be maintained on his salary alone. This illusion may be a fair trade-off for any loss of status experienced by the husband.

In light of the positive transference of Black wives' employment to their mates' sense of job competency, one would expect Black husbands to have more positive attitudes toward wife employment than White husbands. Recent studies show that both race and class influence the proportion of men who have favorable attitudes toward wives working. Among husbands, more lower-income Black husbands have favorable attitudes than any other class or racial group. Given that higher-income Black husbands are half as likely as lower-income Black husbands to favor their wives working, the eco-

nomic-need factor is clearly shaping the working-class husband's attitude.

Further evidence of the economic factor is reflected in
the fact that in the lower-income group, Black wives are more
likely to work than their White counterparts when their husbands have a negative attitude toward their employment (Beckett and Smith, 1981). This can be perceived as a potentially
serious source of tension. Although similar data are not available for Blacks, White husbands whose wives work against
their wishes become depressed, particularly if the husbands'
own wages are low (Ulbrich, 1988). Given the same conditions, we would not expect the same emotional reaction from
Black husbands for three reasons.

If the couple's life-style is raised, Black men appear to
respond positively to the additional income. Second, wives'
employment translates into more egalitarian decision making,
which in turn increases marital satisfaction (although it
should be noted that there is evidence that the highest level of
marital quality occurs in husband-dominant couples). Finally,
unlike White wives, Black wives who enter the labor force
against their husbands' wishes manage to maintain a positive
attitude toward their employment. They are more likely to
see work as not only a right but part of what it means to be a
"good" wife and mother. This attitude no doubt helps defuse
hostility on the husbands' part (Strong and Devault, 1992;
Gibbs, 1990; Harrison and Minor, 1978; Osmond, 1977).

Although Black men's psychological well-being does
not seem to suffer from an employed wife or the shift to more
egalitarian decision making, their own employment is critical
to their well-being and their marriage. Social scientists confirm the popular belief that regardless of race, men define
their well-being through their work; men who see themselves
as successful in the work role will perceive themselves as successful in the husband role (Draughn, 1984). Husbands who
are satisfied with the rewards of their jobs are the ones who
are most likely to express contentment with the amount of
companionship, affection, communication, and understanding they receive from their wives (Scanzoni, 1978). An indica-

tion of this work-family linkage and its process is evident in a study of Black, predominantly male police officers.

According to this study, quality of marital communication, sex, and emotional support is directly traceable to perceptions of job discrimination. The sources of job strain are many; however, feeling that one's skin color is the reason a deserved assignment or promotion is denied creates a sense of powerlessness that spills over into family life. Black workers who feel powerless become ineffective workers and lovers. In its worst manifestation, those who are discriminated against begin to lose interest in their clients, treating them as impersonal objects. Mates who do not care what happens to their clients at work often bring the same attitude home, creating sufficient detachment and disinterest in the relationship to increase the probability of marital separation and divorce (Johnson, 1989).

In the rural Southern regions where discrimination is most apparent, Black husbands appear to have the most dissatisfaction with their marriages. A study conducted in this area during the early 1970s showed that regardless of socioeconomic status, young Black married men reported the lowest levels of satisfaction of all marital statuses (Ball and Robbins, 1986). The alarming reality implied is that income does not overcome the sense of powerlessness for rural Southern Black males. The long history of discrimination may have led to low expectations for marriage for even high-income Black men in the South. In the prime of their working years and on the tide of the civil rights movement, they may expect more from their efforts than the racist Southern social order grants. Their deprived economic position relative to Whites may be more obvious in the South, especially in the rural parts, than in other areas of the country, where the legacy of an exploitative past is not as vibrant. Thus, these husbands may perceive their provider role undercut to a greater degree than others of similar status but who live elsewhere.

Perceived relative deprivation may create frustration that leads to still another outcome—hypertension. Black husbands are well aware that their training and efforts will not produce the same rewards as those of White husbands. Also, about 20 percent of these husbands earn less than their wives (Bureau of the Census, 1983). Thus, they are at the greatest risk for feeling relatively deprived. This deprivation results partly from differences in paths for occupational advancement. Educational attainment is not closely tied to advancement in unskilled and semiskilled blue-collar jobs, in which many Black husbands find themselves. In contrast, many of their Black wives hold jobs in fields like education, nursing, and social work, where each academic degree or unit of advanced education results in higher pay. Data from a recent study of Black parents where the mother was the senior partner (educationally and economically) suggest that apart from hereditary factors, the combination of racial discrimination and relative deprivation within the marriage could create tension that results in hypertension for Blacks, particularly for men (Myers, 1990).

Female Multiple Roles

As far as females are concerned, the triple role Black women perform is assumed to have negative consequences for family satisfaction. Based on the "scarcity hypothesis," early research assumed that there is a fixed and limited quantity of human energy. Therefore, the more roles, the greater the likelihood of stress, overload, and tension from facing incompatible expectations from different people. Those women who are saddled with total responsibility for housework and who are involved in multiple roles are most likely to experience role strain (Goode, 1960).

In this theoretical context, we observe that compared to White wives, Black wives spend less time on housework and receive more help from their husbands, particularly if they are employed. This suggests that the potential for strain as a result of multiple roles is mitigated by husband support. However, employed and unemployed Black wives still perform significantly more child care, cooking, cleaning, and laundry than their husbands (Wilson, Tolson, Hinton, and Kiernan,

1990; Beckett and Smith, 1981). When home duties are repeated at work, they can become stressed out from boredom. The heavy concentration of Black women in domestic work until 1970 emphasizes their historical double duty and the competition between obligations to two households: their own and that of their employer. Yet this duty redundancy only tells part of the story. As we have seen, domestic workers often hold down multiple jobs, thus increasing the potential for stress from work overload (Malveaux, 1988). As the occupational opportunities broadened for women, Black women moved from domestic into clerical, service, and low-level white-collar positions (Swinton, 1991; Harrison, 1989; Jones, 1985). Although role redundancy may be absent, they may still experience work overload. An example is the blue-collar/white-collar marriages.

The shortage of Black males and their limited opportunities means that many of these nondomestic women workers are married to husbands who are below their social status—that is, their husbands work in semiskilled blue-collar jobs. Whereas white-collar husbands have flexible hours for dealing with work-family conflicts, blue-collar husbands' jobs are characterized by inflexible work schedules that allow little time for family business. Thus, blue-collar/white-collar marriages are more likely than dual-career families to organize family household duties around traditional lines, with women assuming the full-time social roles of wife, mother, and worker. In this situation, wives have few escapes from twenty-four-hour duty and conflictual work-family demands.

The negative aspects of multiple tasks are reflected in a recent major study showing those Black women with fewer roles—the unemployed—having among the highest family life satisfaction regardless of their parental status, while married employed women have among the lowest levels (Broman, 1991). The scarcity hypothesis appears to have firm support.

However, scholars are not in agreement on whether multiple roles lead to stress and dissatisfaction. Unfortunately, empirical studies of the last decade primarily give information on Whites, and the few studies on Blacks provide support for both sides of the argument. Counteracting the findings supporting the scarcity hypothesis is a growing school of thought that extols the virtues of multiple roles for women. Rather than assuming that human energy is fixed, greater role involvement is assumed to enhance or increase resources for ego gratification and development of self-worth. The more roles people perform, the greater their ability to maintain positive thoughts about some aspects of self, the greater their resources for trading off negative aspects of each role, and the more legitimate excuses they can use for not meeting obligations in a particular role (Linville, 1987; Thoits, 1983).

Consistent with this line of thinking, a study of the social roles of middle-age and older Black women finds that women who work have higher self-esteem. This is particularly the case for older middle-age women who have high incomes and are in good health. The role combination of work and marriage appears to especially enhance health for middle-age Black women. Given their position in the life cycle, few perform all three roles of employment, marriage, and parenting; most perform only two roles—parental and work. Nevertheless, the evidence shows that certain roles, especially the work role, are important for the psychological and physical well-being of middle-age and older Black women. Given the economic situation of Black Americans and the decreased income and health among older Blacks, being tied to any occupation should enhance self-esteem. Further, in a society of many "manless" and lonely Black women, being married must inflate their self-worth (Coleman, Antonucci, Adelmann, and Crohan, 1987).

Moreover, self-esteem not only derives from the ego gratification experienced from being among the few married or gainfully employed.[1] The contribution women perceive they are making to their community is also important. One study of Black women college students found that those entering nontraditional fields such as law, politics, and medicine did so not for ego needs or competitive urges, but because of their strong drive to serve the needs of Black people. It is reasonable to speculate that for these women, satisfaction derived from contributing to the general welfare of the Black community and financially supporting and nurturing their families outweighed any negatives from performing multiple roles (Harrison, 1989).

In sum, the benefit of multiple roles is controversial. Often the mere existence of multiple roles is assumed to indicate strain or enhancement in Black women's lives. It is possible that those with multiple roles are most likely to be at risk of overload. Thus, it is the overload rather than the number of roles that presents a problem. On the other hand, it is possible that multiple-role strain seldom becomes an issue. Many Black women create strategies, such as childrearing support networks, to avoid work-family strain (Malson, 1983). Also, one must question the appropriateness of self-esteem levels as a sufficient measure of the consequences of multiple roles. Self-esteem does not speak to the issue of general strain. Hypertension and high blood pressure—illnesses suffered by many Black women—appear to be more related to life-style, such as work overload, than to genetic disposition and personality (Myers, 1990). Even within a hostile environment, Black women and men have managed to feel good about themselves. Harsh conditions often encourage self-reliance, self-confidence, a stronger sense of community, and for the religious, a test of their steadfast faith (Harrison, 1989). In sum, self-esteem may rise with increased levels of strain.

We can tentatively conclude that excessive role obligations can impair psychological and physical well-being. However, multiple-role occupancy in and of itself is generally beneficial in a society where "rolelessness" is a social risk factor for Blacks. The paucity of studies and the differences in the study group preclude a definitive conclusion—the jury is still out.

Summary

It is often stated that regardless of race, marriage has provided an abundance of rights for husbands and numerous duties (often simultaneous) for wives. The peculiar history of Blacks, however, has distributed the duties somewhat more evenly. Nonetheless, the few recent studies suggest that Black women are more likely than Black males to feel overworked and dissatisfied with their lot (Strong and DeVault, 1992; Broman, 1988, 1991; Zollar and Williams, 1987).

Scanzoni (1978), who studied middle-class Black families, goes so far as to say that the marital union rests strongly on the wife's subjective definition of the family's economic situation. What seems to matter most is her family's consumption potential in comparison to other Blacks. The more positively wives define their economic situation, the more likely they are to be satisfied with the emotional aspects of marriage. Further, since American wives are the emotional housekeepers of their marriages, Black wives are more likely to evaluate these aspects less positively than their husbands—making the husbands' economic success critical.

Although Black husbands express greater satisfaction with marriage than their wives, economics is also critical to their happiness. Black employed husbands have greater family life satisfaction than unemployed men and employed wives. A report on Black husband-fathers finds that those who experience unemployment or feel discouraged because they are not living up to their image of a "good provider" are at the greatest risk of unhappiness (Bowman, 1989). While provider role failure is bothersome to younger men, it is a more sensitive issue for the middle aged, who have less reason to remain hopeful in face of bleak upward-mobility prospects.

Black husband-fathers who are frustrated by inadequate schooling and postindustrial labor market barriers are finding it necessary to come to terms with the prospect that their provider role problems may be irreversible. They must face the stark realization of the widening gap between Black working- and upper-class families, and the even greater economic gap between Black and White families. Unfortunately for Black husbands, wives, and children, this inequality has become a "permanent" part of the American economy (Swinton, 1991; Bowman, 1989; Wilson, 1980).

In his concern for the Black workers who filled the jobs

left by White workers during World War II, Marcus Garvey (1967, pp. 36–37) warned that "Negroes are still filling places, and as time goes on and the age grows older our occupations will be gone from us. . . . We will gradually find our places among the millions of permanent unemployed." Although he was anticipating the loss of jobs when the White war veterans returned home to reclaim "their" jobs, his words are prophetic, given the chain of events that has shut a significant number of Blacks out of the shrinking job market in contemporary American society.

All in all, it appears that both Black males and females have reasons to venerate or scorn work and marriage. Unfair labor practices have had negative consequences for marital formation and functioning. However, regardless of gender, Blacks who are married are generally happier than the unmarried (Zollar and Williams, 1987). The long historical pattern of role sharing and mutual support continues to serve as an indispensable buffer against the harsh reality of work and income discrimination.

Since money derived from work is the basic determinant of the way families survive, maintain self-esteem, and acquire social prestige within their communities, the contemporary condition of Black families is disturbing. Slavery was demoralizing in its minimum subsistence of individuals and its system of work without pay. But without work in a postslavery society, even minimum subsistence is improbable, presenting numerous Black families with a bleak future.

4

Patterns of
Sexual Intimacy

One can speculate that throughout human history, sexual behavior has been the subject of inordinate interest, and that all cultures have attempted to explain its nature. Understanding human sexual behavior, however, has been complicated by the fact that physiological and sociological factors are closely intertwined. Among nonhuman species, inborn tendencies prevail. But in human society, although the basis for sexual motivation is physiological, sexual behavior is never determined solely by physiological factors.

In looking at the painful history of race relations in America, it seems clear that much of the discrimination that Afro-Americans have encountered is due to the existence of White American stereotypes about their moral character. As a number of polls have revealed, a large number of White Americans see Blacks as a morally loose group. In fact, the sexual stereotypes about Blacks become the ultimate justification for their exclusion from White schools, jobs, and neighborhoods. Many of the ideas held about Black sexuality in particular are exaggerated versions of general attitudes toward the poor. American society was founded on the Protestant ethic, which equated poverty with sinfulness, idleness, vice, and a belief that the poor are sexually indulgent (D'Emilio and Freedman, 1988).

The image of Blacks as sexual beings is deeply rooted in American history, culture, and religion, and we can only

72

touch on this complex problem here. In the early twentieth century, respected scholars imputed a genetic basis to the alleged hotter sexual passions and richer fertility of the Black population (Wyatt, 1982). Subsequent research has done little to invalidate the earlier generalizations about Black sexual drives or to illuminate the sociocultural forces that differentiate between Black and White sexual behavior. The result has been the fostering and reinforcement of stereotypes about Black immorality and hypersexuality. Such false images serve to fuel the fears of those people who remain psychologically wedded to America's puritanical view of sexuality and strengthen their resistance to Black demands for equal opportunity in American life.

Historical Background

Unlike most White Americans who came to this country as voluntary migrants, the majority of Blacks were brought to the New World as slaves. The experience of slavery brought about significant changes in black sexual attitudes and behavior. The diversity of African cultures precludes any generalizations about African sexual behavior. But in the past, African sex life could only be understood in relation to the kinship groups, which provided the basis of the mores and folkways that regulated sexual relations. One difference between the African and American concepts of sex is the lack of religious strictures among Africans. Throughout Black Africa there is a concept of a supreme being and creator, but the supreme being issues no edicts concerning sexual morality. The violation of sexual laws is an offense against individuals and not against God (Diop, 1987). All the available evidence indicates that sexual behavior in Africa before and after marriage was under strict community and family control (Bennett, 1981).

In the experience of slavery, pronounced alterations in Black sexual behavior took place. Whereas community and kinship groups had regulated sexual relations in Africa, most of the control over the Black sexual impulse during the American slave era was exercised by the White slavemaster. The attitudes of most slave owners toward the slaves was that they were property, a commodity to be bought and sold. During this period, reproduction among the slaves had a certain value to the slave owners, and free sexual activity was tolerated. In some cases, Black females, at the onset of puberty, were mated in the same way that the livestock of the plantation were mated. Black women were compelled to breed children—to be the breeder of human cattle for the field or auction block (Franklin, 1987).

This practice of human breeding was one factor that encouraged a permissive code of sexual conduct among the slaves. Where there was no coercion, free sex practice was followed as an end in itself. More important, the nexus between sex and marriage was attenuated among America's Black population. Although some slave owners permitted and even encouraged the legal union of their slaves and regarded marriage as a permanent association, many others expected slaves to mate without the formality of a marriage ceremony and did not regard the union as necessarily permanent. With this attitude of the slavemasters and the harsh conditions of slave life, a permissive type of sexual behavior developed (Ducille, 1990).

The role of organized Black religion was very different from that of the White religions. Although Blacks adopted the religions of their White slave owners, the puritanical traditions that influenced White sexual standards never took hold as strongly among them. The Black church's function related more to tension reduction rather than the setting of sexual standards. Premarital and extramarital sexual behavior has never been countenanced by the Black church, but neither has there been any strong attention paid to America's moral code and its violation by their parishioners. Possible exceptions, of course, could be found in certain middle-class and fundamentalist churches in the Black community (Bennett, 1981). After slavery ended, Afro-Americans probably did have a more permissive sexual code than many Euro-Americans, but that fact has to be placed in the proper historical context. In accordance with Freudian theory (Freud, 1938), we can assume that the sexual drive exists in all individuals and has to be expressed in some form. Historically, males in this culture have been allowed unrestrained libidinal expression. Greater restraints have been placed on women, especially bourgeois women. Even among working-class White women, the norm of chastity has been honored more in the breach than in its observance. A major reason for the class difference is the greater use of economic resources by middle-class males to exact sexual chastity from the women in their class. Where there was no exchange value of sex for material reward, the libido thrived in a more liberated way (D'Emilio and Freedman, 1988).

Thus, because the Black masses enjoyed a greater sexual equality than was possible for Whites in the postbellum era, a more permissive sexual code developed. Moreover, some of the controls on Euro-American sexuality did not exist to the same degree among Afro-Americans. Black males did not classify women into bad and good groups on the basis of their virginal status. White men did make these distinctions, and women were eligible for the respectability of marriage according to their classification in one group or the other. During an epoch in which the majority of White women were economically dependent on men, this was an effective censor of their sexuality. Black women, in the main, were more economically and psychologically independent (Simpson, 1983).

Socialization into Sexual Behavior

While the legacy of slavery and the effect of racial inequality strongly influence the sexual practices of Afro-Americans, there are many other social forces that impinge on the sexuality of Blacks. Among those forces is their socialization into sexual behavior. The process of socialization is designed to condition people to accept the behavioral patterns of their society. This is the way individuals acquire their knowledge of sex and the particular values their society expects them to hold in relation to it. Blacks face a unique situation, in that the sexual values inculcated in them by their parents are coun-teracted by the conditions under which they live (Wyatt, Peters, and Guthrie, 1988). There is little doubt that Black parents teach their female children to remain sexually chaste before marriage. When Pietropinto and Simenauer (1977) asked a group of Black adults how important it was that a girl be a virgin when she gets married, almost 30 percent of the men stated that it was very important, compared to 31.5 percent of White males.

Some parents reinforce this standard by using negative sex education techniques for Black children. Sex is made to appear horrible and extremely dangerous. Some females are warned by their parents (usually the mother) that any sexual relations before marriage will automatically result in con-tracting a venereal disease. This type of sex education often creates severe anxiety in females about their sexual impulses and responses. They become afraid to have sexual intercourse and are convinced that all sexual behavior is sinful (Fox and Inazu, 1980). However, some Black mothers encourage daugh-ters to seek contraceptives (Nathanson and Becker, 1986). Those parents who maintain an awful and complete silence on the subject of sex, yet harshly punish any form of sexual play, are no better. When the children's interest in sex becomes stronger, they frequently discover that their parents do not wish to discuss sex in a way that is significant to them. Therefore, it is not strange to find that many Black children acquired their knowledge of sex through the folklore and myths of their peers. Most of the Black females in the sexual surveys learned about sex through a source other than their parents (Shah and Zelnick, 1981).

The peer group constitutes an important source of sex information for the Black female. A typical pattern is for most ghetto children to discover sex for themselves, then dis-cuss their discovery with close friends or relatives. Many Black females choose an older sister for this purpose. Thus, much of the Black female's socialization into sexual behavior takes place among same-sex peer groups (Shah and Zelnick, 1981; Billy and Udry, 1985). One reason for the importance of the peer group is the absence of the parents from the home. The prevailing marginal economic status of Black people is an important factor in determining their sexual behavior. A high rate of unemployment and underemployment among Black males forces many Black women into the labor market, leaving the children in many families without parental supervision. Thus, the present social conditions and economic deprivation under which Black people are compelled to live create a salient difference in the sexual socialization of Black and White women in this society.

The conditions of poverty mean that Black females are often subjected to the many dimensions of sex long before White middle-class females become aware of its existence. It is understandable, then, to find that Black females have their first full sexual intercourse some years earlier than the typical White female. According to the Centers for Disease Control (1991), the level of exposure to premarital sexual relations is higher for Black females in their teenage years than for White females. Thus, at age twenty a much larger percentage of Black women report having had premarital sexual relationships than White women. In fact, at the age of fifteen, more Black females have experienced sexual intercourse than White males of the same age ("New Study of Teenage Sex," 1991).

Several studies reveal that Black males are more likely to use condoms at a later age than White males (Pleck, 1989). White males learn about sexual intercourse at a later age than Black males. Due to poorer nutrition, the Black male reaches puberty at a later age than his White male counterpart. A critical distinction between Black and White males is the tendency of White males to use substitutes of masturbation, fellatio, and fantasy for direct sexual intercourse. Masturbation, for instance, is more likely to be the source of the first ejaculation for the White male, while intercourse is for the Black male (Belcastro, 1985). A larger percentage of White males reported being sexually aroused by being bitten during sexual activity, seeing a member of the opposite sex in a social situation, seeing themselves nude in the mirror or looking at another man's erect penis, hearing dirty jokes, reading sadomasochistic literature, and viewing sexy pictures. Conversely, Black males tended to engage in premarital intercourse at earlier ages and to have intercourse and reach orgasm more frequently. As Bell (1978) notes in his analysis of these data, the Black male's overabundance of sexuality is a myth. The sexuality of Black and White men just tends to take different forms, and neither group has any more self-control or moral heroism than the other.

The fact that sexual activity among young Black American males begins at an earlier age, is more frequent, and involves more partners than among their White counterparts may partly be a function of differences in social class. Although some studies have focused on college-level males, the studies among Blacks tend to be of individuals who have been shaped by their class of origin's values regarding sexual matters. One racial or cultural factor is the greater involvement of the young Black male with women at a younger age. Apparently, White males are more likely to confine their associations in adolescence to other boys. Westney, Jenkins, Butts, and Williams (1991) found that Black male adolescents were likely to be romantically involved with girls as early as age ten. The kind of rigid gender segregation found in White culture is largely absent from Black society. For example, Blacks are less likely to have the extensive number of all-male clubs, organizations, or colleges.

The sexual code of young Black males is a permissive one. They do not, for example, divide Black women into good (suitable for marriage) and bad (unsuitable for marriage) categories. In the lower-income groups, sexual activity is often a measure of masculinity. Thus, there is a greater orientation toward premarital sexual experimentation. In his study of premarital sexual standards among Blacks and Whites, Staples (1978) found that the White male's sexual permissiveness could be affected by a number of social forces, such as religion, but the Black male was influenced by none of them. Hendricks (1982) found that few Black male adolescents were aware of the increased risk of teenage pregnancy, but there was an almost unanimous wish not to impregnate their sexual partner. In another survey, Black male high school students reported their group believed that a male respects his partner when he uses a condom (Pleck, 1989).

More important than their sexual education are the larger values some young Black men learn. Often this involves buying into a well-defined system for manipulating and controlling women. Early in the life cycle, they realize that money and women are the two most highly valued objects that they can gain in our patriarchal system. Women can supply a male with money or what it can buy and are also a means of satisfying his sexual desires. Hence, a competitive system emerges among men to make as many sexual conquests as possible. It is a dog-eat-dog system whereby the man with the best rap, clothes, or style wins—with women as the spoils. Lost in this struggle for one-upmanship is a feeling of relatedness toward women and an articulated awareness of women's human qualities (Benjamin, 1983).

A most blatant indicator of the woman qua property ideology among many Black men is the violence that often accompanies the sexual experience. This can be seen in the common and legendary practice of "taking sex." The strong-arming of Black women into sexual submission is pervasive, and it is not confined to working-class Blacks but is equally represented among the bourgeoisie (Anderson, 1989). A number of cases involving sexual assaults by prominent Black males against Black women have made headlines (Norment, 1992). And just as White males have traditionally been able to use their privileged economic resources to force sexual submission on White women, there is increasing evidence that a few Black men are not reluctant to use the perquisites of high office or wealth to accomplish the same end. One of the few studies of the attitudes toward rape found no racial differences in these attitudes. However, Blacks anticipated more negative reactions from the police and expressed greater distrust of other institutional agencies than did Whites. Consequently, Black women were more likely to anticipate turning to parents or family members for support (Howard, 1988).

The Influence of Gender

Although we recognize that much of Blacks' sexual behavior is a function of forces beyond their control, there must be some accountability for these individual actions. In every study comparing Black and White sexuality, the greatest conflict exists among gender roles—not racial groups. Black and White men are much more united in the meaning of sex than are Black men and Black women. Men of both races are similar in the very selfish peer-oriented nature of their sexual behavior (Wyatt and Lyons-Rowe, 1990). Male-female disparities in sexual attitudes and behavior are so obvious, and pervade all strata of the society, that it would be easy to assume that this is the natural order of things. However, any historical or cross-cultural analysis would challenge many notions concerning innate differences among males and females in sexual attitudes, desire, or behavior. From both a historical and a cross-cultural perspective, societies and epochs may vary greatly as to the kinds of behavior approved for different gender-role groupings. These variations reflect the fact that gender has both biological and social components (D'Emilio and Freedman, 1988).

Male-female differences in sexual attitudes and behavior, then, are probably influenced by both biological and cultural factors. Females, to a greater degree than males, are oriented toward the responsibilities of parenthood. In patriarchal societies, greater controls are also placed on female than on male sexuality. Women are constantly taught that their self-respect and the respect of others for them are contingent on their use of restraint and discretion in sex matters. On the other hand, patriarchal culture condones, and even encourages, the expression of the male libido. Sexual relations may have various meanings and functions for men. One of those functions is the maintenance of a male virility cult.

What we mean by the male virility cult is that within the male's peer group, status is based on the number of women with whom one is able to have sexual relations. Thus, the male who has a variety of premarital sexual experiences occupies a prestigious position within his peer group. Sexual conquest of women becomes strongly associated with the definition of masculinity (Anderson, 1989). It is sex as a symbol of manhood that supposedly motivates the male's sexual interest as well as physical desire. The virility cult is supposed to have its strongest adherents among Black males. Because the ordinary manifestations of masculine identity were all but impossible for large numbers of Black men, sex became a major instrument of power and status. Black men are supposed to be emasculated and must resort to emphasizing secondary aspects of masculinity, such as the sexual exploitation of women (Anderson, 1989).

On the verbal level, some Black men do view themselves alternately as lovers and exploiters of women. As Liebow (1966) found, these men are eager to present themselves as exploiters to women as well as to men. Within the lower-class group, men not only see themselves as exploiters of women, but expect the same of other men. When the behavior of other men does not meet their expectations, they cannot comprehend their actions. In reality, however, the tendency to use women to gain sexual and economic ends is counteracted by other feelings and goals, especially the male's need to have a meaningful relationship with a woman that he loves. Despite the self-image of many Afro-American men as users of women, many Black women find in Black men very supportive individuals, in both an emotional and an economic sense. Schulz (1991) discovered that many of the women in female-headed households were receiving support from boyfriends.

The discrepancy between the rhetoric and the reality can best be explained by the kind of image Black men wish to sustain, both within the peer group and in their community. Many males do not want to be seen as emotionally dependent on the "weaker" sex. Thus, they counter any suspicions that they are a weakling, sucker, or patsy by projecting an image of being a user of women, a person whose interpersonal involvement is based only on the economic and sexual gain that accrues from such a relationship.

Contrary to prevailing beliefs, Black men are showing increasing concern for the needs of women. The Pietropinto and Simenauer (1977) study reported that only 7.5 percent of Black men found engaging in foreplay an unpleasant aspect of sex. About a third of Black men felt the sex act ended when they had one or more orgasms, and another third believed it was finished when they both had an orgasm. While 29.6 of Black men expressed belief that women should take responsibility for birth control, 22.9 percent said men should have protection ready and 28.3 percent agreed that both should use some sort of protective method. Almost 71 percent of Black men said they deliberately try to delay their orgasm as long as possible, until their partner has an orgasm or seems satisfied. A majority of Black men reported thinking of their current partner during intercourse or masturbation. Approximately a third of Black men said they believe being in love is the most important thing in life, and another third felt if you are in love, sex is better.

Much less research has been done on the sexuality of Black women. Consequently, the cultural beliefs about Black female sexuality run rampant, while the facts remain unexamined. In no other area are there so much speculation and so many stereotypes and myths. The image of the Black woman is that she is the most sensual of all female creatures. One Black writer has even described her as "potentially, if not already, the most sexual animal on this planet" (Hernton, 1965, p. 136). While his description was meant as a compliment, the mainstream view of Black sexuality is rife with negative connotations. The lusty sexuality that White Americans impute to Blacks represents to them the most abnormal, vulgar, and base instincts of mankind. The image of the Black woman as innately sexual is a combination of fact and myth. But that image has been used as a justification of ethnocentric practices, because it suggests unrestrained sexual urges that civilized people do not possess (Ducille, 1990).

Cultural beliefs about Black women's sexuality emerged out of the experience of slavery. The sexual availability of slave women allowed White men to put White women on a pedestal, to be seen as the goddesses of virtue. In a way, this became a self-fulfilling prophecy. For this reason, and also because of general Victorian assumptions about female purity, White women were held aloof from the world of lust and passion and in many cases became more inhibited emotionally and sexually. But while the White woman's experiences and status inhibited sexual expression, the Black woman's encouraged it.

The Black female's sexual morality was at least partly shaped by the experience of slavery. As the violation of her body became routine, she could not value what was unavailable to her—virginity (Davis, 1983). She sometimes even came to look on herself as the South viewed and treated her. In fact, she often had no other morality by which to shape her womanhood. From a review of the conditions under which Black women lived, it is easy to understand why the rigid sexual regulations so prevalent in the dominant American society failed to emerge in the Black culture.

Considering the different history of Blacks, and the different conditions under which they now live, mainstream sexual standards may not be applicable to Black females. While Blacks are influenced by the majority culture's moral code, it does not necessarily guide their behavior, especially in the lower-income group. According to Ladner (1971), premarital sex is not regarded as an immoral act but rather as one of those human functions that one engages in because it is natural. The Ladner study (1971) revealed that working-class Black women basically have two responses to premarital sex: indulgence or nonindulgence. These responses are motivated by pragmatic considerations. Those who do not indulge in premarital coitus are concerned with avoiding pregnancy and often do not condemn girls who do not abstain. The abstainers are more likely to be upwardly mobile and are worried lest a premarital pregnancy prevent them from achieving a higher status than their parents. The middle-class element in the Black population has been very conscious of its unique position in relation to the masses of Black folk. In earlier periods, they placed an exaggerated emphasis on moral conduct and developed a puritanical restraint, in contrast to the free and more liberated sexual behavior of the dominant Black population (Giddings, 1984).

The Class Dimension

As these remarks suggest, some of the gender-role differences we find are related to class values. In the lower classes, the expression of masculinity receives a great deal of emphasis. The lower-class male, for example, is distinguished from the middle-class male in that he moves sooner into heterosexual relationships. In the lower-class environments, distinctions between masculinity and femininity are sharply drawn. The male frequently sees sexual conquest as a strong sign of his masculinity. In many cases, the sexual act is defined as satisfying only the male, thereby providing him with an activity considered exclusively male. The double standard of sexual conduct is much stronger in the lower-class group. Both sexual rights and sexual pleasure are perceived as male prerogatives. In most cases where a double standard of sexual conduct prevails, it allows males more sexual freedom than females (Anderson, 1989; Wyatt and Lyons-Rowe, 1990).

Smith and Udry (1985) found, for instance, that Blacks have more knowledge about sex at an earlier age than Euro-Americans. This is the result of certain elements in Black culture and other variables that are related to their class location. For instance, the greater socialization by peers leads to a heightened awareness of sex at an early age. Also, the fact that Black children become more involved in adult activity affects their sexual socialization. They are more likely to live under overcrowded conditions where they can observe sexual behavior at first hand. This they attempt to imitate, thus making an earlier entrance into heterosexual relations than do Whites. This does not necessarily involve sexual activity, just male-female social interaction. For instance, despite the psychosexual development theories of Freud (1938) and some others that "normal" boys should become interested in girls in early adolescence, in many Black neighborhoods, Black children are socialized at a younger age into heterosexual relationships (Westney, Jenkins, Butts, and Williams, 1991).

There are fewer class differences among females. One difference, however, is very salient to this discussion: the age of first intercourse. In general, the higher the class, the later the age of initial coitus—a relationship that is also true of first marriages. This fact is often attributed to the greater propensity of middle-class females to use substitutes of fantasies and masturbation for intercourse. Among working-class Black females, there is a high probability that the first sexual experience will be a violent one. Wyatt (1985) reports that a Black girl has a good chance of being exposed to rape and violence. Fifty-seven percent of the Black women she interviewed reported at least one incident of sexual abuse prior to age eighteen. After the age of twenty-five, however, race and gender differences disappear. According to a nationwide study by Simenauer and Carroll (1982), only 4 percent of men and 9 percent of women between the ages of twenty and fifty-five have had no sexual partners while single. With such a large proportion of Americans engaging in nonmarital sexual activity, there is little room for race and gender variations.

One sees the operant effect of class as a differentiator of sexual expression by looking at variations in the Black community itself. While the Black bourgeoisie has, until recently, represented only a small segment of the total Black community, its sexual values and behavior have often been a reflection of the White bourgeoisie's. Fairly conservative sexual attitudes have been typical of middle-class Blacks. Many bourgeois Afro-American males prefer that their wives stay at home rather than work. Frazier (1961, p. 771) once observed that "there is much irregularity in this class. The importance of sex to this class is indicated by their extreme sensitivity to any charge that Negroes are more free or more easy in their sexual behavior than whites." In its most extreme manifestation, this sexual conservatism was reflected in the in loco parentis stance of Black colleges in earlier periods. In the 1920s, Fisk University had printed regulations that "it was forbidden for two students of the opposite sex to meet each other without the presence and permission of the Dean of Women or of a teacher." A girl and boy could be sent home for walking together in broad daylight (Walters, 1975, p. 37).

During their college years, until the late 1960s, most Black females adhered to a rather conservative sexual code. Many of them remained virgins until after graduation or confined their sexual experiences to a man with whom they had a committed relationship. A typical example is a thirty-two-year-old social worker, who comments: "My point of comparison would be college—ten years ago. Since then I was a young adult, living in a college dorm, there were some very major changes. Probably sexual expectations are the biggest change; since back then we were still in the 'virgin' syndrome" (Staples, 1981, p. 95). The changes she speaks of have, indeed, been most significant, as attested by a thirty-five-year-old female educator who lost her virginity at the age of twenty-two. She declares that "a sexual relationship is a very normal part of an ongoing dating relationship. It may be an early part of the relationship or may develop over a period of sustained non-sexual contact" (Staples, 1981, p. 96).

Prolonged singlehood has imposed a more liberal acceptance of nonmarital sexual activity on the overwhelming majority of middle-class Black women. Whether they wanted to be participants in the sexual revolution or not, the conditions of single life have required a significant alteration of their previously conservative sexual values. Only a small number of them could hold to a traditional stance on nonmarital coitus. That small group also exhibits a high degree of religiosity (Wyatt, 1982).

That few middle-class Black women hold a negative attitude toward nonmarital sexual activity is partly due to general societal changes toward that behavior. The women's movement has helped by legitimizing the right of women to participate in and enjoy sex on an equal basis with men. Yet the sexual revolution as such was much more in conformity with male than female values. As Hite (1976, p. 449) notes, "The sexual revolution is a male production, its principles still concentrated on male values." Many Black women are not comfortable with the new sexual morality. They would rather have a relationship develop along other lines than just sexual ones. Being an unattached single woman and wanting to date means having to deal with the sexual expectations of men. Due to their differential socialization, most men view dating as an instrumental (that is, goal-oriented) activity. What they do on the date is not so important as the aftermath. If the outcome is a sexual experience, the evening is a success. For women, the date is more of an expressive goal, to enjoy the activity and the companionship (Wyatt and Lyons-Rowe, 1990). One pensive position is that of a forty-year-old male political scientist: "Your first interest in a woman is sexual, so that you tend to discover what else (some would say everything else) there is to her in the course of the relationship originally stimulated by sexual attraction" (Staples, 1981, p. 96).

Sexual Practices

The 1960s and 1970s gave birth to what is popularly called the sexual revolution, accompanied by a greater sexual candor in public discussions, books, film, television, art, and dress. Some sexologists claim that sexual behavior did not change— that only the attitudes toward it and the openness surrounding it were affected. However, there are indications that Americans now engage in premarital intercourse at an earlier age, with more partners, and in different ways. One thing has definitely changed: people remain single longer, and—at least until the AIDS epidemic emerged—being a mature single adult became synonymous with sexual experimentation (Simenauer and Carroll, 1982).

One more example of the changing sexual scene is the variety of sexual practices in which Blacks engage. Acts that were once taboo have become commonplace. Probably the greatest change has been in the practice of oral and anal sex. In one study (Pietropinto and Simenauer, 1977), Black men expressed their sexual desires. Their response to the question "what would you most like to do more often" indicates that different sexual positions were desired more, along with their second choice of oral sex. The second choice is most interesting, since oral-genital sex was long considered taboo in the Black community. Yet Wyatt and Lyons-Rowe (1990) discovered that 55 percent of Black women have performed fellatio on a man. Those figures, while a dramatic change for Black women, are considerably lower than the percentage of White females who engage in such practices. Pietropinto and Simenauer report that 57 percent of all Black men find cunnilingus acceptable. Thus, it would appear that cunnilingus has become acceptable among Black men in just one generation—a truly remarkable change.

Unlike White females, who often progress into premarital intercourse after extended periods of petting—that is, sexually stimulating behavior—Black females face an all-or-nothing situation. In fact, the word *petting* is almost unknown to Black people. For instance, many White females have allowed sexual intimacies other than intercourse with the male to preserve their virginity. Such women are known as technical virgins (Belcastro, 1985). A technical virgin in the Black population is very rare. One reason is that some of the petting practices, such as oral-genital relations, were unacceptable to many Black women (Smith and Udry, 1985). Another factor is that sexually enticing behavior can provoke the Black male into physical violence against a Black woman who engages in such acts without the intention of sexual consummation (Staples, 1982).

Homosexuality may be more or less prevalent in the Black than in the White population. There are few available data on the subject for Blacks. Some writers have claimed that Blacks have a greater incidence of male homosexuality than Whites. They hypothesize that female-headed households in the Black community have resulted in a lack of male role models for Black male children (Vontress, 1971). But there is no evidence to support this supposition. As part of their studies of sexual practices, the Kinsey group investigated Black homosexuality. They found that Blacks were more comfortable than Whites around homosexuals and did not perceive them as any kind of threat to their manhood. Consequently, Black homosexuals (male and female) were not as isolated from the Black heterosexual population as was the case among Whites. They were not relegated to their own bars or social cliques. Also, Blacks were more likely to be bisexual than exclusively homosexual (Bell and Weinberg, 1978).

Considering their greater involvement with women, it would be reasonable to conclude that the incidence of homosexuality among Black males is less than among White men. Yet there are no reliable or consistent data on the number of male homosexuals. Kinsey and others (1953) reported that 37 percent of men have had one or more homosexual experiences. Other sexologists have estimated the number of exclusively homosexual men to be between 1 and 4 percent. The Kinsey associates conducted an extensive study of male homosexuals in 1970 that included Blacks. While the Black male gays made up 11 percent of the male homosexual population surveyed, the study did not use an objective selection process. The Kinsey researchers had difficulty finding Black male gays, because they were not as openly engaged in the gay world as their White counterparts (Bell and Weinberg, 1978). But they discovered that Black homosexual males have their first homosexual experience earlier than do White homosexual males, were less likely to hide their homosexuality from family and friends, and reported more female friends (Bell and Weinberg, 1978).

One of the most extensive surveys of Black male sexuality was conducted by Pietropinto and Simenauer (1977). Their results are not directly comparable to Kinsey's, although they asked some of the same questions. They sent out questionnaires to 4,066 men, of whom 240 were Black. Black men represented less than 5 percent of the total group studied and tended to be unrepresentative in other ways. They had lower incomes and less education than the White males studied. In a question on sexual preferences, 9.2 percent of the Black males claimed to be bisexual, compared to 2.6 percent of the White males. Only 1.1 percent of the White males reported they were exclusively homosexual, as opposed to 2.5 percent of the Black males.

The Black lesbian, like her White counterpart, is a hidden figure. Some have even suggested that Black lesbianism is on the increase because of the shortage of Black males. However, Black women's response is often to become bisexual (Mays and Cochran, 1991). The lesbian's experiences with other Blacks do not confirm the earlier observation that Blacks are more tolerant of homosexuality. Lesbian couples complain that their families are not too accepting of their relationship. They also have to move from their residences because of crank calls and constant threats, indicating that Blacks are more critical of lesbianism than of male homosexuality (Hooks, 1988).

The one sexual perversion that many Black women encounter is rape. Contrary to popular belief, most rapes committed by Black men are committed against Black women, not White women. Many of the sexual assaults of Black women by Black men go unreported. There is a significant number of date rapes that occur daily, especially in lower-class life. It often happens when a woman leads a man to believe that she will have sexual relations with him but protests when he reaches the point of vaginal penetration. Sometimes she simply is ambivalent about sexual relations. Other times it may be forcible intercourse. Most rapes do involve friends or acquaintances of the women involved (Lloyd, 1991; Anderson, 1989).

When it comes to the sex book industry, Blacks are simply not involved at all. Despite the many books written on White sexuality, many of them best-sellers, there is not yet one book on Black sexual patterns. White authors have written several books on interracial sexual activity, but few, if any, have the intimate understanding of Black culture and values to handle this difficult and controversial subject. There is probably more Black involvement in pornography. Quite a few of the recent porno films have featured Black female actresses, most of them in interracial sexual action. The same is true of pornographic books and magazines. The *Report of the Commission on Obscenity and Pornography* (President's Commission, 1971) reported that the typical patron of porno films is a White, middle-aged, middle-class married male. The same commission theorized that there is nothing particularly harmful in viewing sexually arousing films. However, many of the regular patrons of these materials are sexually frustrated. One study found that its Black middle-income respondents were uniformly against pornography, and 82 percent believed it to be harmful to society (Timberlake and Carpenter, 1990).

Summary

When the sexual revolution first hit American society in the 1960s, Blacks were slow to adapt to it and did not participate, in any significant numbers, in certain aspects of it. By the 1970s, premarital sexual activity had become the norm for the formerly conservative middle-class Black female. It is impossible to address any issue in Black male-female relationships without taking note of the shortage of eligible and "desirable" Black men. Not only are there about 1.5 million more Black females than Black males in general, but the sex ratio is extremely imbalanced among college graduates. For a long time, Black women have outnumbered Black men.

Consequently, sexually conservative college-educated Black women often meet the sexual demands of their male peers, fully realizing that if they do not, the men can always find women who will. Once liberated, voluntarily or not, middle-class Black women have indulged in a full range of sexual expression. No longer confined to the outdated notions that "nice" women did not enjoy sex, sex outside of marriage, or unconventional sexual practices, Blacks have abandoned traditional taboos. Oral sex, for instance, became something that a majority of Blacks engaged in. But some of the excesses of the sexual revolution have never taken strong hold among Blacks. Few Black women have willingly engaged in one-night stands or changed sexual partners indiscriminately. Some sexual practices—such as group sex, sadomasochism, and father-child incest—are rarely observed among Blacks. Homosexuality, at least on the part of Black males, is more open and tolerated than in the White community, although lesbianism receives a mixed and often hostile reception.

In the 1980s, the news media began to report the end of the sexual revolution, announcing that men and women were looking for commitment and marriage instead of casual sex. This new sexual conservatism coincided with the aging of baby boom women (those born between 1945 and 1960) and the election of a conservative president who supported traditional sexual ideals. Because women were getting older and facing biological deadlines for bearing a child, they started looking for fathers instead of sexual partners.

Adding to the rising tide of conservatism has been the AIDS epidemic. Although AIDS was originally thought of as a White male's disease, the Centers for Disease Control (1991) reports that Blacks and Latinos constituted 30 percent of those diagnosed with AIDS, 70 percent of the heterosexual cases, 70 percent of the cases in women, and 75 percent of all pediatric cases in 1991. However, it seemed to be women who are most frightened of acquiring the disease. Such a fear is disproportionate to the risks women face. About 93 percent of the AIDS victims are men. When the other high-risk group, intravenous drug users, is excluded, the Centers for Disease Control (1991) found that fewer than 1,000 heterosexual Americans have acquired AIDS by intercourse with others who do not belong to one of the high-risk groups (Selik, Castro, and Pappaioanou, 1988).

Any objective examination of Black sexual behavior would reveal that there are many variations in the type and frequency of sexual activity among this group; that the racial differences have their origin in cultural and class differences, not innate biological traits; and that changes over time have brought about a convergence in the sexual attitudes and behavior of the two racial groups. In light of the stereotypical views of Black sexuality that existed in the past, it is all the more amazing to find that in some circumstances, Blacks have more conservative sexual values than Euro-Americans. The motivation behind the previous labeling of Blacks as sexually immoral is quite clear, as we currently witness the redefinition of behavior that was once alleged to be peculiar to Blacks. More euphemistic terms are applied to the same behavior among Euro-Americans. This society apparently restructures its attitudes and practices when the sexual "deviants" are members of the majority group. While we can agree that these events are a mark of human progress, it cannot be ignored that when the same behavior is found among the Black population, the result is the collective indictment of an entire racial group and a concomitant denial of its civil and human rights. As the pace of sexual change makes it difficult to make moral distinctions between racial groups, let us hope that cultural differences in sexual behavior will be recognized as no more than diversity in the spectrum of possible responses to sexual stimuli. Designations of racial groups as superior or inferior on the basis of their sexual values and behavior have no place in a rational and humanistic society.

5

Singlehood and
Partner Selection

Unmarried people have suddenly become this nation's largest minority group. If we count individuals who have never married or are divorced, separated, and widowed, they account for more than a third of America's population over the age of fifteen, and their numbers are growing (Bureau of the Census, 1992). This has been a neglected group in the literature because of their transient status—in earlier years, most would eventually have entered the ranks of the married population. Increasingly, however, Americans are beginning to view singlehood as a way of life. Some will choose it voluntarily, and others will be forced into making the "choice." Afro-Americans are more likely to face the dilemma of singlehood or marriage. As a group, they are proportionately more likely to be unmarried, divorced, separated, or widowed. Approximately 70 percent of the Black female population aged fifteen to forty-four would fall into our singles category (Bureau of the Census, 1992). Moreover, singlehood poses much more of a problem for them because of the shortage of men, the different cultural traditions under which they were raised, fewer institutional supports for coping with unmarried life, and the inevitable complications stemming from their status as a racial minority. Rarely has the family literature directly dealt with this subject, despite the magnitude of the Black singles situation in America.

94

Obviously, those data reflect some unhappiness with marriage as an institution on the part of Black women. One of the largest surveys of Afro-Americans discovered that only 42 percent were married and another 42 percent were involved in a romantic relationship. Of the remaining subjects who seem most disenchanted with relationships between the genders, a third preferred to be in a marriage or roommate relationship (Tucker and Taylor, 1989). In 1985, the Gallup poll reported that 56 percent of Black women considered the ideal life-style as marriage and a full-time job. According to the National Survey of Family Growth, which looked at women aged fifteen to forty-four, 83.5 percent of Black women had married by the age of forty to forty-four, the age range by which most women who will ever marry have already done so (London, 1991).

Although the times are changing, it is hard to imagine a society in which large numbers of people reject the idea of marriage. America's forefathers obviously considered singlehood a threat when they imposed a special tax on men who insisted on remaining bachelors. As we look at contemporary America, we see how far we have come from the days when birth, marriage, and death were the three supreme experiences in life. In 1991, the proportion of never-married adults in the United States reached a new high. In the 1960s, the average American got married between the ages of twenty and twenty-four. The year 1991 finds 61 percent of women in that age range still single. In 1960, only 28 percent were still unmarried. About 78 percent of the men are still bachelors at the age of twenty-four, compared to 53 percent in 1960. It would be easy and comforting to assume that Americans are delaying marriage until a later age. But the proportion of singles has also increased for the age group twenty-five to twenty-nine. While many will eventually marry, it is conceivable that a large proportion will remain single throughout their lives. Moreover, if we consider the number of individuals divorced, separated, or widowed, there are over seventy-nine million Americans who are theoretically in the state of singleness, or about 45 percent of all people over the age of fifteen (Bureau of the Census, 1992).

Blacks were not allowed to have a legal marriage during the period of slavery. Marriage was, and is, essentially a contractual relationship, and the slaves were not permitted to consummate legal contracts for any purposes. However, there were relationships between male and female slaves that were socially, if not legally, recognized. After slavery ended, the freed slaves went to great lengths to have their relationships legalized. A legal marriage was a status symbol to a group deprived of such rights for two centuries. They married in record numbers, and by far the majority of Blacks were lodged in nuclear families by the beginning of the twentieth century (Gutman, 1976).

As further evidence of the Black emphasis on marriage, the census data for about 1900 indicate that more Blacks than Whites eventually entered into marital relationships (Bureau of the Census, 1972). The question that needs to be answered is what has happened and why. It is easier to explain what has happened than the reasons behind it. The statistics cited earlier were for the general American population without regard to race. If we look at Blacks separately, the trend toward singleness and away from marriage is more pronounced. More than 88 percent of all Black males and 75 percent of Black females are still unmarried between the ages of twenty and twenty-four. More significant, 42 percent of Black males are still single at age thirty, and 37 percent of Black women have not married by the same age (Bureau of the Census, 1992). As unexpected as those figures may be, they do not tell the entire story. Individuals who are separated, divorced, or widowed must be counted as single. When we include these Blacks with the never married, we find that at any given point in time, about 65 percent of all adult Blacks are not married and living with a spouse. Hence, this is not an esoteric group of people we are discussing. Perhaps as important as why it happened is how significant it is to the functioning of the Black community.

Before exploring the answers to those questions, we wish to make our own position clear. Some feminist scholars and others have posited singlehood as a viable alternative to marriage. That is not our perspective. Most Blacks do not see their singleness as a viable choice but as a condition forced on them by certain vicissitudes of life in America. This does not mean that Black singlehood is a pathological form or that Black marriages are that happy or functional. What it does signify is that being single and Black is problematic in many cases. It requires coping with certain problems that either do not occur in the conjugal state, or that happen with less frequency. Let us be clear at the outset that not all people are single in the same way. Some may be living with another person and the relationship takes on all the qualities of a marriage, others have children who occupy their time and satisfy certain emotional needs, and a number of them may be wedded to a career. At the same time, there are those who are actively involved in the dating game and ardently pursuing a spouse. Some scholars believe that the bottom line of all these different configurations is conflicts in the male-female relationship. Remaining unmarried, or dissolving a marriage, is the most fundamental expression of an inability or unwillingness to resolve that conflict (Franklin, 1984).

As to the significance of Black singlehood for the functioning of the Black community, there are certain ramifications that are felt collectively. In contrast to the ideology that singlehood is a viable alternative, it must be interpreted as a symbol of role failure in the normative sense. Perhaps we need some redefinition of roles. No person has yet come up with a known workable alternative. Alternative family substitutes such as open marriage, communal living, heterosexual cohabitation, and so on have been tried and found wanting. And Blacks were never into those family substitutes. Being single and living alone is not a role that relates to any other role. It is the ultimate expression of individuality in a society that is based on an organic togetherness. However, as we shall see, many Blacks find structural barriers to their desire to bond with members of the other gender. Concomitant with individual flaws that make men and women incompatible are social forces that are operative in Black life in a more pronounced manner than seen in mainstream society.

..aracteristics of Black Singles

..hirty years, the proportion of Blacks married
..th a spouse has undergone a steady decline. A
..er proportion of men living in the North and
Wc. ..rcent) than of men living in the South (10 percent)
have nev..r married. The reverse is true for Black women living in the North and West (7 percent), in contrast to women
of the South (9 percent) (Glick, 1988). Among Blacks that
have the highest marriage rate—middle-class Blacks age
twenty-five to forty-five—a clear picture emerges. As the
income level rises, so does the number of men who are married and living with their wife. Many are still married to their
first wife, and those who have divorced subsequently remarry.
On the other hand, Black women who have graduated from
college are the least likely to have married. Among those who
do marry, especially those who have five or more years of
college, their divorce rate is higher and their remarriage rate
is lower than for Black women with less education. Ironically,
the Black men who are least likely to marry, or remarry, are
those who have less than a high school education (Bureau of
the Census, 1985). This suggests that marriage rates are a
function of education (or status) for Black men and women,
but in different directions. And it also points out a basic problem for middle-class Black women: the Black men who have
a similar status are married, and the largest number of Black
men in the eligible pool are those who have a much lower
status.

Types of Singles

Singles are not a monolithic group. The categories used by
the Census Bureau are the never married, the widowed, the
separated, and the divorced. Homosexuals will not be discussed here because of the lack of data available on this
group. Among Blacks, for a long time, the largest number in
the twenty-five-to-forty age group has been the separated.
Lower-income Blacks have long used physical separation as a

form of marital dissolution. The expense of a divorce generally deterred many of them from seeking legal recognition of
a union torn asunder. Very few middle-class Black singles
allowed a marital disruption to remain in a legal limbo. The
time between physical separation and divorce proceedings for
that class is typically brief, except in those cases where ambivalence about the termination of a marriage exists. Among
some men, it is often a ploy to ward off pressures for marriage
from a future consort. Those who are only separated do not
differ greatly from the divorced, except that they may have a
reduced desire to remarry again or may have a lower income
status. Since 1980, the lower-income group has married less
often, thus reducing the numbers in the separated category
(Bureau of the Census, 1992).

The divorced form the second-largest category in this
age cohort and may be qualitatively different from the never
married. Usually, they are older and many have children. Actually, the majority of Black singles age fifteen to sixty-two
were previously married. It is only in the age group below
forty that most have never been married. We would expect to
find some difference between the never married and formerly
married with children. The divorced persons with children
often form attenuated families and carry out most of the same
functions as other nuclear families. The pull of marriage may
not be as great as among childless singles.

Very few Black singles under age sixty are among the
widowed. While the average Black widow loses her husband
at an early age, only a very small number (8 percent) of Black
singles have lost a spouse through death. The never-married
group is much larger in numbers and proportion. Men and
women under the age of forty were more likely to be never
married, along with women that had five years or more of
college. While the tendency of the younger group to remain
single is understandable, the high rate of singlehood among
the highly educated women is not. Apparently, the higher the
education level of the woman, the more improbable is her
chance of marrying. The reverse is true for men. In part, we
have already explained how this situation emerged. While

the total number of Black men with five years or more of college exceeds that of Black women, the men have generally married women below their educational level, while the women futilely seek men who are status compatibles. With a very small pool from which to choose, it becomes an elusive goal (Glick, 1988).

While we consider all individuals who are not married and living with a spouse as part of the singles category, not all of them are single in the same way. Stein (1976), for instance, developed a four-celled typology containing the features of voluntariness and permanence. His four types of singles are classified as (1) permanently and voluntarily single, (2) permanently but involuntarily single, (3) temporarily and voluntarily single, and (4) temporarily, involuntarily single. While these categories might be useful as units of analysis, they imply certain value assumptions about singlehood that we do not share. Considering that the median age of Black singles is under forty, to posit their singlehood as a permanent status would seem premature. As for the voluntary nature of their single status, that is impossible to determine. Although a number of Black single women report receiving marriage proposals, the reason for their refusal appears to be the rejection of the particular male, not the institution of marriage (Tucker and Taylor, 1989). The self-concept of Black singles may, instead, reflect their need to avoid cognitive dissonance. That is, when there is an inconsistency between a status and a belief system, the individual may reduce the dissonance by altering her beliefs (Festinger, 1957). To ensure self-acceptance, many single women declare themselves happy and voluntary in their single status.

Any analysis of Black singlehood would be more valid if we used the concept of a singles career. This concept designates objective movements that one may make through the singles world. Within these movements are manifest changes in the self-concepts that accompany relocations in that milieu. The most common, and of greatest interest to us, is the *free-floating single*. This type of single is totally unattached to any other person and dates randomly with or without the purpose of seeking a committed relationship. Another type is the individual in an *open-couple relationship*. This person has a relatively steady partner, but the relationship is open enough to encompass other individuals in a sexual or romantic liaison. Sometimes it is an open-coupled relationship in a unilateral sense, with one of the partners deceptively pursuing other parties. Occasionally, it is merely the failure to define the relationship explicitly by either of the couples. A related type is that of the *closed-couple relationship*. In this case, the partners look exclusively to each other to have their needs for sex and affection met. By mutual agreement, fidelity is expected and the partners are emotionally bound to each other (Staples, 1981).

We could call this next group the *committed singles*. They would be those individuals who are cohabiting in the same household and are engaged to be married or otherwise have an agreement to establish a permanent relationship. In many ways, they do not share the singles life-style. The cohabitants often maintain the same existence of married couples, sans the legal validation. Those committed to a permanent relationship are so emotionally bound to each other, as long as the commitment lasts, that they spend most of their leisure time together and encounter few of the problems that perplex our other singles.

Another singles stage through which people may pass (or that they may stop at) is accommodation. There are two types of accommodation, temporary and permanent. Among the younger group of singles (under age forty-five), the accommodation to their single status will be temporary. They will lead a solitary existence except for friendships. In the case of women, it can mean refusing all dates, and for men, failing to pursue any heterosexual contacts. Certainly, they are asexual and cease all sexual activity. Some accommodationists may temporarily adopt an alternative life-style or sublimate through work, school, or religion. The permanent accommodationist will generally be in an older age cohort. Many Black singles over the age of forty-five tend to be more permanently resigned to their single status. At this age, many single women are widows and do not plan to remarry. Others have been formerly married, have borne children who are now adults, and devote themselves to the grandparent role (Tucker and Taylor, 1989; Staples, 1981).

The Influence of Sex Ratios

Another element that contributes to the large number of single people among Blacks is the sex ratio. In the age range of twenty-five to sixty-four, there are about 1,500,000 more females than males, or 85 Black males for every 100 Black females. The excess females increase the probability of unmarried females, while the scarcity of males reduces the number of possible husband-wife combinations. Historical patterns of racial discrimination affecting health patterns and resources have created a gap between the life expectancies of Blacks and Whites. Blacks can expect to live about ten years less than Whites, and the percentage of Black females who are aged (sixty-five or over) is greater than the percentage of Black males who are so aged. Thus the operation of the normal age-specific and gender-specific death rates reduces the number of males versus females in the population as age advances, modifying the gender ratio in the relevant portion of the population (Department of Health and Human Services, 1985).

The abnormally high mortality rate for Black males of a marriageable age or younger is attributed to the effects of ghetto living. Death rates for young Black males are much higher than for any other sex-race group. This is due in part to the large number of deaths from homicides, AIDS, suicide, and drugs. The pressures of ghetto life, the inability to find work, and the self-directed violence of America's Black males all combine to kill off the youth of the Black community at an alarming rate (Gibbs, 1988b). One unfortunate effect of living in a racially stratified society is the development of a tendency of Blacks to kill Blacks. The highest rate of homicide involving Americans can be found among Black men. They are most likely to be defendants in homicides involving other Blacks. In 1988, one in a thousand young Black males died in a homicide. That rate was about six times greater than that for all people in that age group (Mydans, 1990). The homicidal acts of Black males are directly traceable to social pressures and racial influences. The traumatic experience of being a Black man in a society that does not provide avenues for Black masculine expression apparently takes its toll. This is particularly true for Black males in the fifteen-to-twenty-five age range.

An additional factor contributing to an imbalance of the genders is the large number of Black prisoners in the nation's jails. Most of the Black prisoners are males and most are poor. The percentage of Blacks within the prison population is more out of balance than the percentage within any other population. In 1988, more than a million Black males were incarcerated, on probation, or on parole. Four hundred and twenty-six of every 100,000 American citizens are imprisoned, while 3,109 out of every 100,000 Black American men are incarcerated, the highest imprisonment rate of any country in the world. About one of every four Black men between twenty and thirty is in a state, federal, or local jail. Black offenders spend more time in prison and on parole than Whites convicted of the same offenses, except for kidnapping (Ostrow, 1991; Bureau of Justice Statistics, 1990).

When selecting a mate, Black women must consider the nature of the pool from which they will draw. In 98 percent of marriages with a Black bride, the groom will be a Black male. Hence, her pool consists of the unmarried Black males with a variety of attributes. The most crucial factor in the search for mates is the excess number of women over men during the marriageable years. According to the Bureau of the Census (1991a), there are almost 1,500,000 more Black women than men over the age of fifteen. By the Census Bureau's own account, there is an undercount of about 925,000 Black males who exist but were not added to the Black population total. It should be noted that the uncounted Black males are likely to be transient and unemployed (Joe and Yu, 1991), and thus not viable husband candidates. Since there is an excess number of Black males at birth, the subsequent shortage of Black males over the age of fourteen must be attributed to their higher infant mortality rate and the considerably greater mortality rate of young Black males through such means as homicide, accidents, suicide, drug overdoses, and war casualties (Gibbs, 1988b).

The biggest problem for Black women, however, is not the quantity in the available supply of potential mates but the quality. Whereas Black women may select a mate on the basis of a number of attributes, a minimum prerequisite is that he be gainfully and regularly employed. According to a study by Joe and Yu (1991), almost a majority of working-age Black males fail to meet those minimum prerequisites. After an analysis of the economic and census data, they concluded that 46 percent of the 8.8 million Black men of working age were not in the labor force. Based on 1982 statistics, they found 1.2 million Black men were unemployed, 1.8 million had dropped out of the labor force, 186,000 were in prison, and 925,000 were classified as "missing" because the Census Bureau says it could not locate them.

Their study, moreover, overstates the number of "desirable" and available Black males in the marriage pool. Even with the census undercount, there are still a half million more Black women over the age of fifteen than Black men. Also, we must subtract from the marriage pool Black men with certain characteristics that substantially outnumber Black women. Among those characteristics would be Blacks serving in the armed forces. Approximately 90 percent of them will be male. The Bureau of the Census (1983) reports that there were 422,000 Blacks under arms in 1982, representing 21 percent of all U.S. military personnel. It can be reliably stated that a large number of those Black males had poor prospects for employment in the civilian labor force (Stewart and Scott, 1978). While the salary and other benefits of military personnel have improved in recent years and a number of Black soldiers are currently married, the military does take out of circulation a number of marriage-age Black males by stationing them in foreign posts and isolated military stations.

Furthermore, once their period of enlistment ends, Black veterans experience a higher rate of unemployment, even in relation to Black civilian males with no military service (Stewart and Scott, 1978). Hence, military service only postpones the entry of Black males into the ranks of the unemployed, one reason Black males have a higher rate of reenlistment than their White counterparts.

Included in the factors that reduce the number of desirable Black males in the marriage pool is the high rate of underemployed Black males. The Commission on Civil Rights (1982) reported that Black men are overeducated for their jobs and have greater difficulty translating education into suitable occupations. Even college-educated Black males have an unemployment rate four times greater than their White peers. Among Black males employed in the labor force, one out of three will suffer from unemployment in a given year (Swinton, 1992). In Hampton's study (1980), the respondents who reported the highest number of employment problems had a marital disruption rate three times higher than the overall rate for the sample.

Another group of Black males regarded as undesirable or unavailable are those confined to mental institutions or otherwise mentally unstable. The environmental problems facing Blacks are such that they are more likely than Whites to suffer from mental distress. Blacks also use community mental health centers at a rate almost twice their proportion in the general population. While their exact number is unknown, Black males are more likely to be committed to mental institutions than are Black women. The rate of drug and alcohol abuse is much greater among the Black population, especially males, based on their overrepresentation among patients receiving treatment services (Department of Health and Human Services, 1985). It is estimated that as many as one-third of the young Black males in the inner city have a serious drug problem (Staples, 1991b). Many of the mentally unstable or drug and alcohol abusers will have been included in the figures on Black males who have dropped out of the labor force or are in prison. The magnitude of the problem simply reinforces the fact that Black women are seriously disadvantaged in choosing from the eligible and desirable males in the marriage pool.

Education and gender significantly impact on the opportunities for marriage and risks of divorce. Failure to marry, among Black men, tends to be linked to income and employment potential. Black men whose income is below the poverty level are the most likely to remain unmarried, while college-educated Black males have the greatest chance of being married. As incomes rise, so does the number of Black men who marry. The reluctance of lower-income Black men to marry is understandable, given the fact that they have one of the highest rates of marital dissolution of all sex-race groups in the United States. On the other hand, Black female college graduates are less likely to marry, or to remarry if divorced, than their less educated counterparts, both Black and White (Glick, 1988). It seems that educational and occupational success adds to a man's desirability as a mate but detracts from a woman's. Thus, the low-income Black male has difficulty attracting a mate because of his poor employment and income potential (Goldman, Westoff, and Hammerslough, 1984; Tucker and Taylor, 1989).

Dating as a Process

Each unit of the family begins as a dyad, usually two members of the opposite sex who occupy a range of roles based on the stage of their relationship. The first stage in the process of forming a family has historically been dating and courtship. Changes in attitudes toward the family have brought about variations in the practice of dating and courtship. Among the most marked changes in the dating and courtship system are the different characteristics of its participants, the changing purpose of dating, and variations in its form. Dating, for instance, now involves more than very young people. The increasing numbers of individuals who remain unmarried until fairly advanced ages mean that a dating partner could as easily be thirty-eight as eighteen. The spiraling divorce, and low remarriage, rates created another large pool of dating partners. Dating has also become time contained, often existing only for the moment or sexual or recreational purposes, and is no longer automatically presumed to be a prelude to courtship or marriage. Even the concept of dating has been modified, as men and women get together without making formal arrangements for an evening out in a public setting. Much of the previous description is relevant to the White middle class, which has developed a new ideology about the nature and content of the dating system. When we discuss Black dating, there are limitations to the generalizations we can make due to the limited literature on the subject.

The practice of Black dating can vary by epoch, region, and social class. In the past, when Blacks formed a small, cohesive community in the rural and urban South, what might be called dating behavior was centered around the neighborhood, church, and school. In general, it was a casual process where men and women met, formed emotional attachments, and later married. Most of the participants were members of larger social units, whose members or reputation were generally known to the community. As Blacks moved into urban areas outside of the South, dating patterns modified due to the anonymity of individuals in that setting. The school and house party became centers for fraternizing between the genders, particularly in the working class. In the middle-class group, dating habits took on the characteristics of mainstream culture, as they participated more in activities like movies, dances, bowling, and so on (Dickinson, 1978; Porter, 1979).

Very little is known about dating and sexual behavior in the Black community. Dating patterns may vary from community to community, region to region, and within and between the social classes in either of those areas. As among Whites, dating behavior involves a great deal of image management on the part of both males and females. In general, it is acknowledged that the male attempts to maximize sexual involvement with and minimize commitment to his female date. The reverse is usually true of the female. Success in reaching one goal or the other is often based on the principle of least interest—that is, who is more committed to maintaining the relationship and more likely to give in to the demands of the other partner—for sexual involvement or commitment to a steady relationship or marriage (Burgest, 1991).

It is the process of dating that most markedly distinguishes single from married people. The difference is not absolute, since many married individuals (particularly the males) have a strong presence in the dating game, but their relationships are one of discrete liaisons rather than the structured ritual involved in the dating situation. One often hears that people do not "date" anymore. However, there is some question as to what has taken its place. As one woman reported to us: "I have friends who consider the word 'date' or the situation known as 'dating' passé. They haven't really come up with new words for activities they are involved in which are essentially identical to dating" (Staples, 1981, p. 45).

One thing is certain—that the process whereby the sexes form relationships has substantially changed in recent years. Dating began as part of the courtship process in the 1920s, when the concept of romantic love became increasingly popular among middle-class Whites. Prior to that time, marriages were arranged as a result of negotiations between two families or groups. Once individuals were ostensibly given free choice in the selection of a mate, dating became the method whereby unmarried men and women mutually explored each other's strengths and weaknesses as a potential spouse. In most cases dating partners were young and met each other in their respective communities. As a result, most Americans married persons who lived within six miles of them (Whyte, 1990).

Nowadays, dating—or whatever we choose to call it—is an entirely different matter. For some singles, it is the most valuable aspect of their life and provides them with an active social life, new experiences, a variety of new and interesting people to meet, freedom to sexually experiment, and so on. To others, it ranks as the most undesirable element in singlehood. However one responds to the dating situation, the one predictable element in it is its unpredictability. Once it ceased to be part of a structured courtship system, it became literally a form of social anarchy. The people in today's dating game are not necessarily young people who grew up together and who are searching for compatible mates. They form a diverse group in terms of age, values, background, motives, and experiences. As a result, dating has a different character and dynamics than some thirty years ago. Individuals caught up in the dating game must develop skills and resiliency to cope with its chameleonlike structure (Burgest and Goosby, 1985).

Even in urban areas and among the middle class, Black dating in public places was restricted due to racial segregation in the South and a lack of recreational outlets in Northern Black communities (Dickinson, 1978). Most Blacks met their future mates in school, in the neighborhood, or at house parties. With the increasing mobility of middle-class Blacks, those sources of potential mates are no longer as available. Moreover, they now meet members of the opposite sex as individuals, whereas in the past they were part of a larger social unit. This has certain implications for those who participate in the dating game. It means that people are more subject to image management techniques, since they have little independent verification of a dating partner's character in settings that are new to them both. Also, the controls on negative or antisocial behavior in dating situations are lessened when the social sanctions that can be exercised by relatives or friends are absent.

Not everybody is in the dating game in the same way. At one time or another, an individual may have a serious involvement with one person that takes up most of their time and attention. With the short duration of many relationships, and the awareness by many that "nothing lasts forever," most people fit into what Farber (1964) calls the *permanent availability* model. According to this model, almost everyone is always available to a member of the opposite sex, including those who are presently married. Due to the lack of legal or kin control, individuals go in and out of relationships, including marriage, freely. Hence, being involved in a "serious" relationship and participating in the dating game simultaneously is qualitatively different than being an unattached individual. It affords one a greater selectivity in choosing dating partners, a more leisurely pace in developing the relationship, and the ability to negotiate for higher rewards. No matter how one chooses to participate in the dating game, it still requires the ability to cope with different situations and diverse personalities.

Mate Selection Standards

Most heterosexual Black women have some concept of the ideal man they would like to marry. But, like other aspirations, these aspirations are tempered by the reality of their lives. Since it is working-class Black women who suffer the most from poverty, their standards for a husband are most modified by the availability of such men in their environment. Despite the dilution of their mate selection standards, most Black women prefer the state of matrimony to a life of solitude. Many working-class Black women expect a life of celibacy to be even more ungratifying. Even an imperfect marital relationship is often better than a life that lacks love and companionship. Moreover, most of the wives receive some satisfaction in their relationship with their husbands (Heiss, 1988).

Within the Black middle class, women have a greater opportunity to realize their ideal standard for a marital partner. In selecting a mate, the middle-class Black woman is more likely to follow middle-class norms. There is more emphasis on romantic love and less on economic security. However, romantic love is not the only basis for marriage among the Black middle class. It may be that middle-class Black women make an a priori assumption that their husband can provide for them and seek to maximize the emotional gratification they will receive from a potential husband (Staples, 1981).

Still, most Black women maintain an ideal concept of the man they would like to marry. These idealistic standards of mate selection, however, must often be subordinated to the realities they encounter. A working-class woman frequently will settle for a man who will work when he is able to find employment, avoid excessive gambling, drinking, and extra-marital affairs, provide for the children, and treat her with respect. But even these simple desires cannot be fulfilled by lower-class Black husbands who are unable to find work and retreat into psychologically destructive behavior such as alcoholism, physical abuse of their wife, and so on (Heiss, 1988).

The middle-class Black woman has a slightly better chance of fulfilling her desires for a compatible mate. She is likely to require economic stability, emotional and sexual satisfaction, and male participation in childrearing. One aspect of White marriages is conspicuously missing—Black women do not expect their husbands to support them. Both Black men and women are in agreement that women will work after marriage. And it has been found that the wife's employment does not pose a threat to the Black male's self-image. Black males are more likely to believe that the wife has a right to a career of her own than White males. The dual employment of both spouses is often necessary to approach the living standards of White couples with only the husband working. It also reflects the partnership of Black men and women that has existed for centuries (Taylor, Leashore, and Toliver, 1988).

The basis for selecting male dating partners can vary according to the values and needs of the individual female. A male with money—a rarity in the Black community—is much desired by many Black females. The male's personality is very important, but all things being equal, his physique is rapidly becoming the most attractive element for Black women. The process of ranking males by body build can be called the masculinization of female mate selection standards. For years, males have evaluated females in terms of breast size, shapely legs, protruding buttocks, and other physical features. Now females are also beginning to rank males in terms of their pulchritude (Cash and Duncan, 1984).

Black women demonstrate a stronger preference for a

physically attractive man than her White counterparts. In a
Jet Magazine survey of Black women in Chicago ("Ten Things
Women Notice About Men," 1982), Black women ranked the
ten things they notice about men in this order: (1) dress/
grooming, (2) personality, (3) eyes, (4) mouth/smile, (5)
money, (6) physique, (7) thoughtfulness/walk, (8) intelli-
gence/handsomeness, (9) chest, and (10) buttocks. Only four
of the desirable attributes are nonphysical ones. Unlike their
male cohorts, they place comparatively little emphasis on skin
color. When they express a preference, it is for darker-skinned
men. Many Black women say they do not trust light-skinned
men and find darker men more dependable, settled, and attractive (Azibo, 1983).

Socioeconomic status figures more prominently in a
man's life chances than in a woman's. When women are selecting a man for a husband, they generally consider his level of
education and income first; since a woman is not only choosing a companion but is determining her standard of living,
his physical assets are less important (Tucker and Taylor,
1989). That does not mean a man's physical attributes are
totally insignificant. Men over six feet tall are more likely to
obtain high-level executive positions than shorter men. Bald
men suffer in employment opportunities and other areas relative to their peers with all their hair. The media has a preference for handsome men in visible positions. Certain social
forces may account for the Black female's greater interest in a
male's physical appeal. Partly, it may be a function of the
shortage of Black men with any tangible wealth. Given that
they may not find a high-status Black male in any case, they
will choose one on the basis of his looks. Perhaps more important is that many Black women are not economically dependent on a man for economic support. As a result, their
standards for an acceptable mate have become oriented more
toward the body.

Unfortunately, Black women seem to be heading in the
same direction as Black men: rating people by their physical
features rather than by the content of their character. When
personal characteristics that are genetically influenced make

such an important difference in a person's status, a genetic determinism emerges that is very similar to the operation of racial attitudes. Since the standards of physical attractiveness are set and dominated by Euro-Americans, it could presage an increase in group self-hatred.

Apart from racially determined physical characteristics, standards of beauty have varied over time and in different cultures. France, for instance, has regarded feet as a sex symbol. The United States has long been obsessed with female mammary glands, an anatomical asset that would seem senseless in precolonial Africa, where women did not wear clothing above the waist. While America currently worships the thin woman, opulent females were more highly regarded in African societies because this connoted high status and good health. Certain factors seem almost universal in determining physical attractiveness. One is the rarity of a physical trait in its most exacting form. The more abundant a trait is, the less it tends to be highly regarded. Another is whiteness. Even in predominantly white cultures, blonds are the preferred coloration. They are especially valued by Mediterranean Whites (Hatfield and Sprecher, 1986; Staples, 1989).

As far as Black men are concerned, lightness of skin color is a dominant criterion in determining beauty among women. The rhetoric about Black is beautiful notwithstanding, that has been the yardstick of beauty for Black women for the last 400 years. According to Villa (1981, p. 202), "For many decades the lighter skinned females of the Black race were most preferred by Black men, because their color was closer to that of the white race, and the Black American had been conditioned for centuries by White Americans to believe that anything or anyone who resembled the whites had to be better. Any Black man who had a light-complected female (known in slang as a 'high yellow') possessed a status symbol of sorts."

The evidence for this cultural attitude is not forthcoming from the mouths of Blacks. In any survey of mate selection standards among Blacks, skin color is rarely mentioned. When Berkeley psychologist Juanita Papillon did a study of the effect of skin color on the emotional makeup of Blacks, she found the higher the self-esteem, the darker the color (Stewart, 1979). Given that many Black men prefer their women light or White, the supply of such women is limited for a number of reasons. What, then, do Black males consider in their search for a desirable mate? A survey informs us on this question. When *Jet Magazine* ("Ten Things Men Notice About Women," 1982) surveyed Black males in Chicago on the ten things they notice about women, they listed them in this order: (1) face, (2) legs, (3) bust, (4) eyes/hair, (5) personality, (6) dress/intelligence, (7) smile, (8) buttocks, (9) walk, (10) hands/feet/voice/conversation/sincerity (Staples, 1989).

It is obvious from that ranking that a woman's primary assets are physical traits. Other sterling qualities such as personality and intelligence rank fifth and sixth, respectively, and the ability to hold a conversation and sincerity come in dead last. Moreover, the first four physical traits are generally those most common to White women. The face should be light and keen in features, legs and bust should be big, eyes round, hair long and straight. It is an ironic twist of fate that physical traits originally designed for other functions, to allow a group to adapt effectively to its physical environment, have become a benchmark of beauty. Black women actually need a combination of beauty and brains to attract a high-status husband, but it is still their looks that are the decisive factor. A sociologist did an empirical test of whether a woman's physical attractiveness was a predictor of her husband's status. He reported that if a White woman does not go to college, her attractiveness has a strong bearing on whether or not she gets a high-status husband. If that same White woman goes to college, her looks bear no relationship to the status of her husband. But for the Black woman, attractiveness is influential in getting a high-status husband whether or not she goes to college. It plays a stronger role if she goes to college than if she does not, though (Udry, 1977).

The relationship between beauty and intelligence is a complicated one. In White culture, an attractive woman has less need to cultivate her intellectual potential because she can obtain a high level of self-esteem and class mobility (through marriage) without it. The same is not entirely true of attractive Black women. Most Black families, for instance, socialize all their female children to get a good education and not depend on a man for satisfying their material wants. Furthermore, to obtain high-status husbands, most beautiful Black women have to attend a college where they can meet them. Unlike Whites, the wealthiest Blacks are generally those with the most education (even Black athletes generally attend college). Many of them will be medical doctors and dentists who attended either Howard University or Meharry Medical School. Since both Howard and Fisk University (the undergraduate school next door to Meharry) have historically had high academic standards, women of limited intellect would experience difficulty in matriculating at those schools.

Alternatives to Monogamous Marriage

Throughout our discussion of singlehood, we have emphasized that it is a complex phenomenon. To understand its multiple dimensions, we need to distinguish the condition of being unmarried from singlehood as a way of life. The historical data tell us that the overwhelming majority of Americans do marry at some point in their life. Only 4 percent of Americans have never married, and of those who get married and divorced, 79 percent remarry (Bureau of the Census, 1992). Those figures, of course, are based on past patterns and do not reflect the attitudes of single men and women who are under the age of forty and have never married. Yet it is possible that, antimarriage attitudes notwithstanding, most of the Black singles will eventually marry. And they will eventually marry for a very simple reason: the social structure does not provide any viable alternative.

This assumption may be regarded as heresy by the antimarriage proponents. Literally hundreds of articles and a number of books have been written that endorse alternatives to the traditional marital union. There are several journals, academic and popular, devoted to exploring and justifying these alternative life-styles. Support for them comes primarily from Whites, women, and gays, for reasons unique to those groups. Black endorsement of alternative life-styles has been noticeably absent. This may not last long.

There appears to be a generalized discontent with marriage among those who are married and an anticipation of unhappiness in the conjugal state among those who are not. The unhappily married tend to be concentrated in the lower stratum of the social classes. Still, middle-class Black women do not escape the disaffection with marriage, although for slightly different reasons. They are often unable to find husbands of comparable status and have to face keen competition, both before and after marriage, should they find one. The official divorce rate is actually higher among middle-class Black women, although marital breakup is greater among working-class women, who do not use the divorce courts as frequently. At any rate, there is considerable dissatisfaction with marriage as an institution. But this dissatisfaction will not be translated into large numbers of Black women who never marry. Among Black Americans born in 1954, 86 percent of the men and 70 percent of the women are expected to marry by the time they reach forty-five years (Rodgers and Thornton, 1985).

As for the men, they also voice antimarriage attitudes, particularly lower-class Black men. Studies show them to fear public and private fights between spouses; to see marriage as creating problems of how to feed, clothe, and house a wife and child; and to experience anxiety about being able to ward off attacks on the health and safety of their children (Cazenave, 1983). These men are the most likely of all Blacks to remain legally unmarried. Middle-class Black men, on the other hand, are less inclined to voice antimarriage perspectives. While claiming to enjoy the single life, they will eventually settle down in a permanent union. Unlike the other groups, they see themselves as having much to gain from marriage. They have an abundance of women from which to select, of different races and educational levels. Because of the shortage of men in their category, they can make very favorable matches from the variety of women in the eligible female pool. Since society, and their own values, allows them considerable flexibility in choosing the woman to marry, their pool is infinite, actually ten times larger than the middle-class Black woman's. Moreover, marriage for them provides an image of respectability, steady and free sexual relations, regular and better meals, and so on. Within marriage, they maintain a certain freedom to pursue their careers and other activities, even to continue dating other women. Small wonder that they see marriage in a positive light. They are the group of Blacks most likely to marry, and when divorced, to remarry (Glick, 1988; Tucker and Taylor, 1989).

Given the shortfall of Black men of a similar educational and income level, it can be assumed that many Black women will have to settle for an alternative life-style. The question remains, is it really an alternative and how viable is it? For Blacks in general, many of the alternative life-styles advocated are nothing new. Having a child out of wedlock has long been known to the Black community. The latest figures show that 60 percent of Black children born in 1988 were conceived out of wedlock (Bureau of the Census, 1991a). Most Black women hardly consider raising a child alone an alternative life-style. About 51 percent of all Black households are headed by women, and they have the lowest income and most problems of all Blacks (Bane and Jargowsky, 1988). Harriette McAdoo, quoted in a *Newsweek* article, warned, "These types of families should not be romanticized out of context. They exist for sheer survival in the face of real and threatening problems and the problems may be becoming overwhelming" ("Blacks Fresh Trials," 1978, p. 77).

In any examination of alternatives to the conventional monogamous marriages, few, if any, appear desirable or viable. Some cannot be regarded as legitimate alternatives for Blacks (Williams, 1990). Dedication to a career seems irrelevant to a group of Black women who have been in the labor force for the last hundred years. Raising a child alone has become a traditional and often undesirable life-style of too many Black women. Those who realize the burden it imposes on both the mother and child are hardly inclined to view single motherhood as something they want or happily choose. Other alleged alternatives contain flaws because they do not address the basic cause of Black singlehood: the shortage of Black males and the conflict between the genders. Heterosexual cohabitation, for instance, does not increase the number of males available, nor does it alter the ability of men and women to live in a harmonious relationship. Ironically, two of the most commonly mentioned alternatives, homosexuality and interracial marriages, are used more often by men, thus compounding the problem of Black women seeking a heterosexual mate within the race (Bell and Weinberg, 1978; Tucker and Mitchell-Kernan, 1990).

Black people have had to deal with the shortage of men for a number of years. Through a variety of coping mechanisms, they have been able to marry and raise children. Much of this has been accomplished through the pattern of serial polygamy—that is, a male marries more than one woman in his lifetime and vice versa. Whether this will continue or not depends on how many Black women choose to redefine their options and priorities. Rather than use the misleading term *alternative life-styles* to describe the behavior of middle-class Blacks, it is more appropriate to call them *family substitutes* or, even better, *coping styles*.

The expression *alternative life-styles* implies that individuals are free to choose within an array of available options. But middle-class Black singles, especially women, are choosing within the limits of the existing social structure. They are free to choose between alternatives, not what the alternatives should be. In looking at the family substitutes available, we will see that people are products of their culture and cannot free themselves of it for greater individual freedom unless they first understand the constraints that culture imposes. Monogamous marriage is the only sanctioned institution in which the needs of most adults are met in the United States. The family substitutes are, at best, inadequate ways of satisfying these human prerequisites. Many of these family substitutes have been tried and found to be of short-term duration. They often are a revolving door rather than a family.

Summary

Relationships between Black men and women have had a peculiar evolution. Unlike the White family, which is typically patriarchal and sustained by the economic dependence of women, the Black dyad has been characterized by more egalitarian roles and economic parity in North America. The system of slavery did not permit Black males to assume the superordinate role in the family constellation, since the female was not economically dependent on him. Hence, relationships between the genders were ordered along sociopsychological dimensions rather than reflecting an economic compulsion to marry and remain married. This fact, in part, explains the unique trajectory of Black male-female relationships.

The growing trend toward singlehood among American Blacks is reflected in the fact that a majority of Black women over the age of fifteen are no longer married and living with a spouse. While the institutional decimation of Black males is the primary factor in this unprecedented number of singles, other sociocultural forces impact on the relationships between Black men and women. Among them are the changes in Black institutions and values that create barriers for Blacks in finding and keeping a mate. The conflict between Black men and women also stems from incompatible role enactments by the two genders. The older societal prescription that women are to be passive and men dominant is counteracted by other forces. Black women resist Black men's dominance, and Black men who wish to be in charge cannot fulfill the economic provider role, which supports the dominance of men in American society (Franklin, 1984).

The situation of Black singles is much too fluid, and the research on them too sparse, to pontificate about the direction of their family life-styles. Given the present circumstances, it is difficult to hold out much hope that the majority of Black women will marry and stay with one man their entire lifetime. Alternative life-styles are conceptually flawed, however, because they do not take into account the effects of social forces over which most individuals have minimal control. Not only does American society fail to provide structural supports for persons engaged in alternative life-styles, but it can and does punish individuals who violate its norms. Furthermore, the greatest punishment is administered by the individuals themselves when there is any incongruity between their life-styles and the values they have internalized. In the past, the Black community provided some support for the coping mechanisms of its members. Whether the reality of the Black community can be accommodated to this new situation remains an open question.

6

Gender Roles
and Male Sexism

In recent years, gender identities and roles have received a great deal of attention. While the debate in mainstream society has centered on the issue of female subordination and male dominance and privilege, Blacks have very different problems and priorities. They have to first overcome certain disabilities based on racial membership—not gender affiliation. However, that does not mean that gender roles within the Black community fail to carry advantages and disadvantages. In many ways, they do. But Blacks must contend with the insistent problems of a high unemployment rate, the declining life expectancy rate of Black men, rises in drug abuse, suicide, and crime, and educational failures. These problems do not inspire much support for a movement to equalize the condition of men and women in the Black community (Staples, 1991a).

Gender and Historical Forces

From a historical perspective, the Black male's role has changed as he has moved from the African continent to the shores of North America. This span of time has introduced the forces of slavery, discrimination, and wage exploitation in the determination of his masculine identity and role. As we have seen, women had an important place in African society; they often exceeded their European counterparts in the authority they wielded and the contribution they made to their respective social units (Terborg-Penn, 1991). But most areas of Africa were patriarchal, and males had a variety of influential roles. This changed with the appearance of slavery.

Under slavery, the role of the father was, in essence, institutionally obliterated. Not only was the slave father deprived of his sociological and economic functions in the family, but the very etiquette of plantation life deprived him even of the honorific attributes of fatherhood, since he was addressed as "boy"—until, when the vigorous years of his prime were past, he was permitted to assume the title of uncle. If he lived with a woman in a "married" relationship, he was known as her husband (for example, as "Sally's John"), which again denied him a position as head of the household (White, 1985).

The structural barriers to Black manhood were great. In a capitalistic society, being able to provide basic life satisfactions is inextricably interwoven with manhood. The opportunity to provide for his family, both individually and collectively, had been denied the Black man. After emancipation, the economic role of the Black woman was strengthened as Blacks left the rural areas and migrated to the cities, where it was difficult for Black men to obtain employment. Increasingly, the Black woman was thrust into the role of the family provider. Although Black men had previously held jobs as skilled craftsmen, carpenters, and so on, they were forced out of these occupations by a coalition of White workers and capitalists. In some instances, they found employment only as strikebreakers (Giddings, 1984; Davis, 1989). The jobs that were available lacked the security and level of income necessary to maintain a household. Additionally, certain jobs historically performed by Black men (for example, waiter, cook, dishwasher, teacher, social worker, and so on) often carried a connotation in American society of being "women's work" (Davis, 1989).

After slavery officially ended, the kind of role flexibility that existed during slavery continued for Black families.

Despite theories to the contrary, male-present households were the norm in poor Black communities in the period between 1880 and 1925. Families headed by women were hardly, if at all, more common than among comparable Whites (Gutman, 1976). These two-parent black households were often dual-worker families, since many wives often worked alongside their husbands to obtain land and an education for their children. In the harsh economic conditions of the late nineteenth century, a certain egalitarianism developed within Black families, and the sharp dichotomy between male and female gender roles so common to antebellum Southern White families failed to develop (King, 1990; Davis, 1989).

Socialization into Gender Roles

Central to the understanding of Black gender roles is an investigation of the process of socializing them into their gender identity. The literature is full of assumptions—but little proof—about how Black males are reared in their families. A dominant, though unproven, theory is that the nature of the male role is not adequately conveyed to them because of absent or weak father figures. Others have contended that Black mothers raise their sons to be docile because of the risks to life and limb that an aggressive Black male would be exposed to. Another common assumption is that Black mothers have traditionally favored female children over male children. All these hypotheses need to be carefully tested by an examination of the socialization processes in the Black family and how they shape gender-role identity (Hale, 1982; Peters, 1988).

Because many Black men have been absent from the family due to welfare regulations and an inability to obtain regular employment, the Black mother has played a strong role in the ongoing care of Black children. Many Blacks have vivid memories of their mothers scrubbing floors in White households to put food on the table or to send them through college. Research studies that have attempted to study the matter unanimously find that Black children have a closer relationship with their parents than White children do. While Black parents may use physical discipline, they rarely practice the technique of withdrawing love from the children. This eliminates some of the anxiety and resentment that often result from that childrearing method. And it is generally the mother that both male and female children feel closest to. In his study of Black families, Scanzoni (1978) found that both Black males and females were more likely to view their mothers as being a help to them in getting an education than their fathers. However, the fathers were more likely to provide tangible material assistance, while the mothers gave counseling and encouragement to stay in school.

Given this history, it is puzzling as to why the Black mother has come under such strident attack in recent years for having a negative influence on Black male children. Such prominent Blacks as columnist William Raspberry (1984) and writer Shahrazad Ali (1989) have criticized Black mothers for their role in creating a host of undependable and low-achieving Black males. Since a near majority of Black families are headed by only a female parent, it is crucial to determine how well male children are raised when the mother is the sole parent.

Certainly, classic psychoanalytic theory assumed the existence of a strong father figure in the development of a healthy male identity. Sigmund Freud (1938), the father of psychoanalysis, believed the male child's first love object is the mother. When the son becomes aware that he cannot compete with the father for the mother's love, he subsequently identifies with the father and acquires his masculine characteristics. If this resolution of what Freud termed the Oedipal complex does not occur, the attachment to the mother persists and the male child develops an ambivalence toward the father and the masculinity he represents. Freud's theory has been criticized for not considering the social and cultural context in which male personalities develop. This theory was based on his therapy with White middle-class women in Europe during the nineteenth century. Other observers of Black culture have noted that the Black male child can form an attachment to and identify with other male figures in his environment, such as his uncles and grandfathers, when the male parent is absent (Taylor, 1986). Moreover, Lewis (1975) has noted that in Afro-American culture, children are considered sexual beings. Thus, the Black child's sexual identity is more easily tied to his definition of himself as a sexual being than to behavior that has arbitrarily been defined as masculine. In Black society, she claims, traits such as independence, nurturing, assertiveness, and so forth do not distinguish between males and females. A boy understands he is male on the basis of his sexuality, and a girl realizes her femaleness on the basis of her sexuality and her ability to bear children.

Much of the recent controversy over the Black mother's role was ignited by the publication of the widely criticized Moynihan report (1965). In it, Moynihan attributed much of the blame for Black problems to the existence of the so-called matriarchy. It was, he said, the dominance and influence of Black mothers over their sons that was responsible for their lack of achievement, especially in relationship to Black daughters. The premise itself might be questioned, since Black women still earn considerably less than Black men. Still, it is noticeable and verifiable that Black women exceed Black men at all educational levels (National Center for Education Statistics, 1991a). Increasingly, the same is true of Euro-Americans.

Other social scientists have claimed that Black mothers cannot give their sons a positive role model, so that the female-headed family hinders them in the development of a masculine identity. Some have gone so far as to assert that a large proportion of the Black male population are latent homosexuals, as the result of being raised in father-absent or mother-dominant households (Allen, 1981; Peters, 1988). The evidence for this assertion is very questionable. One widely quoted study found Black males scored higher on the femininity index of the Minnesota Multiphasic Personality Inventory test. Their femininity score was higher than that of White males, because they were more likely to agree with statements such as "I would like to be a singer" and "I think

I feel more intensely than most people do" (Hokanson and Calder, 1960). Such evidence reveals no understanding of Black culture—specifically, of the traits that define masculinity among Black people. There is, in fact, no validation of the theory of massive homosexuality among Black males, and certainly no evidence that Black mothers are responsible for it (Baldwin, 1987).

The whole question of how Black males can acquire an appropriate masculine identity in a household headed by a woman is answered by other research. There is ample evidence that a mother can communicate to her son the way men act. He can be shown the way men cross their legs, how they carry their books, the way they walk, and so on. Furthermore, there are few Black male children who do not observe men in their environment. The Black community is much less sex stratified and segregated than mainstream society. Blacks have few all-male or all-female clubs, associations, or schools. Men and women mingle easily in all walks of life (Hale, 1982). Hence, the Black male child has a number of male role models to choose from. Even in two-parent homes, the father may not be the person he will choose to emulate. Whereas he may idolize the male parent in early childhood, his later role models can be glamorous personalities such as movie stars, athletes, or fictional characters. During his late adolescence, the most admired role models will often be attractive and visible men who demonstrate certain valued competences or skills and who are generally admired in the community (Taylor, 1986).

We can better understand the problems of the Black mother-son relationship by reviewing Black history and culture. As Lewis (1975, p. 221) has observed, "Many of the behaviors which Whites see as appropriate to one sex or the other, Blacks view as equally appropriate to both sexes or equally inappropriate to both sexes. The sex differences that do exist are more in the nature of contrasts than of mutually exclusive traits." Unlike some of the ancient societies of Asia, and even of Europe, Africa did not have a strong gender preference among children nor the need to sharply differentiate men from women (Binion, 1990). Female independence coexisted with the recognition of male authority in many African societies (Sudarkasa, 1981). However, there were unusual circumstances that caused Black mothers to raise their sons differently in the postslavery era of the Southern United States. And it is that male socialization practice that is the subject of much criticism of Black mothers today.

Where such differential socialization has existed, a more likely explanation is the Black mother's fear for the safety of her son. In the pre–civil rights era in the South, a Black man with too much temper and too much ambition would have had his life shortened if he acted too aggressively toward Whites (Dollard, 1957). As a result, the Black mother had to teach her son to be obedient and compliant (Allen, 1981; Peters, 1988). White society would tolerate the independence of Black women but not that of Black men. Where this socialization practice continues, the Black mother's overprotection of her son can foster dependency in him and hinder his ability to make important decisions as well as erode his sense of manliness and the ability to achieve and accomplish (Staples, 1984).

Young Black girls also have a close relationship with their mothers. At a fairly young age, they assume heavy household responsibilities such as cooking, cleaning, and child care. Many of them, by the age of nine, are given the charge of their younger siblings. The sharing of household responsibilities builds a positive relationship between mother and daughter. The close relationship Black mothers have with their daughters has led to the charge that Black mothers express a preference for female over male children. But such allegations are unsupported by any evidence (Bell-Scott and others, 1991).

Young Black females are usually socialized in different ways than the males. Probably one of the most salient differences is in their sexual education. Since some Black mothers realize that the avenue to sexual gratification will be an open one for their children, they instruct them early in matters of pregnancy and "social" diseases. It is alleged that Black girls are socialized to be more independent, disciplined, and cautious than Black boys. There is some evidence that there are fewer social conformists among Black females at a fairly early age (Peters, 1988). One reason for this differential socialization is the belief that Black men are basically worthless and irresponsible; consequently, less is expected of them. The other side of this theory is that Black women are morally and intellectually superior to Black men, and hence one can expect more from them (Franklin, 1986).

Historically, Black families (not mothers alone) were more likely to send their daughters to college because the sons were needed to help on the farm. Another compelling reason for sending the daughters to college was to help them avoid becoming domestic servants in White households. While household work can be, and is, a noble occupation, in the pre–civil rights movement era it often entailed the risks of sexual harassment for many young Black women. During that period, only two occupations were generally available to Black women: domestic worker or schoolteacher. Thus, it was more important that they go to college and avoid those risks, since the sons had a greater variety of occupations, with less risk, available to them. Moreover, much of this gender difference can be traced to the higher dropout rate of Black men in the secondary schools. And the reason for the Black male's higher dropout rate is aptly noted by Hale (1982, p. 66): "Traditional classrooms," she says, "are generally oriented toward feminine values. Teachers are disproportionately female, and the behaviors tolerated and encouraged are those that are more natural for girls."

Black Male Sexism

Most men are conditioned through the socialization process to believe that they are endowed with qualities of leadership and that women should play a subordinate role in human affairs. Black men cannot help but be affected by the stereotyped roles of men and women. To some degree, they internalize the same values of male supremacy that White men do.

However, various social forces have prevented them from carrying out the oppression of Black women to the same degree that White males oppress White women. Black people have had little control over the enactment of their roles. Black males have not been as overbearing with their women because White society has more severely restrained the behavior of Black men than of Black women. This partly accounts for the very important role of Black women in American history (Collins, 1990; Hooks, 1984). Yet historical records also reveal a number of Black male sexists during the postslavery period. After the Civil War, there were numerous cases of Black men demanding a superior position in the family. Even during slavery, the freed Black male became a patriarch because he had purchased his wife and children from their slavemasters. But most Black men were in chains and had no authority over any individual; in fact, they lacked control over their own lives (Giddings, 1984; King, 1990).

In reviewing the attitudes of Black male leaders, writers, and scholars toward Black women, one finds a mixture of affection, a recognition of their contribution to the Black struggle for liberation, and a desire to protect them from the ravages of White racism. Different Black men have exhibited these feelings in diverse ways. One needs to understand how the times they have lived in have shaped their attitudes toward women. When we analyze the views of the Black nationalist leaders, we find a return to the traditional male position: that women should occupy a subordinate role. Most of these nationalist groups have based their position on historical experiences. In particular, the Republic of New Africa advocates a return to the African patriarchal system, where men make most of the decisions. They also want a reinstatement of the system of polygyny, in which Afro-American men could have more than one wife (Williams, 1990).

The Nation of Islam (commonly known as the Black Muslims) also relates its present position on the role of women to past experiences, when Black men could not support and protect their women, thereby abdicating any role of leadership. Also, Muslims base their attitudes toward the role of women in the Islamic religion. In traditional Muslim society, it is believed that men have a natural right to act as overseers of women. The Black Muslims teach that no marriage can succeed if the woman does not look up to the man with respect. A man must have something above and beyond the wife in order for her to be able to look to him for psychological security (Ali, 1989; White, 1991).

When Malcolm X was a member of the Black Muslims, he echoed the same views. But he had a very close relationship with his wife. In his autobiography (Haley, 1965), he states that he depended heavily on her for the strength to endure some of the crises he faced. Malcolm believed that Islam was the only religion that gives both husband and wife a true understanding of love. According to him, when a woman loses her physical beauty in Western society, she loses her attractiveness. But Islam teaches individuals to look for the spiritual qualities in each other (Haley, 1965). Malcolm's views changed radically after he left the Nation of Islam. In his twelve years as a Muslim minister, he preached so strongly about moral issues that even Muslims charged him with being misogynist. In retrospect, he admitted that every aspect of his teaching and all of his personal beliefs derived from his devotion to the Nation of Islam's leader, Elijah Muhammad. After Malcolm broke from the Muslims in 1963, he steered away from morality and addressed himself to current events and politics. His position on Black women just before he was assassinated was very supportive of their equal rights (Cone, 1991).

Even revolutionary nationalist parties such as the Black Panther Party had questionable views on gender roles. At one time, the official position of the Black Panther Party was that the attempt to repeal the abortion laws was a genocidal plot. One of the former leaders of that party, Eldridge Cleaver (1968, p. 158), stated that "Black women take kindness for weakness. Leave them the least little opening and they will put you on the cross. . . . It would be like trying to pamper a cobra." At least this sentiment was offset by Cleaver's other tributes to Black women. The position of writer and cultural nationalist Immamu Baraka (Sisters for Black Community Development, 1971) was a clear-cut call for Black female subordination. His organization had a doctrine concerning the Black woman's role in it. Women should not smoke, drink, wear slacks, or have abortions. They should not be involved in men's discussions except to serve refreshments. While the men are busy making decisions, women should occupy themselves with ironing, sewing, and cooking. The rationale for this gender segregation of effort was the need to develop a unique Black culture that was bereft of all White concepts.

Reviewing some of the books written by Black men, one finds a certain ambivalence in them about Black women. Although the concept of the Black matriarchy emerged from the writings of E. Franklin Frazier (1939), he held a generally favorable opinion of Black women. He saw the slave woman as the protector of the race. Although he believed the matrifocal family to be undesirable, he was appreciative of the sacrifices Black women had made for their families over the years. His most negative criticism of Black women was reserved for women of the middle class, a group he felt did not measure up to the intellectual and cultural abilities of middle-class White women (Frazier, 1957).

Literature on Black women in the late 1960s was very negative. One of the most virulent criticisms of Black women can be found in Grier and Cobbs's book *Black Rage* (1976). Their treatment of Black women led one Black female reviewer to label them ignorant and stupid. The book, she asserted, is "a clumsy but effective attempt to modernize old stereotypes to explain topics of current interest" (Saxe, 1970, p. 58). Basically, Grier and Cobb's thesis is that the Black woman has been made to feel that she is not worth much and that she arrives at this conclusion through the teachings of her mother, who is also filled with self-hatred. The book also contains other questionable assertions, such as that "Black women lack self-confidence, they are more skin color conscious, preferring those of light-skin, than Black men, and they have abandoned any interest in their feminine appearance" (p. 39). The authors go on to say that the Black woman aspires to the cosmetic

beauty of White America. Since she lacks the qualities of attractiveness and feeling loved, her self-confidence is impaired.
Instead of directing her hatred toward the object of her oppression, she directs it inward.

Presently, many Black male authors summarily dismiss
women's liberation as being irrelevant to Black women. Some
call it a part of America's contradictions, and any contradic-
tion in America should be seen as a White-against-Black
movement ("The Black Sexism Debate," 1979). A Black male
psychologist labels women's liberation as a diversion, an activ-
ist way to ignore racism, and has charged that it is merely
another self-hate and self-destruct mechanism imposed by the
White middle class. Many of the women in this movement,
he says, are trying to substitute the latest revolutionary identity for an unfulfilling personality (Hare and Hare, 1984).

Ironically, the most recent negative assessment of the
Black woman's role in the family has come from a Black
woman. Shahrazad Ali's book *The Blackman's Guide to Understanding the Blackwoman* has generated strong anger among
Afro-American women, who feel it attacks them and blames
them solely for problems in the community and in relationships with Black men. Probably the most provocative statement in the book is Ali's suggestion that Black women who
question the Black male's authority should be soundly
slapped in the mouth. This has led the respected columnist
Dorothy Gilliam (1990, p. D-3) to write: "It's a sad commentary on the state of Black folks in white America when a book
written by a Black Muslim woman that tells Black men to
slap Black women is selling like hot cakes in some areas of
Washington." Still, the appeal of the book to some Black
men is cogent testimony to their belief that they have been a
victim, not a beneficiary, of the independence and strength of
Black women.

The views of those leaders and authors represent a few
Black male opinions out of millions. But they have reached
many people. A Black female author has retorted that Black
men are largely interested in liberation for themselves and are
not sympathetic toward Black females. Indeed, she claims

that Black female subordination is one of their chief goals. Black women should not be lulled into believing that the liberation of Black men is their greatest priority. Few Black men, she says, are their captives, and fewer still seek to be their liberators (Wallace, 1990).

To further refute the notion of a castrated Black male, Hooks (1981) raises the issue of Black male sexism. She contends that male superiority is an institutional value into which Black men are also socialized. While Black men are denied many of the ordinary perquisites of manhood, they are still elevated above the status of Black women on the basis of gender affiliation alone. Using the statements of certain Black male leaders, she advances the argument that Black women must not allow Black men to define the role of women as subordinate and unequal. The conclusion is that Black women should hold their men accountable for their actions and demand parity in decision making and leadership organizations.

As for gender-role attitudes in the larger Black community, research has indicated a greater split between attitudes and behavior for Black Americans than for other groups. A number of studies discovered that Blacks have more traditional beliefs regarding family values and roles than comparable White respondents (Ransford and Miller, 1983; Rao and Rao, 1985; Uzzell, 1986). But Blacks score higher on the liberal or egalitarian behavioral dimensions of marital roles like women working and sharing child care and housework (Taylor, Chatters, Tucker, and Lewis, 1990). Many Black marriages involve greater female autonomy, individualism, role sharing, and decision making (Ross, 1987). Despite the gender inequalities and stereotypes of Black male-female conflict over their gender roles, research shows that the overwhelming majority of Black women are either married to or in a relationship with Black men (Tucker and Taylor, 1989).

The Rise of Feminism

Black women are, of course, victims of sexist values and practices emanating from within and outside the Black community. In part, it is a different brand of sexism than that faced by White women. There is less inequality of income between Black women and men. In general, Black women earn 84 percent of the income of Black men (White women only earn 62 percent of White male income). College-educated Black women actually have a higher median income than college-educated White women and earn 85 percent of the median income of college-educated Black males (King, 1990). Also, Black women are actually better educated than Black men at most levels (National Center for Education Statistics, 1991b).

This, however, has not prevented Black men from gaining ascendancy over women by virtue of their gender. Despite having more education, Black women consistently earn less than Black males. In addition, they suffer many of the same liabilities faced by White women due to the pervasiveness of sexism in this society. Like all other American women, they face a formidable level of violence and harassment from males. Black women are the victims of gender stereotyping, are expected to cater to male desires and assume a subordinate role, and are forced in many cases to bear the responsibility for family planning alone.

Feminism as an organized social movement has attracted few Black women, but its impact on attitudes toward women's roles has been noticeable and on the increase. In part it is responsible for a reluctance to marry. Whatever the virtues of marriage, it is evident that it is an institution that favors men. Although some Black single women express the need for an egalitarian marriage, it is a demand that can hardly be placed before Black men who operate as buyers in a buyer's market. Thus, some single women refuse to consider joining an institution where their needs have a low priority (Heiss, 1988). Whereas Black women's main concerns relate to the problems of racism and economic survival, they are increasingly becoming preoccupied with the issues of gender per se. As a result, we have witnessed a burgeoning of black feminist organizations to tackle women's issues (Collins, 1990).

One group of Black women issued a manifesto that declared sexism to be a destructive and crippling force within the Black community (Combahee River Collective, 1982). Black feminism is not always a protest against male political and economic domination. Instead, it may reflect tension in interpersonal relationships. In referring to male joblessness and female-headed households, one woman writer has asserted that "these conditions are the result of economic transformations. They change gender relations as they change the marital, family, and labor arrangements of women and men" (Zinn, 1990, p. 262). This economic disenfranchisement, says C. W. Franklin (1987), is a gender phenomenon of such magnitude that it affects the meaning and definition of masculinity for Black men.

Many techniques used in forging the women's liberation movement were borrowed from or paralleled those of the civil rights movement: all-Black organizations, creation of Black consciousness and identity, the changing of names that signified their unequal status, and so on. Women adopted some of these practices because they had been successfully used by Blacks. But they also asserted that their situation was very similar to that of Blacks (Giddings, 1984). It is to be expected that any group that defines itself as the object of oppression will share similar traits with other oppressed groups. One of the most obvious similarities between women and Blacks is that both are discriminated against on the basis of their physical characteristics. Blacks suffer because of their skin color, and women encounter discrimination because of their gender. Both are said to be innately inferior, less intelligent, more emotional, dependent, and so on. With both groups, their physical traits are said to create certain barriers to their social achievement. This fact, then, becomes the explanation for their unequal status in society (Wolf, 1991).

Many specific parallels have been drawn between the situations of women and Blacks. For example, women are socialized to fit into certain occupational roles, such as secretary, waitress, schoolteacher, and so forth. They are discouraged from entering traditionally masculine jobs and denied training for those jobs. As with Blacks, women are then deprived of employment in certain fields on the ground that they are not skilled. Both groups are consigned to low-paying, monotonous jobs where a high rate of absenteeism and turnover is typical. It is then said that both groups are too unstable to trust with more responsibility (King, 1990).

One can make an analogy between the different terms applied to women and Blacks. Women are frequently called "girls," while Black adult males are referred to as "boy." In both cases, the term implies that the individuals under discussion are not capable of full adulthood. The same reasoning applies in distinguishing women by their marital status (Miss or Mrs.), while men are not so differentiated. Blacks were the only racial group or nationality referred to by a Spanish word for their color (Negro), while others were known by their land of origin (Hooks, 1984).

Probably one of the most interesting similarities between women and Blacks is that membership in their group may transcend all other attributes they possess. Among Blacks, for example, their skin color is the one bond that ties them together. Even the wealthiest Black man faces some problems because of his blackness. For women, the double standard in society's attitudes toward age in men and women represents an obvious liability. Older women represent the lowest-prestige group in American society. Since the value of women is closely associated with their sex appeal and reproductive capacity, the aging process gradually diminishes their worth—both socially and personally. One result of this fact is that middle age can be much more stressful for women than men (Wolf, 1991).

Despite the commonalities just discussed, the nature of Black oppression is very different from that of women. Blacks are, as a group, confined to separate quarters, where they suffer the worst of social ills. Women may be the only oppressed group in history that lives with their adversary. Yet, because of their close ties to men, they do not share the economic deprivation of Blacks. The problems of substandard housing, poor nutrition, inadequate services, and lack of other essentials that affect Blacks do not affect White women to the same degree (Joseph and Lewis, 1981). Many of the conditions that middle-class White feminists have found oppressive are perceived as privileges by Afro-American women, particularly those with low incomes. The option not to work outside the home, for example, is a luxury historically unavailable to most Black women. According to King (1990), the desire to struggle for that option can, in such a context, represent a feminist position, precisely because it represents greater liberty for certain women.

Whether women's liberation is relevant to Black women is a subject of considerable controversy in the Black community. White women assert that Black and white women share a common oppression: that Blacks cannot be free until women are free. Hooks (1981) questions whether certain women, particularly those self-identified feminists who are White and middle class, are truly oppressed as opposed to discriminated against. Others have charged that the race-sex analogy is exploitative and racist (King, 1990).

Summary

The Black male's response to the charge of sexism has been slow in forthcoming. To a large extent he believes, as do many White males, that the women's demand for equal rights is a threat to whatever masculinity he has been allowed by the larger society. There is some resentment, particularly among middle-class Black males, about what is considered the preferential treatment of Black women in the workplace, since they may be used as a double minority in affirmative action hiring. But the impact of feminism is forcing some changes in Black male behavior. One notes a discernible erosion of the sexual double standard, more men participating in child care, and the sharing of housework and decision making. One factor retarding these changes in male behavior is the excess number of women over men in the Black community. Because of the severe competition for the small pool of eligible Black males, many Black women are still forced to take marriage on male terms.

The machinations of American society have placed Black men in a position where one-half are without jobs, they are the only sex-race group whose life expectancy actually declined in the last decade, many are not keeping pace with the educational progress of other sex-race groups, and they have made less progress in white-collar areas relative to White males than Black females have made relative to White females (Staples, 1991a; C. W. Franklin, 1987). Thus, it is clear that for them, the problems caused by the legacy of racism will continue to take precedence over the need to address sexism. Although many middle-class Black males will increasingly have to concentrate on the changing role of women, Black males of the working class must continue to confront the challenge of economic survival. Many Black women, however, will refuse to permit men to dominate the definitions of Black womanhood and will demand parity in the home and in all other aspects of life.

What will happen in the future is hard to determine. Many Black men will continue to fall behind Black women in their educational and economic progress. The result may be a Black female dominance of high-status positions. Some segments of American society will be pleased with this result, because they perceive Black women to be less threatening to their racial hegemony. At the same time, large numbers of Black women—and men—will continue to occupy the bottom rung of the socioeconomic ladder. Whether either is better off than the other is an academic question; the need is for both racial and gender equity. The issues of gender and of race are too interwoven to separate at this time. Significant changes must await a serious effort by this society to eliminate both racism and sexism from American life.

7

Marital Patterns and Interactions

The popular song of the 1950s declaring that "Love and marriage go together like a horse and carriage" expresses the Western variety of love. Among Americans, love is almost exclusively celebrated as feelings of passion, excitement, and closeness. It is expected to precede marriage and thereafter to be the foundation for marriage. In its purest or ideal form, husband-wife love is monogamous, eternal, and forsakes all other relationships (Crosby, 1991; Strong and DeVault, 1992; Blood and Wolfe, 1960). Black Americans' acceptance of this Western form of marriage is inconsistent with the customs of their African heritage. A historical understanding of Black marriages helps to illuminate the transformation that has taken place since preslavery days. Since Chapter One provides a broad historical account of Black families, we will only briefly select key aspects of this history that highlight the evolution of the love-marriage linkage, the primacy given to the husband-wife relationship, and monogamy.

History of Black Marriages

Traditional African societies gave low priority to expressions of love prior to marriage and higher priority to the economic and other functional interdependency between husbands and wives. If love and deep affection developed, they grew largely from living together and from the cooperation of husband and wife in the struggle for a livelihood. Love as a prerequisite to marriage was considered potentially disruptive, for it involved individual choice, thus increasing the risk of bringing together individuals from different backgrounds. Marriage as a utilitarian device served to perpetuate family tradition and wealth along socially prescribed lines. Consequently, marriage and divorce in Africa were strictly regulated by the families of the bride and groom. They controlled it by arranging child marriages, isolating the genders premaritally, placing severe limits on the field of eligible mates, and of course matching the bride and groom. The elders made these arrangements without even seeking approval from the state or religious bodies. In this latter sense, common law marriages in the United States that have the approval of the concerned families are directly in line with African custom (Herskovits, 1941).

African marriages were organized around two contrasting bases: *consanguinity*, which refers to blood kinship, and *affinity*, which refers to kinship created by law. In contrast to European custom, the consanguine group and not the conjugal pair was paramount (Sudarkasa, 1988). As an example, the wife's tie to her own family was presumed to exist in perpetuity, whereas her tie to her husband could be dissolved. Despite the fact that the groom paid a bride-price in compensation for taking away a member of the family, the bride's family continued to maintain an active interest in her welfare. In matrilineal societies, the newlyweds lived in the compound of the bride's blood relatives and the husband was considered an in-marrying spouse. In such societies, the wife's brother exercised so much authority, particularly over the children, that some anthropologists considered the husband a stranger in his own home (Stephens, 1963). Consistent with the importance placed on consanguinity, in a crisis most brothers and sisters took sides with their siblings against their wives or husbands. This is not to say that conjugality was totally discounted. The bride's husband was expected to guarantee good treatment, and wives were expected to reciprocate by working hard. However, the extended blood kin remained paramount.

Conjugality did not include the element of exclusivity found in Euro-American marital dyads. In the context of polygamy, men and women frequently had sexual liaisons with more than one partner. These liaisons did not necessarily threaten marital stability. Children from such unions only served to strengthen the lineage, particularly in patrilineage systems where men aspired to have as many children as possible.

This pattern of family organization meant that the stability of the family did not depend on the stability of the couple. When marriages dissolved, this did not have the ramifications of contemporary American divorce. Remarriages usually followed, and children remained with members of their lineage even if the in-marrying parent left the village (Sudarkasa, 1988; Omari, 1965; J. H. Franklin, 1987; Herskovits, 1941).

Slavery changed the African pattern of marriage formation and function. The greatest loss in this change was not the denial of legal marriage, because in Africa the state was not an active agent. Rather, it was the loss of strict kinship control over the marriage institution, which drastically changed the meaning and character of marriage. The slavemaster replaced consanguine authority. His ultimate interest was in economic profit from his slave investments; he had no regard for the slaves' African mores and kinship relationships.

Ironically, with regard to mate choice, slaves had greater individual freedom in colonial America than in Africa. Many slavemasters allowed their slaves to pick their mate and only required them to ask permission to marry. On occasion, the master allowed them to pick a mate from another plantation or from the free Black population. After gaining their master's consent, the couple could live together without further formality. However, in most cases the slaves themselves conducted their own rituals. A typical account of this ritual is given by an ex-slave: "When you married, you had to jump over a broom three times. 'Dat was de license" (Meltzer, 1964, p. 46). "Jumping the broomstick" was usually done in front of other slaves or a slave minister, who included in his remarks the phrase "until death or distance do you part" (Simms-Brown, 1982). In some cases, a White clergyman would conduct a solemn ceremony. While free slaves generally secured state licenses and had a civil religious ceremony, this was generally not the case when they married a slave. Masters generally intervened in the process when slaves were slow in picking their own mate: "Marsa used to sometimes pick our wives fo' us. If he didn't have on his place enough women for the men, he would wait on de side of de road til a big wagon loaded with slaves come by. Den Marsa would stop de ole nigger-trader and buy you a woman" (Meltzer, 1964, p. 46).

Greater freedom existed in marital formation than in its dissolution. Although slavemasters generally kept couples together for the sake of morale, the couple knew that the permanency of their marriage depended on the economic stability and interest of their master: in this they had no control. Because masters separated families for economic profit, some slaves found themselves in polygamous arrangements. Slave women and men were first and foremost full-time workers and breeders for their master, and only incidentally a parent or spouse. Thus, whether slaves were in monogamous or polygamous marriages was of little concern to profit-hungry slavemasters (Steckel, 1980; Brouwer, 1975; J. H. Franklin, 1987; Stampp, 1956).

Emancipation restored only a modified version of the African marriage formation. Families regained their control, but the state gained authority, polygamy eventually lost its appeal, and love as a precondition for marriage replaced the decision of the elders. The importance of the state became evident as thousands of former slaves who had "jumped the broomstick" in slavery formally renewed their vows. Acquiring a marriage license was tantamount to declaring one's freedom. However, not all ex-slaves embraced monogamy.

Retention of African polygamous practices was observed by nineteenth-century abolitionists working in the Sea Islands off the coast of South Carolina. They noticed that men who worked on more than one plantation often had wives and families in various locations on the islands. These polygamous arrangements were noted to be quite stable. Thinking that this "immoral" practice was rooted in their former slave life or their African culture, the abolitionists sent missionaries to convert these ex-slaves to monogamy and to the model of provider-dominant husband and domesticated-submissive wife. They appeared to be successful in bringing about the demise of polygamy. However, the need for cotton production during and after the war years as well as the continuing necessity for two incomes among Black families meant that the traditional submissive wife could only be accepted in principle, if at all.

The dilution of the African tradition is also evident in the way contemporary Black Americans and African-educated young people differ in their definition of love or what they consider to be desirable traits in a mate. But before we consider this difference, we should note that no one study compares the marital expectations of modern African and Black American young adults. Our information is gathered from a few scattered studies that provide information on one or the other group. While these studies are not directly comparable, taken together they give us a glimpse of the possible differences that exist.

Like American Black youth, modern educated African young adults have been influenced by the Western concept of love. Nevertheless, love has different meanings for these two groups. Unlike American Blacks, for Africans nonemotional factors outrank emotional and affectionate feelings. For both genders, affection is ranked ten on a fifteen-point scale for Africans, whereas for American young people, affection is not only a prerequisite for marriage, but among the majority of American Black females it is considered a prerequisite for premarital sexual intimacy. Furthermore, for Africans, obedience is explicitly stated as an important aspect of love, but not for Americans. Based on their ranking of mate selection traits, both genders in Africa are identical in their desire to find a mate who will place love for their children before their love for their spouse. Children are seen as critical to the continuity of the lineage, and without children, a substantial number feel they would either leave their spouse or lose their love for them. Children are not even ranked as a component of love for Black Americans. Given the central place of children in traditional African society, it makes sense that what is generally considered to be "love" in the Western world is deemphasized in Africa in favor of the love that centers around children (King and Griffin, 1983; Griffin, 1982; Reiss, 1976; Johnson, 1978; Omari, 1965).

Few Black Americans enter marriage without declaring their love for their mate. Yet marriages are not based solely on love. There are external forces or societal norms that dictate the relative characteristics of the couple. In general, males are expected to be superior in age and also in terms of social, economic, and educational status. However, there is a limit: a certain amount of *homogamy* or similarity is also expected. A male married to a female over four years his junior may be accused of "robbing the cradle," or if she is several years his senior, he may be accused of marrying for her money. *Heterogamy* refers to couples who have substantial differences in characteristics such as these. In addition, couples are expected to share the same marital history. For example, it is expected that divorced females will marry divorced males, and never-married females will marry never-married males.

Overall, society does not support substantial differences between couples, particularly if these differences are in racial or religious membership. Exogamous norms that forbid intermarrying on color and religious lines are often based on deep-grained prejudices. However, these norms also reflect society's belief about the important ingredients necessary for a successful marriage. Couple similarities in demographics are deemed important because they are believed to be an indication of shared values, interest, and mutual friendship networks—all of which support marital stability.

Societal norms for mate selection are not as easily met in the Black community. Since an imbalanced gender ratio exists, it is not surprising that relative to Whites, Black couples violate these norms more frequently. According to one national study, compared to White females, Black females are far more likely to marry someone at least four years older, and those females married once are more than twice as likely to wed formerly married men. Moreover, whereas 24 percent of White wives have higher educational status than their husbands, 36 percent of Black wives are higher. Among the college-educated husbands, the ideal in male educational superiority is most likely to be realized. Fifty-nine percent of husbands with some college have higher education than their wives, whereas only 11.6 percent of husbands with no college are higher. Half of the husbands with no college education have wives with the same amount of education (Spanier and Glick, 1980).

Obviously, those with higher education have a larger field of marital partners. From their advantaged position, most choose to conform to societal norms by maintaining a superior educational position in their marriages. Black college men are a rare breed and are in the best position to pick and choose.

And pick and choose they do. High preference is given to light-skinned women regardless of whether the men married before, during, or after the "Black is beautiful" season of the 1960s. The Black nationalist movement may have changed Blacks' preoccupation with trying to become White through processing or straightening their hair, lightening their skin with commercial cosmetics, or tightening their lips to reduce their size, but it did not significantly change the preference for light-skinned women.

As far as the light-skinned women are concerned, dark-skinned men have become more desirable mates since the 1960s. Apparently, the Black pride of the 1960s coupled with the greater job and educational opportunities made dark-skinned men more ambitious than their lighter-skinned brothers. Darker-skinned men are more willing to sacrifice everything to get a better job, and in the height of the civil rights movement, they were more likely to achieve occupational mobility. Darker-skinned men prior to the 1960s may have had the same ambition, but there were few opportunities (Udry, Bauman, and Chase, 1971). Since women tend to select men on educational, occupational, or income attributes first, light-skinned women become color blind when offered a marriage proposal from an educated dark-skinned suitor.

Unfortunately, because many Black men still prefer light skin, dark-skinned women remain at a disadvantage in the marriage market. Despite Black males' light-tone preference, many still marry dark-skinned women for three reasons. First, dark-skinned women outnumber their lighter sisters. Second, since the 1960s, dark-skinned women have reduced some of the educational advantages light-skinned women had over them, thus increasing their desirability as suitable mates. Third, despite the darker males' earlier progress, a recent study reveals that lighter-toned males are disproportionately located in higher economic and occupational positions (Keith and Herring, 1991). Apparently, the economic recessions and political conservatism that began in the 1970s continue to impede equal opportunity for all minorities, especially for dark-skinned men.

When light skin color is the dominant criterion for mate selection, Black women of all shades must deal with the competition from White women. With White women also available to Black males, they realize that Black males of higher status will no longer have to settle for light-skinned Black women when they can get the real thing. As Calvin Hernton (1965) puts it, now light-skinned women will have to stop "playing White" in the Black community and prove themselves as desirable females.

Interracial Couples

White women as competition is not a new phenomenon. Many believe that the gateway to the public display of affection between White women and Black men began with the 1966 *Loving v. Virginia* U.S. Supreme Court decision, which declared laws prohibiting interracial marriage unconstitutional. This is a logical turning point: since then the number of all interracial marriages has increased 2.5 times, from 310,000 to 827,000. Today, about 1.5 percent of all marriages are interracial (Strong and DeVault, 1992). Miscegenation laws are powerful, but throughout American history there have been periods where they were ignored or did not exist. In the beginning, America made little social distinction on account of race (J. H. Franklin, 1987).

Some scholars hypothesize that regardless of legal statutes, uneven sex ratios serve to encourage the formation of interracial unions. According to the "sex ratio" theory, people will marry more within their group if their own group has a relatively well-balanced distribution of the genders. Imbalances push the disadvantaged gender into scouting in the outgroup's territory (Guttentag and Secord, 1983). Three points in history demonstrate this notion. As noted earlier, in the beginning of American slave history, there was a shortage of Black female slaves. Consequently, the number of sexual relations between Black slaves and indentured White women was fairly high. Black males were even encouraged to marry White women, since the children from such unions would also be enslaved, thereby increasing the property of the slavemaster (Staples, 1992).

A second period occurred during and after the Civil War, when the passage of antimiscegenation laws had already taken place. The shortage of White males created by the war resulted in an upsurge in White women who either married or cohabitated with Black men. The death and maiming of millions of White males meant that White women had to violate caste boundaries if they wanted a male mate (Blassingame, 1972). This was not a difficult mate choice for the many White women who had internalized the prevailing myths about the Black man's extraordinary strength and exhaustless sexual desire. Also, the social reforms during Reconstruction increased the Black man's social and economic status and heightened his appeal (Spickard, 1989).

Just as these sexual stereotypes may have stimulated White women, the Black male may have been attracted by the White woman's higher social standing as well as her forbidden-fruit status. The penalties for having sex with a White female were severe, and as far as some Black males were concerned, this created an aura of mystic enticement around all White women. Against this backdrop of taboos, lies, and stereotypes about Black sexuality and sacred White woman-hood, the stage was set for mutual attraction. For the first time in American history, Black and White women openly competed for the attention of Black men. Obviously, racial relations did not significantly change as a result of these few unions. They do, however, demonstrate how demographic changes, apart from the law, can alter mate selection choices.

Finally, during the late 1960s Black males found them-selves returning the White females' attention. Recruited for their athletic ability, they often found themselves on predom-inantly White campuses, where Black women were few or nonexistent. Given the more liberal atmosphere of college campuses, the 1960s hype on civil rights, and White women's push for sexual and economic liberation, interracial dating and marriages took a sudden upswing. Black males and White females were meeting for the first time as equals with shared educational values and goals. White females found themselves emancipated from parental control and enmeshed in a network of friends that was more liberal than the one they left at home. Part of their newfound freedom was expressed through crossing the color line.

As the proportion of Black female students increased, they again found themselves competing for a scarce number of Black men. For them, a real crisis is created when Black college men cross the color line. College-educated Black women have a narrow field of eligibles. Not only do Black men become more scarce, but the qualities Black middle-class women look for become even harder to find. There is a genu-ine fear among Black bourgeois women of the competition from White women for Black men that dates back to E. Franklin Frazier's observation some years ago. He noted that Black middle-class women attempt to justify their fear by stating that the Black man always has an inferior position in relation to the White woman or that he marries much below his social status. Frazier believes that such rationalizations by Black women conceal their deep-seated feelings of insecurity and inadequacy, since they have no objection to the marriage of a White man to a Black woman, especially if he is reputed to be wealthy (Frazier, 1957).

Recent studies show that while interracial marriages do not shield the Black partner from his lower position in society, Black men, like Black women, tend to marry in the expected socioeconomic direction: Black men down, Black women up. There is no evidence of hypergamy—that is, a situation where a White female gains more status in terms of education if she marries a Black man than if she marries within her own race (Tucker and Mitchell-Kernan, 1990; Heer, 1974).

On predominantly White campuses, the intensity of the competition between Black women and White women deceases as the size of the Black student population increases. This situation has caused some students of race relations to observe that the absolute size of the group also influences the rate of intermixing. On those campuses where Blacks are found in small numbers, interracial mating increases; conversely, as the Black student body increases, the cross-racial mating decreases. On one large Western state campus with a Black student population of 100 males and far fewer females, over 90 percent of the Black males said they had dated interracially. This high percentage partially reflects the prestige many women students attach to dating an athlete (Sebald, 1974; Willie and Levy, 1972). Regardless of sports involvement, the evidence shows that a significant number of Black males have dated interracially (see Staples, 1981).

This pattern of group size and cross-racial mating appears so consistently that when it was first observed in the larger society, it was regarded as a sociological truism or a law of intermarrying. These theories based on sex ratios and group size do not explain, however, why so few Black women date and marry interracially when so few Black males are available. In many ways, Black women face a more complex and enigmatic situation. Black women suffer from a split image. In the eyes of Whites, she is a mixed bag—sexually alluring, romantically passionate, animalistic, motherly, and unattractive. Throughout history, White men believed that White women belonged on a pedestal and Black women in their bedrooms. Filling historical annals are numerous accounts of forced sex between White masters and female slaves, White bosses and Black workers, and rape by White men not acquainted with their Black victims. Few White men married Black women, for marriage assumed a degree of equality that White society would not accept. This background of exploitation makes Black women suspicious of any advances from White men. When Black women accept the dates from White males, they seldom give in to sex, particularly on the first date. According to one study, 70 percent of Black males and only 25 percent of White males reported having intercourse on at least one of their interracial dates. No White male reported having a one-night fling, whereas 50 percent of Black males had at least one (Sebald, 1974). Further, many Black females are made to feel guilty by Black men when they jump the color line. This seems hypocritical, since many of the males making the criticism date interracially themselves. This double standard works in the Black males' interest, since most of those who date White will only marry Black (Willie and Levy, 1972).

Another element holding back Black female–White male unions is the social expectation that the male be the aggressor. White males are not generally motivated to date or marry Black women. Those who are interested feel that their motives may be misunderstood in light of historical exploitation, while others fear social retribution, family disinheritance, or damage to their career. Further, Hollywood has been a powerful force in promoting the European standard of beauty—long blond hair, blue eyes, thin noses—over negroid features. While women are more likely to select on the basis of "earning power" or "ambition," men continue to be enticed by physical attractiveness as defined by White society (Tucker and Mitchell-Kernan, 1990; "The Black Male Shortage," 1986).

Although these forces have and do operate, Black women–White male marriages may be increasing. But given that

Black male–White female pairings are decreasing, the reverse coupling may be an illusion. In other words, if the typical pattern continues to decrease and the atypical White male–Black female unions merely remained constant, it would eventually appear as if the atypical is now typical. Regardless of the possible change, many Black women have altered their position on dating White males as they find it increasingly difficult to find a Black mate with status equal to or higher than their own ("The Black Male Shortage," 1986). Their attitude coincides with attitude changes in the general population.

There is growing acceptance of interracial marriages. In a national survey, 20 percent of all Americans reported that they had dated interracially. Naturally, there were regional differences. The South had the lowest incidence of biracial dating (10 percent), while the West had the highest rate (one out of three) (Staples, 1992). Blacks and Whites are not only meeting as equals on college campuses, but also in the workplace, in neighborhoods, and in the last bastion—the churches.

However, prejudice still exists. Some White parents still disown or isolate their children if they intermarry, and some Black families will only accept a White in-law if they show some appreciation or understanding of Black people. In addition to encountering the common discrimination against Blacks in general, such as in housing and the workplace, some interracial couples become estranged from their family and lifelong friends. Many interracial couples still claim that they are shut out of much of the social life in Black circles and do not fit perfectly within White social groups.

Contrary to popular wisdom of the early 1970s, children from such unions were found to be no worse off than Black children in general. They were considered Black by both communities, and found themselves adjusting to Black problems and Black customs (" 'You Can't Join Their Clubs,' " 1991; Aldridge, 1978; Porterfield, 1973). However, as these children have reached young adulthood, some have begun to express discontent with their social status. There are those who claim that they are forced to choose between Black and White and wish for their own "beige" category. Many multiethnic Americans are forming support groups to help them deal with their unique issues (Atkins, 1991; Donloe, 1987; Porterfield, 1973).

Other popular accounts show biracial persons adjusting well to both their White and Black heritage (" 'You Can't Join Their Clubs,' " 1991). Without a large survey of biracial adult children, it is unclear whether interracial unions produce the "tragic mulattoes" or the "love children" who will be the catalyst for future racial harmony. More than homogeneous ones, interracial couples must undoubtedly rely on their own determination to continue the marriage when social support fails.

To optimize social congeniality, interracial couples generally search out communities that are more tolerant: the West as opposed to the South. The Tucker and Mitchell-Kernan (1990) study shows that a disproportionate number of mixed couples living in the West have migrated from the North, a foreign country, or to a far lesser degree the South. Their study also suggests that it is not sufficient for the host environment to be more tolerant. The likelihood of an interracial union is generally maximized if the individuals grew up in a racial environment where race relationships are somewhat more permissive, such as in urban areas or in the North or where they did not experience firsthand knowledge of racial tensions, such as in a foreign country (Tucker and Mitchell-Kernan, 1990; Aldridge, 1978).

Whether moving to a more tolerant climate puts interracial couples on the same marital stability footing as Black-Black or White-White marriages is unclear. The few published studies are inconsistent (Heer, 1974; Monahan, 1970). Obviously the race difference is not in their favor. Not so obvious is the fact that many of these marriages violate other social norms—homogamy in marital history and age. Compared to those in homogamous marriages, either or both women and men in interracial marriages are more likely to be older, previously married, or significantly different in age from their partner (either older or much younger than their partner). For example, White men married to Black women in Los Angeles are on the average 6.7 years older than their wives, whereas husbands in White marriages and Black marriages were only 1.5 and 1.0 years older on the average (Tucker and Mitchell-Kernan, 1990; Bass, 1982).

All these demographic differences are associated with a lower chance of marital stability. Yet some argue that mixed marriages begin with greater commitment, and so they can overcome these odds. Others believe that interracial couples are doubly doomed because they violate societal norms on several fronts and they marry for the wrong reasons—rebellion against society or parents, sexual curiosity, and status. A popular motive ascribed to Blacks is that they hate being Black and marrying White is a way of compensating for their feelings of inferiority. The fact that many of those who remarry were formerly married to members of their own race casts some doubt on this motive. There is no question that a significant proportion of all American marriages are formed on neurotic and irrational bases. However, ascribing such judgments to all interracial couples does serious injustice to the healthy individuals who have the courage to ignore social norms and live out their love convictions. Further, ascribing these negative motives feeds the racist concept that Blacks and Whites are unable to live together in loving relationships. There is no scientific evidence to show that these motives differ by racially homogeneous and heterogamous marriages. If you ask interracial couples why they married, most will eventually say they married for love (Bass, 1982).

About 22 percent (3.4 percent of all Black couples and 0.3 percent of all White couples) of interracial marriages are between Blacks and Whites. Even when considering other possible racial mixtures, interracial marriages only represent 1.5 percent of all marriages in the United States (Strong and DeVault, 1992; Glick, 1988). Thus, in the remaining portion of this chapter we will focus on commonalities and variations among typical Black marriages—that is, where both husband and wife share the same racial heritage.

Marital Sexuality

The literature on marital sex among Black couples is sparse. As noted earlier, the assumption is that Blacks have a relaxed attitude toward sex. This assumption is primarily based on limited data on working-class blacks as well as on extrapolations from data showing higher rates of liberal premarital sexual behavior and attitudes among Blacks than among Whites. It is true that Blacks have a more relaxed attitude toward premarital sex. But given the negative experiences many Black women have after their first premarital experience, there is no reason to totally romanticize Black marital sex. Whether liberal attitudes and sexual behavior prior to marriage translate into affectionate and healthy sexual performance within marriage is also unclear. Few studies exist to help in separating fact from fiction.

There is no large-scale empirical study to test whether Frazier was correct in characterizing the middle class as having sexually starved women and glamorous sexually restless men who seek sexual promiscuity as a compensation for their impotence in the White world. Undoubtedly, their dual-earner life-style results in battle fatigue that adversely affects the frequency and quality of their sex life. We suspect that like White dual-earner couples, the frequency of their sexual activities is lower than among couples who are not dual earners. For sure, the marriage chambers of Black couples are not devoid of the complaints of insensitivity, sexual inhibitions, and unimaginativeness that echo through the bedrooms of Whites.

According to one study, 10 percent of Black wives said that their husbands were never affectionate, and another 27 percent felt they were only affectionate once in a while. A quarter of these wives also indicated that their husbands perceive them as affectionate never or only once in a while (Addison, 1983; Wheeler, 1977). Although a quarter to a third represent a minority, it certainly does not add fuel to the various sexual stereotypes surrounding Black sexuality.

Of course, affection is not the same as sexual performance. However, for many, particularly females, it is an important precondition for heightening sexual pleasure. As far as performance is concerned, therapists are reporting that Afro-American couples, primarily the nonpoor, are increasingly seeking therapy for a variety of sexual problems. This is due partly to the greater acceptance and availability of sex clinics, as well as to the increased ability to pay for such services through sliding-fee scales.

Sex therapists are reporting that they are getting couples with performance anxiety and poor sexual communication because a significant number have internalized the myth of their own super sexuality. Typifying such couples are Ann, a twenty-three-year-old shy and slightly overweight wife, and John, her tall and thin twenty-seven-year-old husband. Ann had been uninterested in sex during all of their six-year marriage. The problem intensified after the birth of their two children. John expected her to have sex every night during the two hours they were home together. Within these hours, family dinner also had to be served. John clearly felt he was "taking care of business," as was expected of a Black man. He even wore a badge sewn on his jeans that read "superstud." Ann was filled with guilt because she did not live up to the image of the "sexy Black woman," either physically or mentally (Wyatt, 1982). Clearly both partners attempted to emulate the stereotypes, despite the fact that their schedules and individual needs were not being met. Unfortunately, we do not know what proportion of Ann-and-John couples exist among all Black couples. But there may be as many as a quarter, and that is cause for concern.

Marital Conflict

Marriages are not without their conflicts. The amount of disagreement or hostility that may exist without breaking up a marriage varies. Some marriages thrive on constant bickering and violent behavior; in others, the marriage is threatened by the least bit of disagreement or hostility. The issues argued about range from the way the toothpaste is squeezed to sex and decision making, from in-laws and music to political and religious issues. And as the emotional housekeepers of marriage, women see conflicts as being both more intense and more frequent than men. We cannot possibly cover the myriad of conflict areas, so we will focus on those on which scientific information is available.

Conflict over decision-making style is the cause of much tension for working-class Black families. In those few cases when wives make unilateral decisions, the marriages tend to break up. Husbands who insist on using this style create a great deal of negative feelings between themselves and their wives, but their behavior is less likely to result in separation or divorce. Undoubtedly, their behavior is more tolerated because it fits into the culturally prescribed role of a male being in control of his family.

Interestingly, as important as decision making is to the Black working-class, it is much more important in White families, where strict "male" and "female" roles are most often observed. Crossing over into the husbands' domain just does not have the same impact in the Black family, where role assignments are more flexible. On the other hand, Black working-class families are sensitive about how conflicts are resolved. Wives who perceive that their husbands "give in" often during their arguments are more likely to stay in the relationship than those wives who believe that their spouse never or seldom gives in. Further, "giving in" has its greatest benefits in democratic marriages, as opposed to those that are nondemocratic (Strong and DeVault, 1992; DeJarnett and Raven, 1981; Osmond, 1977; Scanzoni, 1978).

When "blow-ups" occur, they are most likely to be about sex (Osmond, 1977). Sexual fights are not so much about the sexual performance of their mate, since many Black women are assumed to have relaxed and accepting attitudes toward sex. Rather, tension is most likely to be sparked by extramarital affairs, which are fairly common. Several years ago, when Robert Bell (1970) asked his Black working-class female subjects if a wife should expect running around, 56 percent of them answered yes. Over the years, this expectation has not changed.

Lower-class men, particularly those who have a marginal relationship to both jobs and community organizations, have difficulty developing intimacy. Although many factors undermine their efforts for marital harmony, it is their struggle with two competing sets of values that weighs heaviest. Most desire stable long-term marriages, but they also want relationships with women outside of the marriage. Their first image is that of a good husband and father who works hard to provide for his family. The second self-image is that of a single young man who is attractive to many women and is perceived by them as a swinger and good lover. Lower-class communities hold both images in high esteem, but the second image is seen as more heroic. When there are problems with work that leave them feeling vulnerable and incapable of filling the provider role, they seek compensation in the image of the swinger and lover (Gooden, 1989). Often, extramarital affairs involve using grocery money for drinking, gambling, new clothes, and entertaining the many available women in the Black community. Consequently, fights over money become a secondary issue in the marriage.

The fact that money is seldom the dominant issue may seem odd, since a nationwide survey showed 54 percent of American families frequently argue over money (Strong and DeVault, 1992). Perhaps these lower-class couples seldom fight over it because there is little discretionary money available. Both partners clearly understand that their limited financial resources must go for survival—food, shelter, and clothing. When the money fails to reach home because of the vices of one or the other spouse, it becomes a source of serious conflict. Because many lower-class couples possess ineffective conflict resolution skills, many arguments degenerate into physical fights that are often interrupted by the police (Gooden, 1989; Bell, 1971; Rainwater, 1966).

Within the middle-class family, the conflicts are more likely to be centered around money. Husbands often accuse their wives of excessive spending (a subject explored more fully in Chapter Three). Other reasons given for marital tension are preference in social activities and extramarital affairs.

Unlike their lower-class brothers, their commitment to marriage and the companionship and attention marriage provides makes them work harder at resolving conflicts in a constructive way. Further, when marital conflict arises, they are more likely than lower-class couples to be guided in effective conflict resolution by successful parental role models or the active intervention of maternal or paternal advisers.

This is not to say that extramarital affairs do not exist. In contrast to their lower-class counterparts, middle-class husbands do not make such affairs public if they can help it. But like lower-class husbands, they have experienced a double self-image. In college, many lived out the playboy image by having women friends on campus who they planned to marry and others in town who they dated just for fun. But once they got a "good-paying" job and established linkages with community organizations, they were able to live out their primary dream of husband-father who not only provides for his family, but receives positive affirmation both at home and in the community. The difference between the lower-class and middle-class husbands primarily reflects their socialization and relationship to the outside world (Gooden, 1989).

Family Violence

In the past two decades, family violence has emerged as an urgent social problem in American society. Determining an accurate rate of violence is hampered by poor record keeping—especially by inconsistencies in the way violence is measured by courts, police, shelters, clinics, social service agencies, and researchers (Gordon, 1988). Our best national data indicate that each year, one in six couples experience at least one violent act, one in eight involves serious injury, and one in twenty-five marriages is plagued with perpetual violence. Per year, nearly two million wives and husbands physically abuse their spouses (Lockhart and White, 1989). Verbal abuse is even more prevalent. Popular wisdom indicates that marital violence is endemic to Black families. In movies, books, plays, newspapers, and television documentaries, the fussin' and fightin' theme is constantly repeated.

The Color Purple, an Academy Award–nominated movie, powerfully portrays male-female relationships around the early 1900s as turbulent, hostile, and bitter; major scenes involve incest and spouse abuse. This early portrait of male-female tension has contemporary relevance. Today, many Blacks believe that over the last fifty years a growing distrust, even hatred, between Black men and Black women has emerged (Wallace, 1979; Cazenave and Smith, 1990). Their hatred is provocatively conveyed in Ali's book *The Blackman's Guide to Understanding the Blackwoman* (1989). Ali, a Black Muslim, claims that Black women's unwillingness to submit to men of their race is the cause of Black men's poor condition and the Black family's destruction. Moreover, she does not limit her charges of insubordination to working-class women. All Black women are said to be guilty of complaining, whining, and disrespect. Ali's disdain for "uppity" Black women is forcefully made when she instructs the Black man to give his woman a solid, open-handed smack in the mouth when she is disrespectful (Ali, 1989). It is important to keep in mind that Ali's Muslim background biases her nonempirical and polemical thesis toward extolling the virtues of female submissiveness and male dominance.

Despite this popular image, there is little reason to believe that Blacks are inherently more violent than Whites or that Black men and women have declared open warfare. First, a discrepancy exists between rhetoric and reality. While the majority of Blacks believe that Black male-female relationships have deteriorated over the years, few characterize their own personal relationship as essentially negative. Moreover, those with the most positive attitudes are married, whereas the most negative feelings are expressed by the nonmarried (Cazenave and Smith, 1990). If beliefs are not based on personal experience, then they must derive from popular myths. Undoubtedly, these myths are internalized, rhetoric is repeated, and little thought is given to the incongruence between personal experiences and popular belief.

Further, Black females recognize that Black males face occupational discrimination that makes them less responsible and trustworthy and generally not in control of their destiny. For this reason, they rate Black males relatively low on their ability to adequately provide. But this does not mean that Black men are rejected. Over forty years ago, Frazier noted that Black males compensate for not being able to play the "masculine role" by cultivating their "personalities." Black females respond positively to Black males' expressive qualities, ranking these qualities far higher than White women and men rank the expressive qualities of White men. Thus, despite the fact that Black females expect to be disappointed in the provider role, they continue to find Black men lively, gregarious, vigorous, and exciting partners (Turner and Turner, 1983; Frazier, 1957).

Any violence existing in Black families reflects to a considerable degree the particular social and economic predicament in which Blacks find themselves. The reality of Blacks' differential exposure to violence must be acknowledged. They are overrepresented among youth dying from nonbiological causes, or what is known as the "new morbidity": accidents, homicide, and suicide. In 1977, the number of young Black men dying from homicide (5,734) surpassed those killed from 1963 to 1972 in the Vietnam War (5,640) (Gibbs, 1988a). Black psychiatrists Pouissant, Grier, and Cobbs stress the intense frustration Black men face as a result of being shut out of the mainstream of American life. They suggest that the high incidence of Black-on-Black homicide reflects subliminal anger that is vented on convenient victims within their immediate environment (Grier and Cobbs, 1976; Pouissant, 1983). It is certainly true that Black crime is more a reality of the underclass (Star, Clark, Goetz, and O'Malia, 1979). Yet Blacks in general face constant assaults on their self-worth that may not be physical but that nevertheless produce scars that cripple psychologically and create subliminal rage. This has the potential of exploding within the family.

Whether Blacks are caught in a "culture of violence" that permeates their family life is debatable. Scientific knowledge is hampered by the tendency to exclude Blacks from the analysis, even in those cases where they are represented in the sample. The greatest flaw in the studies, particularly the early ones, is the failure to account for the effect of social class when comparing rates of violence among Black and White families. Blacks are overrepresented in official marital violence statistics not only as a result of racial bias but also because of their overall low socioeconomic status. Thus, social class is a key factor to consider.

Not surprising, high income and employment are the best shield against family violence. Conflicts around family decision making are strongly related to social class. Not only do working-class couples report more conflicts in this area than the upper and middle class, but these conflicts are more likely to result in violence (Cazenave and Straus, 1979; Lockhart and White, 1989; Uzzell and Peebles-Wilkins, 1989). This is not surprising, since traditional gender roles appear more frequently within Black and White working-class marriages (Jackson, 1991). Many working-class husbands have few material resources that translate into power within the family. Thus, they may embrace society's prescription of male dominance in the home. Hampered by communication skills that are often vague and limited, they frequently resort to nonverbal messages and control (Foley, 1975; Uzzell and Peebles-Wilkins, 1989). Opposition from the "little woman" challenges their self-esteem, masculinity, and demand for authority. In the heat of an argument, they are most likely to sense a loss of their family power and to react violently.

This relationship between social class and violence breaks down when type of abuse is considered. Working-class families are more likely to not only report abuse, but to be victims of severe violence. On the other hand, a higher proportion of middle-class women compared with their counterparts in the lower and upper classes report being pushed, grabbed, and/or shoved by their husbands. Despite their higher rate of "mild violence," they are less likely than their upper-class counterparts to report their abuse to the police or professionals (Lockhart and White, 1989). It is important to note that mild violence is not only more typical than severe violence, but less likely to reach the attention of authorities.

The high level of "mild violence" within the middle class may reflect their high work ethic and social marginality. They have been called "strivers and strainers" and "conspicuous consumptionists." Their emphasis on appearance, as demonstrated by excessive spending on clothing and cars, often reflects status panic and anxiety. Their newly achieved status is precarious. The lack of a solid economic base within the Black middle class was noted as early as 1957, when E. Franklin Frazier published his classic thesis on the Black bourgeoisie. They are dependent on Whites for their very salaries and wages and are just two or three paychecks removed from the working class. This situation heightens tension and potential for violent behavior.

Financial insecurity is no doubt intensified in those Black families living the middle-class life-style on one person's salary. This is certainly suggested by the higher degree of abuse reported by unemployed wives within the middle class, as compared to their employed counterparts. The causal direction of the effect of employment is unclear. Perhaps the added income from dual earners enhances the economic security of the family in general and reduces the environmental stress that often results from financial deprivation. Or the effect may be more direct—that is, the mere fact of employment enhances a wife's family power position and independence, making her less vulnerable than the dependent unemployed wife (Uzzell and Peebles-Wilkins, 1989).

Adding to this lack of power is an isolation factor. A Black homemaker will most likely not find companionship with other Black wives, since most are working. If she lives in the suburbs, she is likely to be further removed from the Black community and must create bonds with White homemakers. These bonds, however, are too often superficial. If she is not active in a Black church or other Black organizations, she experiences social isolation. In the eyes of some in the Black community she is an anomaly: too "uppity" or lazy to work. Consequently, relative to employed wives, unemployed wives may be minimally integrated into the community, lacking the friendship networks that could provide support and protection during extreme stress (Cazenave and Straus, 1979).

When attacked, Black wives are significantly more likely than White wives to retaliate and to kill their mate after repeated and long-term abuse (Uzzell and Peebles-Wilkins, 1989). One should not assume, however, that this reflects higher family violence among Blacks: just the opposite is true. In a 1979 national probability study, Blacks as compared to Whites reported a lower rate of spousal slapping at every income level except those in the $6,000-to-$11,999 bracket (Cazenave and Straus, 1979). If a "culture-of-violence" explanation has any merit, it may have more relevance for Whites than Blacks. Through the ages, the family has served as a haven from extrafamilial abuses Blacks must endure. It is likely that this family function has not been severely weakened even in the context of escalated violence against Blacks in American society at large.

Marital Dissolution

Prior to 1974, "until death do us part" reflected the reality of most marriages. By 1974, a watershed in American family life was reached, when more marriages ended by divorce than death. Today, if the trend continues, 49 percent of all individuals between the ages of twenty-nine and thirty-five will divorce by age seventy-five. A disproportionate number of these divorces will involve Black couples. Combined data from several national surveys indicate that between 1973 and 1980, 37.2 percent of Black males and 22.2 percent of White males who had ever married were divorced. Among females, 42.2 percent of Blacks and 23.5 percent of Whites were divorced (Strong and DeVault, 1992). Whereas three-quarters of all Black marriages were intact in the 1960s, barely half are so today. The proportion divorced is highest among Black females (Bureau of the Census, 1991a; Glick, 1988).

The divorce trends are clear, but the underlying reasons for divorce are not as clearly understood. Economic factors rank high among the reasons given for divorce. These are covered in greater detail in Chapter Three. Briefly stated, it is well understood that divorce is highest among low-income couples. Obviously, however, not all working-class couples divorce, nor do all middle-class couples remain married. Other demographic forces as well as personal factors come into play. Among the demographic factors related to divorce are length of courtship, age at time of marriage, presence of children, education, differences in husband and wife's background, parental marital history, geographical location, marital noncohabitation, and religion. These factors provide valuable information on groups; however, we gain little to no knowledge about the individuals involved. Unfortunately, even individuals do not always know their motives, and sometimes the intensity of their pain leads them to blame others or deceive themselves. In this chapter, we review noneconomic demographic forces as well as some of the individual reasons Black couples give for separation and divorce (Rindfuss and Stephen, 1990; Strong and DeVault, 1992).

Black marriages end in separation, divorce, or widowhood with far greater regularity than do the marriages of Whites or Spanish-origin couples. This pattern is true regardless of class. Yet, although Blacks do not rank marriage as highly as Whites, most define marriage as being very important to them personally and an overwhelming number plan to marry. A trouble sign for marriages is the significant number of Black youth who indicate that their desired age for childbearing is earlier than their desired age at marriage. Many begin their childbearing in their teen years. Ten percent of the births to Black teenagers in the mid 1980s were legitimized by marriage. Unfortunately, for two major reasons these marriages are struggling against the odds (McMurray, 1990; Moore, Simms, and Betsey, 1986).

First, many teenagers who marry interrupt their schooling in order to work. Black and White individuals who do not complete a unit of education (that is, elementary school, high school, or college) increase their chances for marital dissolution. As an example, Blacks who only have one to three years of college are more likely to divorce than those who complete high school. This pattern has been observed so frequently that it is called the *Glick effect,* named after Paul Glick, who first observed it. Glick suggests that dropping out of both school and marriage has a common root—lack of persistence. Thus, those who do not persist in school are not as likely as those who graduate to persist in their marriage. Yet it could also be argued that the differences in dissolution rates between dropouts and graduates result from the teenagers' immaturity (Glenn and Supancic, 1984; Bauman, 1967).

For both Blacks and Whites, adolescent marriages are more likely to end in divorce than marriages that take place when people are in their twenties, particularly if they marry after age twenty-six (Glenn and Supancic, 1984). This is primarily because among the younger set, neither partner has the economic skills to maintain a stable family, the commitment to stay together while most of their friends are enjoying the freedom of singlehood, or the maturity it takes to resolve marital conflicts constructively.

To strengthen their economic position, some join the U.S. Army in order to earn that steady check needed for supporting their families. The number of Blacks—particularly females—who select the services as an escape valve from economic deprivation and lack of jobs is partially reflected in their increasing enlistment since the 1970s and highlighted by their disproportionate presence in the 1991 Persian Gulf War (Pinderhughes, 1991). As the doors of job opportunity are closed in the private sector, many turn to Uncle Sam.

Ironically, this solution places those married in a Catch-22 situation. While the reasons are not entirely clear, Black soldiers are three times more likely than their White buddies to be separated from their spouses while serving in the U.S. military. Perhaps this situation is caused by the fact that Black military spouses find it more difficult than their White counterparts to find a job when their spouse is relocated overseas. In the military as in the civilian population, Black married couples are heavily dependent on a second income to make ends meet. Rather than give up a job in hand and risk unemployment abroad, some choose to live apart. Unfortunately, those Blacks not living with their spouses are twice as likely as cohabiting Black couples to experience marital disruption (Rindfuss and Stephen, 1990; McCubbin, Patterson, and Lavee, 1984; Harrison and Minor, 1978). Thus, these Black soldiers not only place their lives on the line, but their marriages as well.

Second, three is a crowd when a couple is first married. Time is needed for adjusting to life as a couple. For teenagers whose previous single life involved minimum responsibilities and high social interaction with peers, the time needed for adjustment is even more critical. When a crying demanding baby is an immediate addition, the husband-wife adjustment time is greatly reduced. Even in the best of stable marriages, children tend to lower marital satisfaction. Childbearing families and families with preschool children experience a rate of marital disruption way above the national average. Moreover, the pressure from children exceeds that from economic forces (Hampton, 1982).

It is understandable then that about half of all premaritally pregnant marriages end in divorce within five years, about twice the rate for those in which the woman is not pregnant at the time of marriage (Strong and DeVault, 1992). The proportion of divorces is even greater for Blacks, who have higher rates of premarital pregnancies than Whites. Despite their poor chances at a long-term marriage, a small proportion of lower-class teenagers continue to venture into matrimony, thinking that they can improve on their deteriorating economic existence.

A significant proportion of all race-sex groups marry in their twenties. While they do not face the disadvantage of early marriage, there are other factors that may work against their marital stability. Those who have known their mate the longest before marrying are more likely to have a successful marriage (Chavis and Lyles, 1975; Jewell, 1989). Also, although not a strong factor, there is a slight tendency for the rate of divorce to increase if the parents of either spouse have been divorced. However, it is unclear as to whether it is the parents' divorce that is the culprit or the fact that children of divorced parents tend to marry earlier.

Another aspect of parental characteristics that weighs on the stability of Black couples, particularly those in the working class, relates to the parents of the bride and groom. If the husband's father has a higher occupational status than his wife's father, the marriage has a better chance of remaining intact. Interestingly, the effect of this disparity seems to hold regardless of the husband's own mobility (Osmond, 1977). This pattern is evidence of the power of gender norms that prescribe that the wife be inferior in status to her husband.

Heterogamy is another type of disparity that increases divorce probability. It refers to the selection of a mate whose personal and group characteristics differ from one's own. Many Black women find themselves in heterogamous relationships because of the male shortage. In broadening their field of eligible males, they often include men significantly older or younger, with lower educational achievement, and who have a history of at least one divorce. Many individuals who have been married previously have not worked out the problems from the previous marriage when they enter subsequent marriages. Thus, second marriages tend to be high risk (Bumpass, Sweet, and Martin, 1990; Glenn and Supancic, 1984; Kitson, 1985; Spanier and Glick, 1980). Age, educational, and marital history differences reflect divergent experiences that may indeed result in marital conflict. If heterogamous couples do not have an appreciation for these differences or if these differences get in the way of reaching desired goals, the marriage is headed for rocky shores.

A major strength of Black family life has been its social support system. Many marriages have weathered the storm through the active participation of extended family members and community support. As Blacks have become more urbanized or as they have moved from tightly knit Black communities, some of that support has been weakened. This is one reason why we see regional differences in divorce rates. Black couples, particularly those over thirty-five, are more likely to divorce if they live in the North and West than in the South. Southern living is characterized by a high degree of social integration, with extended families, ethnic neighborhoods, low levels of residential mobility, and numerous church congregations. Such forces are weaker in other regions, especially in the West.

Religious affiliation as a deterrent to divorce is difficult to determine, since over 80 to 90 percent of Blacks are Protestants (Bureau of the Census, 1991a; Chavis and Lyles, 1975). However, it is the social support quality of religion that becomes important in maintaining marital stability. Of course, for the small number of Blacks in conservative religions such as the Catholic church, the Seventh Day Adventists, and Jehovah's Witnesses, the ecclesiastical pressures for marriages to remain intact are probably very strong. All these forces interlock to create spiritual, emotional, and instrumental support—the key social controls that tend to keep marriages intact.

Summary

Divorce is a harsh reality, and many forces operate to pull marriages apart. Sociologist Mervyn Cadwallader calls marriage "a wretched institution," unworthy of salvaging. Others claim it is outdated and unnecessary (Melville, 1977). Still, nearly half of those Blacks who divorce will remarry, particularly the males (Bumpass, Sweet, and Martin, 1990). While an increasing number of Blacks in their twenties are remaining single, Blacks continue to desire the state of marriage. When the marriage dissolves, a majority seek still another. Among those over age sixty-five, only 5.3 percent of Black women and 5.7 percent of Black men have never married, in contrast to 4.9 percent of White women and 4.0 percent of White men (Bureau of the Census, 1991a). Even among the younger, the desire to marry continues.

In sum, millions of Black people, despite the odds, continue to seek intimacy and fulfillment within the marriage institution. Only one in ten persons agrees that society could survive just as well without the institution of marriage (Billingsley, 1990; Melville, 1977). Rather than abandon the institution, there is a need to understand it and defend it against the external and internal forces that cripple its ability to absorb the shock of a changing and—for a sizable minority—hostile society.

8

The Challenges
of Parenting

Only Black families and other minorities socialize their children under conditions that are in stark contrast to the American creed of life, liberty, and the pursuit of happiness. Despite social and economic advancements, a Black child still lacks a fair opportunity to live, learn, prosper, and contribute in America. Tragically, the Black infant mortality rate in the 1980s was the same as the White infant mortality rate in the 1960s. Today, Blacks are twice as likely as Whites to die during the first year of life. Although both Black and White infant mortality rates have fallen, there is no indication that Blacks will ever reach the level of Whites (Leffall, 1990; Edelman, 1988).

One reason for this continuing disparity is the growing poverty rate among Black children under age eighteen, a rate that is higher now than at any time since 1967. The relative economic deprivation of Black children is even more striking when one realizes that nearly one in two Black children is poor, compared to one in five of American children in general. About 70 percent of Black children live in families with incomes less than twice the poverty level, while nearly two-thirds of all White children live in families with incomes more than twice the poverty level. Simply stated, Black children are more likely to get sick or die, because they are three and one-half times more likely than Whites to be poor (Bureau of the Census, 1991a; Swinton, 1991; Edelman, 1988, 1985; Peters, 1985).

On the other hand, the economic and educational status of some Black children and families has improved. While the proportion of Black families with incomes less than $5,000 has increased by 38 percent, those with incomes greater than $50,000 has increased by 38 percent. Since the 1960s, the Black-White racial gap has narrowed considerably for both high school graduates and those with one to three years of college (Swinton, 1991; Bureau of the Census, 1991a, 1991b, 1989; Reed, 1988).

Despite the undesirable rates of Black dropouts, the 1980s ended with the largest and best academically prepared high school graduates of any Black group in history. In addition, the decline in minority enrollment in graduate schools halted for the first time in the 1980s (Wilson, 1989). Although a substantial gap remains between Blacks and Whites in higher education, a small but significant number of Black parents have acquired upward mobility at this level. For these parents, higher education has empowered them with more resources for mediating the impact of the wider society's attack on their children.

But regardless of their particular socioeconomic circumstances, varying degrees of subtle and overt prejudice and discrimination threaten to destroy the self-concept, self-esteem, and aspirations of Black children. This threat is certainly more ominous among those with fewer economic and social resources. Yet even the most affluent cannot totally escape the negative fallout of a racist-oriented society.

Since slavery, Black parents have been preparing their children to become "somebody" in a White world that continues to treat them in various ways as "nobody." As we will see, with few exceptions, Black parents continue to labor for their children's future, and they have never ceased dreaming of their children living out the American creed—the pursuit of knowledge and happiness.

Emancipated Parents

Perhaps the cruelest aspect of slavery was the way in which it crushed the hopes parents had for each child they brought into the world. For dying slave parents, it had to be agonizing to know that they were leaving their children in bondage. It did not matter how hard parens worked; they could not change the lot of those dearest to them. However, with the demolition of the slave system, hope came alive. For emancipated mothers and fathers, freedom did not mean release from backbreaking slave labor. Rather it meant they could use their labor to improve the family's spiritual and material welfare and thus chart the upward mobility of their children.

The discipline and values imparted to children reflected the parents' retention of African survivals, disdain for their past bondage, and the need for all members to labor for family survival. While parents disciplined with the liberal use of the rod, they refused to whip their children on the directive of White folks. Such a chain of command reeked of slavery and was totally intolerable. Older children were responsible for younger ones while parents were working outside of the home—a practice consistent with that of their African progenitors.

When preschool children were unable to be cared for by older children or extended family members or if housing and board were inadequate, parents were creative in balancing work and family responsibilities. Some hired out their children to White employers to lessen overcrowded conditions at home and to increase family income. Others who worked in the homes of White families took their young children with them so that they would not only have supervision, but they would get at least one square meal a day. Still others resorted to having their youngsters of five or six picking cotton with them so that they not only could be supervised but could add to the family income. When possible, mothers took in washing and worked at home, assisted by older children who if left to their own devices would get into mischief (Jones, 1985). Of course, there were those who found it impossible to simultaneously supervise children and work for their survival. Both W.E.B. Du Bois (1908) and E. Franklin Frazier (1939) attributed Black juvenile delinquency and child neglect to the inability of parents to supervise their children while working outside the home.

The devastating results of poverty are evident in the demographic profile of Black families. In the period from 1880 to 1910, Black women's fertility declined about one-third due to disease and poor nutrition. A twenty-year-old woman could expect to see one out of three of her children die before age ten, and to die herself at age fifty-four, before her youngest left home (Jones, 1985; Blassingame, 1972).

Despite their poverty, parents instilled in their children the importance of self-dignity. As an example, fresh in their memory of slave days was the humiliation of being handed plain, drab, heavy clothes (two pieces a year). Thus, poor but proud parents instructed their sons and daughters to go without before accepting immodest or ill-fitting clothing from White folks. As a sign of their freedom, some Black fathers spent an inordinate amount of their sharecropping proceeds on colorful and elaborate garments for their children and wives. Of course, most sharecroppers earned barely enough to keep body and soul together, but when possible, clothes were made or purchased for expressive rather than practical wear (Jones, 1985; Escott, 1979).

Even today, Black parents with little material means are known to sacrifice their own appearance so that their children can be well dressed. Sometimes the importance of clothing is carried to the extreme, as it was for one cleaning woman. Between tuition and dressing her daughter to be one of the ten best-dressed women students at a major university, she did not have enough money to attend her own daughter's graduation. In its immediate context, this mother's action seems inappropriate. Yet, within the historical context of Black slavery, her behavior takes on a different meaning.

The importance of clothing did not exceed the freed mothers' and fathers' hunger for education for themselves, but particularly for their children. Most felt that regardless of their past slave experience, they could die happy knowing that their children would live the balance of their lives in freedom and in pursuit of knowledge. Given the limited resources of parents and their community, it was not easy acquiring an education. Some parents attempted to educate themselves so that they could pass their knowledge on to their children. Their determination is demonstrated by the laundry woman who tied her book to a fence while she scrubbed. Throughout the South, when public and philanthropic support was not forthcoming, Black women joined with their men to build schoolhouses and hire teachers on shoestring budgets. Unfortunately, most communities of parents could only afford these teachers for a couple of months out of the year (Jones, 1985; Franklin, 1974).

As the Reconstruction government took shape, the few Black political officials found sufficient support to establish the American public school system. Through the work of philanthropists, religious organizations, and the Freedmen's Bureau, 4,329 schools were operating for Blacks by 1870. Education, however, was far from equal in caliber to White schools. Lower salaries were paid to Black teachers, and White teachers in Black schools faced social ostracism. Parents had to fight against hostile school boards that provided their children with poor facilities and White teachers who were considered unfit to teach White children.

The shortcomings in the education of Blacks, particularly in attendance, stemmed not from the lack of zeal on the part of teachers, parents, and students, but from misunderstanding the needs of Blacks. Black families were preoccupied with survival. Many had to make tough decisions as to which child could be released from field responsibility to attend. Given that during the late 1800s, the average number of children was six or seven per family, this was a major decision. Sometimes the daughter was chosen to avoid her going to work for White folks. Frequently, however, the daughter's education had to take the backseat to the family's economic welfare. Recorded in history are testimonies from sharecropper daughters who complained that they were uneducated because their fathers felt they were needed far more in the field than in the schoolhouse.

When possible, fathers and mothers took on extra work so that they could send all their children to school and avoid the painful "Sophie's choice." In the worst scenario, parents worked and children were either locked in their homes or left to roam the streets with only occasional supervision from neighbors who had their own youngsters to attend to. More commonly, school-age children as young as eight went to work in the field and either did not attend school or did so only irregularly. In the eyes of freed working parents, the ideal Black family was one in which the father worked full time, the mother devoted most of her time to rearing children and keeping house, and all the children attended school (Jones, 1985; J. H. Franklin, 1987).

The Contemporary Parenting Dilemma

Today, Black parents continue to pass to their children values for effective living and a quest for formal education. However, Black and White parents often differ in the way they inspire their children toward higher achievement. Black parents have often been criticized for "saying one thing" and "doing another." Specifically, they have been accused of having low expectations of their children and providing weak support, while setting unrealistically high goals. There is certainly ample research evidence to show that Blacks' aspirations for their children do indeed exceed their expectations, whereas among Whites, aspirations and expectations are closely matched. Such disjointedness is said to make it difficult for Black children to set realistic goals and to achieve academic success in school. Yet this disjointedness is easy to understand.

For example, three-quarter of Blacks enrolled in college in 1970 came from homes in which family heads had no college education. The fact that in 1985 the family income of more than half of Black college students was under $20,000, compared to only 15 percent of White students, attests to the greater willingness of Black parents to sacrifice financially for their children's education. It also reveals the high level of motivation of Black students.

Recent data show that a large proportion of Black lower-income mothers and fathers not only hope that their children will attend college, but spend time discussing educational options with them. Sixty-four to ninety-two percent limit television watching on school days, have rules for doing homework, and insist on maintaining a certain grade-point average. However, they are less likely than the more affluent Blacks to help their children with their homework—no doubt reflecting their own limited education. But even here, nearly 60 percent report they help with homework. Despite their own lack of educational achievement, many of these parents actually have specific occupations they would like their children, particularly their daughters, to pursue (National Center for Education Statistics, 1991a; Reed, 1988; Robinson, Bailey, and Smith, 1985; Clark, 1983; Jackson, 1975).

In addition, such accusations do not take into consideration the role of racism. Compared to White children, Black children's own desires for achievement are not as strongly determined by the occupation of their parents. Black children are keenly aware of the role racism plays in limiting job mobility and opportunities for their mothers and fathers. Not because they have read the statistics—they do not have to. The most crucial facts for them are the daily experiences of watching the capable adults in their lives struggle with gaining education and work. Thus, Black parental encouragement and behavior per se have as much or more impact on the upward mobility of Black children than what their parents actually do for a living or the amount of education their parents have personally attained (Reeder and Conger, 1984; Carnegie Council, 1977).

Through example as well as words, Black parents must transmit to their children the realities of living in a society that is hostile to Black aspirations. In Scanzoni's study (1978) of middle-class Black families, many parents who were aware of their own deprivation tried to prepare their children for disappointments while encouraging them to set high goals. In striving toward the American Dream, these parents taught their children the value of hard work, the importance of holding on to a job, and ways of preparing for and bouncing back from life's disappointments. Recent studies suggest that fewer than a third of Black parents fail to provide their children with racial socialization messages (Taylor, Chatters, Tucker, and Lewis, 1990).

Partly because of the many sacrifices Black parents have had to make for their families in a hostile environment, Black children have closer relationships with their parents than do White children. Of course, not all children have positive relationships. About one-third of Black adult children claim they do not want to be like one or the other parent—about half of these reject their parents' lack of ambition, inability to provide economic rewards, or dysfunctional personalities. Although negative modeling generally means that parents behaved in an "undesirable" manner (overbearing or lacking aspirations), sometimes such identification developed from caring and intentional acts on the parent's part. Statements such as "Son, work hard and go to school so that you can do better than your old man" demonstrate how some Black parents use their disadvantaged position to motivate their children for upward mobility (Clark, 1983; Scanzoni, 1978).

Cross-Gender Parent-Child Relationships

The gender of the child and parent not only determines how discipline and encouragement are given and received but how parent-child bonding is developed. Unfortunately, the narrow definition given to fatherhood (as provider) and the emphasis placed on boys' need for a male role model for healthy personality development ignore the father's expressive contribution to character development and social achievement in their female children. Likewise, the narrow definition given to mothers (as nurturant) ignores the contribution they make to the occupational attainment of their children. Given that Black fathers and mothers deem it appropriate to interchange or share the provider and expressive roles, the father-daughter and mother-son relationships are just as important for understanding child development and aspirations as are the mother-daughter and father-son relationships.

The limited information on cross-gender parent-child relationships suggests that White high-achieving daughters generally have fathers who make an important contribution to their development. A book about the life and career histories of twenty-five White women in top management revealed that these women were extremely close to their fathers. Their fathers gave of their time, provided encouragement, taught them athletic skills, and most of all gave them strength to reject the opinions of those who placed limits on their ability.

Much the same can be said about the closeness of Black father-daughter relationships. Black fathers are especially close to their daughters. They, more so than White fathers, encourage their daughters' independence. Further, their encouragement has a greater impact on their daughters' occupational and educational attainment than does the encouragement received from mothers. The more educated the fathers, the more likely they are to invest in and support their daughters' upward mobility. In contrast, the encouragement sons get from their fathers or mothers makes virtually no difference in their educational outcome (Reeder and Conger, 1984; Willie, 1988; Scanzoni, 1978).

In the early years of socialization, Black fathers appear to be significantly different from their White peers. They tend to have an authoritarian approach to parenting, in that they expect a set standard of conduct, believe in forceful compliance when necessary, and have few give-and-take discussions. Further, unlike White fathers of daughters who succeed, they do not encourage individuality, independence, or nonconformity in their preschool daughters.

By White social science standards, their style of parenting is undesirable. Surprisingly, relative to White preschool daughters, the Black father's behavior produces daughters with exceptional independence and competence. Apparently, their authoritarian parenting style is not a reflection of authoritarian personality disorder. In contrast, the authoritarian parenting style of White fathers is more likely to reflect an authoritarian personality syndrome—dogmatism and inflexibility motivated by repressed anger, emotional coldness, and a sense of impotence (McAdoo, 1985–86).

Our focus on father-daughter relationships is not to suggest that mothers are inconsequential in influencing the occupational choice of their daughters. In fact, compared to White daughters, Black daughters' occupational aspirations are more likely to be inspired by working mothers. Using their mothers as role models, they are more likely to see gainful employment as a requirement of adulthood rather than an option. The mothers' contribution to sons' occupational success also cannot be ignored, although quantitative research in this area is sparse. Qualitative reports show numerous male statesmen, scholars, lawyers, and physicians who have distinguished themselves in various fields giving credit to their single or married mothers.

Ben Carson was raised in inner-city Detroit by a divorced mother with a third-grade education. He lacked motivation, had terrible grades, and had a temper that threatened to put him in jail. But his God-fearing mother relentlessly believed in his capabilities, pushed him toward excellence, and despite his grades, challenged the school system to treat him as if he had promise. Today, Carson is world renowned for his role in successfully separating Siamese twins joined at the back of the head. He generously gives credit to his mother's guidance (Carson, 1990). Similar stories can be repeated about the divorced mother who raised psychologist Kenneth B. Clark, whose research influenced the 1954 *Brown v. Board of Education* decision; the married employed mother who raised historian John Hope Franklin, former president of the American Historical Association and the United Chapters of Phi Beta Kappa; the single mother who raised Ralph Bunche, winner of the 1950 Nobel Peace Prize for mediating the 1948–49 Arab-Israeli war; and numerous sports stars who proudly call themselves "mama's boys."

In analyzing numerous case histories of mothers of successful sons, Charles Willie (1984) concluded that regardless of whether Black women were single, married, widowed, poor, or nonpoor, they gave their sons constant company, care, early learning opportunities, and partial or full economic support. They expected good academic performance and had ambitions for their sons' high achievement. He even suggests that the more education mothers have relative to fathers, the more education the sons will attain. In Scanzoni's study (1978) of working- and middle-class adult children, nearly a majority of the adult children said their mothers help them materially, and the majority mentioned that their mothers encouraged or goaded them to get ahead. In fact, although fathers are more likely to provide material assistance, it is the mothers who are most likely to be credited by both sons and daughters as inspiring them to get ahead in education.

Single Mothers and Educational Achievement

The greatest challenge in parenting is faced by the mother who must raise her children virtually single-handedly. Because substantial numbers of Black men have been absent or infrequently at home due to welfare regulations, inability to obtain regular employment, or holding down multiple jobs that require long hours away from home, many children find themselves raised by their mothers. This situation has created a special bond between mothers and sons. Black adolescent males do not take kindly to any derogatory comments about their mothers, particularly if the father is absent. In "playing the dozens," a game where manhood is determined by the number of derogatory comments one can calmly withstand, it is often a slur on the mother that causes the player to lose his emotional composure. If these sons become financially successful, they generally will purchase a house or car for their mothers with their first big check. In presenting these gifts, most of the men comment on the hardships their mothers endured for their sake (Staples, 1984).

Given the mother's historical role in the Black family, it is perplexing as to why Black mothers have come under such harsh attack in the social science literature and in the popular media. A review of fifty years of published research in the social sciences found that most of the developmental difficulties in child development were attributed to weaknesses in the family structure. The brunt of the attack has been on Black mothers who are poor, teenagers, and/or unmarried. These mothers have been accused of raising children with limited language, cognitive, affective, and intellectual development, low academic achievement, and low self-esteem. Also, children from these families were said to have a proclivity for delinquency and violence (D. Franklin, 1988; Adams, Milner, and Schrepf, 1984; Harrison, 1988; Baratz and Baratz, 1970; Rainwater, 1970; Jensen, 1969). Moynihan (1965) felt that in the absence of a male head, her influence was so detrimental to male children that he recommended that sons join the army in order to escape the irregular, unpredictable, and female-biased childrearing practices of their mothers.

Moynihan, like many of his predecessors, assumed that Black children from single-parent households "fail and flounder." Their failure is primarily attributed to the children's exposure to female authority when society sanctions male leadership. Further, absent fathers generally mean that children are living in poverty and environments conducive to social pathology. The Head Start programs of the 1960s were postulated on the assumption of ineffective childrearing practices of Black mothers and deficient home environments.

Apart from skin color, the most salient feature of Black children's social status is their speech pattern. Social scientists of the 1960s assumed that children's linguistic competence is closely linked to their intellectual capacity. This assumption was based on another belief—that languages could be hierarchically ordered—and that German was the "best" language for conceptualization. In fact, even today a substantial number of Whites (far fewer Blacks) believe that the way Blacks speak is a strong determinant of their intellectual competency in other areas (Mitchell-Kernan, 1982; Yetman and Steele, 1975). Since the speech pattern of Black children, particularly those of the lower class, differed from those of Whites, a primary task of the Head Start programs of the 1960s was to bring Black children's speech skills in line with White children's.

Observing that in lower-class homes, speech sequences of mothers seem to be limited and poorly structured syntactically, efforts were made to place preschool children in day-care centers where they could learn standard English and thus improve their cognitive skills. Many of these same scientists dismissed any possibility of retention of African habits of thought and speech, and most important, they did not believe that Black Americans had a culture worth protecting. Thus, in their eyes, intervening in Black children's lives presented little or no risk. When they found that their efforts did not alter cognitive thinking, they argued that the mother's influence was so great that Head Start programs must begin at earlier times in the child's life and should be extended from three months to one year.

Such intervention assumes that a difference is tantamount to a deficit. No one can argue that the language system of many Blacks is different and can become a handicap to the child attempting to negotiate with the standard English–speaking mainstream.* It is nonetheless a highly structured system that is adequate for abstract thinking. Black mothers and their children are no less able to think abstractly because of their language pattern than are Japanese children who attempt to speak standard English (Baratz and Baratz, 1970).

In light of insufficient scientific evidence of a link between speech and intelligence, Black mothers were then accused of indirectly hindering their children's cognitive development by not providing enough social and sensory stimulation. When research showed that ghetto children receive an abundance of sensory stimulation, it was argued that ghetto stimulation is excessive and thus causes children to inwardly tune it all out, thus creating a vacuum for themselves. When it was found that the stimulation did not appreciably differ by social class, ghetto mothers' stimulation was considered ineffective because it was not as "distinctive" as that found within middle-class environments.

Finally, the lower-class mothers' teaching styles came under attack. Since so many of these mothers dropped out of school because of pregnancy, it was assumed that they failed to learn proper parenting skills. Black mothers, unlike White mothers, are more likely to value obedience, conformity, and respect for authority as childrearing goals. As an example, they direct their children to learn because the teacher or the parent said so, rather than because learning is intrinsically rewarding. An appeal by Black mothers to external rather than internal inducement is considered inadequate in a White world, which stresses self-direction and individuality. Despite the fact that the evidence does not demonstrate a weaker link between this type of Black parenting style and readiness to learn, the Black style is considered inferior. In sum, it is apparent that lower-class Black mothers are a priori defined as inadequate because they are not White or middle class (Peterson and Peters, 1985; Baratz and Baratz, 1970).

Despite the social science bias against Black mothers, there is sufficient evidence showing problems among single unwed mothers and their children, regardless of race. Only recently have social scientists provided less pejorative and more objective data. The more convincing studies have followed a cohort of teenage mothers and their children over several years. These studies demonstrate that child development and future outcome is not as dependent on early childhood experiences as once believed. Recent research makes it clear that while early childbearing increases the risk of ill effects for mother and child as well as prolonged deprivation, there is only minor support for the popular image of the adolescent mother as unemployed, uneducated, and living on welfare with three or more unkempt, poorly motivated and socialized children (D. Franklin, 1988; Furstenberg, Brooks-Gunn, and Morgan, 1987).

First, most women who begin bearing children five to ten years earlier than their peers conclude childbearing five to ten years earlier than their peers. Thus, in the long run, their fertility is similar to that of their peers who delayed childbearing. Early motherhood is likely to establish a pattern of rapid childbearing if adolescent mothers receive family planning assistance, avoid another birth in the first few years following their first pregnancy, and remain in school. It is this latter requirement that many believe presents the greatest challenge to teen mothers and their children.

It is believed that the teen mothers are unable to effectively transmit educational values to their children because they themselves have dropped out of school. Yet, while a substantial number of adolescent unwed mothers drop out of school following pregnancy, a decade later nearly 70 percent obtain a high school diploma, 30 percent take some postsecondary courses, and at least 5 percent graduate from college. These statistics may not be surprising, in that Black teenagers are less likely to marry or to leave school than are Whites. However, in comparing these early childbearers with older ones, it is clear that if they had postponed childbearing, they would have attained a year more education on the average, as well as avoiding the difficult struggle of raising a child while in their teens. Of course, many were poor students prior to their pregnancy; thus childbearing was less predictive of their educational failure. But more important, those 25 to 30 percent of teen mothers who do not complete high school are the ones most likely to depend on welfare, live in poverty, and produce children who fail academically and socially (D. Franklin, 1988; Furstenberg, Brooks-Gunn, and Morgan, 1987; Moore, Simms, and Betsey, 1986).

For the majority of teen unwed mothers, welfare dependency is not a permanent feature of their lives. By the time teen mothers reach their early thirties, nearly three-quarters have steady full-time jobs. Of these, the majority are either the exclusive breadwinner or the principal source of family income. Unfortunately, a third earn annual incomes below poverty level for a family of four; if they had postponed childbearing, fewer would have been poor and far fewer of their children would have been at risk of school failure. On the other hand, some scholars believe teen childbearing is a trivial side issue, since many teenage mothers are seriously disadvantaged before they ever had children. Thus, regardless of their fertility record, the odds are against their escaping poverty (Furstenberg, 1991).

It is the poverty that presents the greatest difficulty to parenting. The effect of income is translated into poorer-quality neighborhoods. Youth in such neighborhoods have daily experiences with unemployment, illicit employment, and few models of high educational achievers. This milieu encourages early sexual activities and low academic achievement and presents a real challenge to parents who must supervise their children (Furstenberg, Brooks-Gunn, and Morgan, 1987; Moore, Simms, and Betsey, 1986; Adams, Milner, and Schrepf, 1984).

Lower-Income Fathers

Of course, not all lower-class children are without involved fathers. Slightly over half of the children of unwed teenage mothers never live with their biological fathers. However, the limited studies on teen fathers do not support the popular image of them as uncaring and uninvolved. While they often are unrealistic about parenthood, they express affection and concern for the mother and children. Many plan to meet social, educational, and financial expectations for their offspring. Realizing the awesome responsibility of parenting, Black adolescent fathers are more likely than those in other non-Black groups to complete high school. To complete their education or earn money, some delay living with their children for one to two years.

For those few involved in court ordered support, about three-quarters pay nearly 80 percent of the full amount. And although Black mothers are less likely than White mothers to be awarded any type of support, they are more likely to receive smaller payments when awarded. It is noteworthy that despite the fact that in American society few fathers actually have sole responsibility for raising their children, Black fathers are more likely to do so than are White fathers (Watson, Rowe, and Jones, 1990; Hill, 1989; Conner, 1988; Marsiglio, 1987; Furstenberg, Brooks-Gunn, and Morgan, 1987; Johnson and Staples, 1989).

Further, substantial numbers of lower-class Black fathers in intact families work and sweat every day to keep their families together and healthy. Several studies confirm their active involvement with their children. One study of a small sample of poor urban fathers showed 83 percent wanted for their children what they missed most—a good education. They believed that education will provide the best opportunities for their children. In addition, an overwhelming number of these fathers are involved in the daily decision-making and disciplinary responsibilities concerning their children.

In disciplining, lower-class fathers perceive that it is their duty to provide punishment to their children for violating externally imposed rules. Generally this punishment is physical rather than verbal and given in line with the transgression's consequence rather than the child's intent. Given the fact that their children will most likely be involved in subordinate relationships with Whites, child-raising strategies that involve obedience, conformity, and respect for authority provide realistic preparation for life circumstances for low-income children. Interestingly, although these fathers perceive themselves as actively involved with their children and mates, they do not believe that other fathers are as active. This disbelief reflects their buying into the popular myth of unresponsive Black fathers (Furstenberg, Brooks-Gunn, and Morgan, 1987; Conner, 1988; Robinson, Bailey, and Smith, 1985; Peterson and Peters, 1985).

Black fathers and fathers in other racial and ethnic groups value companionship with their children more than the provider role. Perhaps this results from the fact that they have been put in a double bind. If Black men accept the White male culture's definition of what it is to be a man— that is, the sole provider—but are denied full employment, then they may create other alternatives. Of course, the most popular alternative we hear about is drugs and crime. However, the majority of lower-class Black fathers in intact families have merely broadened their definition of masculinity to include expressive parent-child relationships. They have modified the traditional definitions of masculinity and enacted the definition that makes sense for them. This may not just be limited to the lower class (Johnson, 1989; Harrison, 1988; McAdoo, 1985–86; Robinson, Bailey, and Smith, 1985). Cazenave (1979) found in his study of Black letter carriers that the greater the economic security, the greater the involvement of the father in childrearing.

Child Abuse

Some parents are so involved with their own problems that they act with indifference or even hostility toward their children. For example, family violence is known to be more prevalent among parents with major socioeconomic problems—the lower class, unemployed, and uneducated. In some intellectual quarters, it is thought that because Blacks are most likely to reflect these characteristics, they have higher rates of child abuse than Whites. Their position gains support from both the bias in reporting Black abuse and sensational media portrayal.

Socioeconomic status and ethnicity play a major role in determining who gets labeled abused. When children enter hospitals with major injuries, Black children are far more likely to be classified as victims of child abuse than are White children. Further, if Black and White children with identical major injuries are observed, Black children are one-third more likely to be reported to authorities. Five percent of one group of 157 physicians claimed that the race and ethnicity of the child's guardians are so important that they would file a child abuse report on the basis of these traits alone. Lower-class White children experience the same bias when evaluated against upper-class Whites. More affluent families deal with practitioners on a fee-for-service basis, which favors the least offensive diagnosis on the circumstances of a child's injuries (Hampton, 1987; Daniel, Hampton, and Newberger, 1983).

The overemphasis on Black violence is facilitated by the popular media portrayal of Black family life. In the powerful Broadway play *For Colored Girls Who Have Considered Suicide When the Rainbow Is Enuf* (Shange, 1977), the frustrations of Black men are taken out on Black children. The play's most shocking portrayal of Black family violence occurs when a father, angry at his woman, intentionally drops their child out of a high-rise low-income apartment window. Consistent with this scene, Black parents who abuse their children are frequently those who suffer from severe economic adversity and stressful relations with their kin and find that they have no one to turn to for help (Daniel, Hampton, and Newberger, 1983).

Yet, despite the hardships of Black parents, it appears that there are cultural norms and structural conditions that protect Black children in a way that they are not protected in the White community. In a major national study on child abuse and neglect, it was found that Blacks are less likely to report the occurrence of either child, sibling, or parent abuse. Parental abuse is so rare or unacceptable that less than 5 percent of Black parents in blue-collar occupations report it, and none of those in higher occupations report behaving violently toward their parents. Even though the majority of both Black and White parents slap or spank their children, Blacks are least likely to do so. This is especially the case for Blacks in white-collar occupations.

It appears that a major deterrent to child abuse is the number of children in the family and the number of years lived in the neighborhood. Family violence is far less likely in families with five or more children than in those families with one or two. This is particularly true for Blacks. The more years in the same neighborhood, the lower the rate of child abuse. Both observations strongly suggest that isolation is associated with abuse. They also suggest that parents of larger families may not only value children more, but may receive more child care from within the family. Among Blacks, the relatively high degree of family-kin network and social ties serves to buffer against the even higher rates of violence one would expect from their socioeconomic circumstances (Cazenave and Straus, 1979).

The proliferation of drug abuse in Black communities threatens to seriously escalate violence against children. Already, the news media are giving regular accounts of children being abused or killed by drug-addicted family members. Combatting drug abuse should be a high priority in every community because it promises to destroy the most innocent of human beings—children.

Self-Esteem in Black or White

Black children must deal with two realities—the Black community and the larger society dominated by Whites. In their interaction with Whites, they are told in various ways that they are socially, educationally, physically, and culturally inferior. The mass media constantly bombard Black children with images that suggest to them that White is preferred. White models and heroes are predominant in television, movies, music videos, billboards, magazines, and children's stories. A clear message is sent. One ought to be White if one is to be powerful, beautiful, economically successful, and socially acceptable ("Why Skin Color Suddenly Is a Big Issue Again," 1992). The prevailing assumption in Euro-American social science is that the image Black people receive of themselves from the White community is the major determinant of Black self-concept. This perspective—derived from C. H. Cooley's "social looking-glass" theory—assumes that one's self-concept is primarily determined by how one is seen by significant others. Thus, Black children are assumed to despise themselves and their race because the White community devalues them. Once social scientists rejected the Black community and Black parents as viable active agents in socializing Black children, it was easy to accept the thesis of Black self-hatred.

The most often cited support for Black self-hatred comes from Kenneth and Mamie Clark's experiments (1950, 1958). From 1939 to the early 1950s, they presented children with Black and White dolls and discovered that Black and White children showed a preference for White dolls and described Black dolls in negative terms. It was assumed that Black children were suffering from low self-esteem and indirectly demonstrating disdain for Black people in general. This study began a long tradition of reporting lower self-esteem among Black children as compared to White children. Regardless of whether researchers used fantasylike projective mea-

sures involving dolls, pictures, or line drawings, their conclusion was the same: Black self-hatred.

Recently these studies have come under attack. Criticism centers on the fact that most of the studies showed very
little consistency. The responses of children varied from one
day to the other, shifted depending on the race of the experi-
menter, and showed reverse results when a "mulatto" doll
was introduced. Further, prior to the late 1960s, Black dolls
were a "novel stimulus" to most children. Unable to find
Black dolls, some experimenters had to construct their own.
Even today, the majority of parents do not buy Black dolls for
their children. Thus, many children may have been reacting
to an unfamiliar stimulus. Also, shortly after children make
negative statements about cross-racial groups or their own
race, they can be observed moments later playing with both
same-race and cross-racial friends (Ramsey, 1987; Hare, 1985;
Harrison, 1985). This disparity shows that children may prefer lighter dolls without rejecting others like themselves. More
profoundly, the interpretive framework of these studies has
been rejected.

It is argued that the "social looking-glass" theory has
been erroneously applied. The assumption that the significant
other persons are White ignores the fact that the most salient
and direct contacts for Black children are the Black adults in
their Black community. It is these individuals who are the
most significant others in the life of Black children. If Black
children have healthy self-esteem, it is because they perceive
that they are well regarded by parents, relatives, peers, and
church members (see Chapter Nine), or are skilled at highly
valued activities.

In addition, the traditional interpretation assumes that
Black people consider the evaluation of them by Whites as
objective (Jackson, McCullough, and Gurin, 1988; Hare, 1985;
Baldwin, 1979). In practice, Black parents begin quite early
teaching their children, particularly their daughters, the
importance of maintaining a love for self and pride in being
Black in a racist society (Taylor, Chatters, Tucker, and Lewis,
1990). The testimony of two mothers in a study of racial

socialization of Black children clearly makes this point: "I'd like them [the children] to have enough pride, because if you have enough pride or self-confidence in yourself, you'll let a lot of things roll off your back." The second mother explains that she is instilling pride in her children "so nobody can put them down" (Peters, 1985, p. 165).

This early socialization appears to have its effect. The bulk of recent scientific studies, based on more representative and larger samples with social-class controls, have ranged from detecting no racial differences to showing that Blacks score higher on self-esteem measures. One study of 3,000 children found the self-confidence of Black girls to be higher than that of White and Latino girls (Daley, 1991). Black children learn to prevent negative racial attitudes from influencing their self-evaluation. Black teenagers and young adults, for example, give more credence to negative feedback from Black evaluators than to the identical feedback from Whites. These findings clearly show that knowing children's racial identity or preference does not provide a good indication of how they feel about themselves.

This protection of their self-worth is also evident in other areas. In school, for example, Black children are able to maintain high self-esteem even when faced with low academic achievement. If Black boys are performing poorly in school, they transfer their concepts of self-worth to areas where they are doing well, such as in sports or school popularity. Although research on area-specific Black self-esteem by gender is in its infancy, it appears that Black girls and boys differ in the areas in which they show high self-esteem. Whether this is primarily the result of community or family gender socialization is unclear (Jackson, McCullough, and Gurin, 1988; Hare, 1985; Clark, 1982; Baldwin, 1979). As we await more definitive information, it is encouraging to know that despite the fact that Black children must interact in a White environment that devalues their worth, their Black parents and significant others in their community have provided them with the spiritual and cognitive power to feel good about themselves.

Summary

All parents are challenged to prepare children to become productive citizens. Regardless of economic status, parents must strive to instill in their children enough self-reliance and self-esteem to successfully confront life's challenges. Impoverished families certainly face the greatest difficulties. However, despite its obvious disadvantages, poverty can provide benefits that may escape the more affluent. This is best illustrated by an Anglo-Saxon Protestant male, age twenty-seven, who was raised by two highly educated parents in an affluent American suburb. Recounting the hardships and tough times of his father's childhood, he asked his father, "How could you raise me in the lap of luxury and expect me to develop character. . . . Didn't it occur to you that by sparing me from the hardships, . . . sacrifices, . . . hard work, and . . . fights you were robbing me of the chance to become the kind of man you are. . . . You know you are tough. . . . You know you can make a way for yourself and that you deserve to be where you are" (Campolo and Campolo, 1989, pp. 7–8).

While at least a third of all Black families encounter the character-building hardships and sacrifices that this son missed, the present opportunity structure will not necessarily provide them with the success realized by his father. Being Black and poor is double jeopardy. Black parents face not only the task of building strong character in their children, but the challenge of making them understand that character alone may be insufficient for overcoming discrimination, prejudice, and other negative life circumstances.

In her study, Marie Peters (1985) asked Black parents what the most important thing is that they give to their children. Material wealth was not mentioned. Love and security, however, were deemed essential ingredients for overcoming the harsh realities of being Black in America. Lifting each other as they climb, many impoverished families generate these ingredients. Numerous successful Blacks look back on their childhood and realize that at the time, they did not realize they were impoverished. They only understood the love and security that derived from laboring together. Black love continues to be Black wealth. Unfortunately, too often even this precious asset is insufficient for achieving upward mobility.

9

Kinship and Community Support

If it were not for strong kinship bonds, Black men and women could not have survived the physical and psychic atrocities of slavery as well as the hardships of the Reconstruction and Depression eras. The slave community dramatically demonstrated affection and reverence for its families. Only deep affection could motivate runaway slaves to repeatedly risk their lives by returning to slave territory in the hopes of rescuing blood and in-law relatives. The devastation of the Civil War and upheavals during Reconstruction revealed the far-reaching boundaries and elasticity of the family circle. Despite their own meager resources throughout this period, young and elderly adults adopted kin and nonkin children who were left homeless and destitute. Active compassion was repeated during the Depression of the 1930s, when thousands of families doubled up with aunts, uncles, cousins, and other relatives to weather the economic storm (J. H. Franklin, 1988; Jones, 1985; Gutman, 1976).

Many of those who experienced the dreadful events prior to the twentieth century are now buried beneath the circular flat rocks that typically mark their graves. Occasionally, these stones can be found weathered and eroded; most are lost forever (Haley, 1986). However, the memory of these ancestors' upward struggle has left an indelible mark on contemporary society. Today, relative to Whites and even to some ethnic groups of color, the Black community shows a higher level of multigenerational households, fosterage of kin and nonkin children, care for dependent family members, respect for elders, religiosity, and sacrificial efforts for the upward mobility of its members.

How much of this sense of family obligation is African survival and how much developed in the New World has been debated by various scholars (D. Franklin, 1988). The most vocal of these scholars have been Herskovits, Frazier, and Du Bois. Herskovits (1941) argued for continuity between African-American traditions, Frazier (1939) insisted that the African-American link broke under slavery, and Du Bois (1898) had more confidence in the survival of African religious practices than family traditions. Uncertain of African family survivals, Du Bois called for further research to settle the debate. His call was masterfully answered by the historical revisionist Herbert Gutman.

Gutman's revolutionary study (1976) provides sufficient evidence that African slaves continued to view kinships and the obligations flowing from them as the normal expression of social relations. To understand what survived in the New World, it is necessary to understand the nature of African family organization. In traditional African society, families are seen as enveloped in a large circle. Within this circle are smaller circles representing the ancestors, elders, the fathers, the mothers, and the children. Even gods are envisaged as a series of family groupings. The use of circles can be seen in the physical arrangements of family compounds and the round huts within many traditional African villages. In essence, circles served as a constant reminder of interdependence, unity, humility, and the absence of greed (Diallo and Hall, 1989).

Typical features of African extended families include strong religious orientation, keen awareness of kinship obligations that extend beyond the nuclear family and the living, kinship based on consanguine descent rather than marital ties, economic cooperation and family-owned property, affectionate and material exchanges among relatives, respect for elders and age-grade groupings, shared residence, joint activities, and children reared by a large number of relatives and community members (Diallo and Hall, 1989; Kayongo-Male and Onyango, 1984; Herskovits, 1941).

It is clear that the unique circumstances of bondage meant that certain kinship patterns were not fully recreated on American soil, some found new meaning, new ones were created, and the origin of others is unclear. Regardless of the specific features, kinship obligation has served as the pivotal point for social organization for Black people since preslavery days. In the following section, our description of precolonial Africa reflects many of the characteristics of contemporary African families. For African colonialism was even less able than American slavery to destroy African traditional familial practices. Thus, much of what is written in the past tense could very well be stated in the present.

The Circle of African Elders

Perhaps the most striking feature of African families was the large number of individuals rearing children. In traditional African communities, any adult had the right to discipline and order children to do simple tasks. To assess their precision in following orders, elders tested children by asking them to perform detailed tasks, such as gathering and bringing to them certain medicinal herbs. If the children proved themselves responsible, the elders would reveal to them the secrets and knowledge of their ancestors.

Failure to follow orders in every detail could incite the elder's anger. In light of the importance of oral tradition, this anger was well placed. Oral communication was the primary medium for transmitting medicinal, ceremonial, and cultural traditions. When children were instructed in ritual practices and herb secrets, any deviation in carrying out instructions could result in future generations being led into practicing false traditions, or more seriously, lives could be endangered by passing on an incorrect medicinal prescription (Diallo and Hall, 1989; Kayongo-Male and Onyango, 1984).

Grandparents served as important agents of socialization. They introduced young people to the sensitive topics of husband-wife relationships and sexual behavior as well as the values and traditions of the larger society. For example, each girl was assigned one grandmother who was responsible for training her to become the nucleus and educator of her future family. The grandmother gave training in the strict rules of conduct during pregnancy and helped her to develop the inner strength necessary to make personal sacrifices for the protection and well-being of her children (Kayongo-Male and Onyango, 1984).

There were spiritual as well as practical reasons for pleasing the circle of elders. Apart from the supreme being, God (Nyame among the Ashanti; Kle among the Minianka), it was the ancestors who had the greatest power and commanded the greatest respect. Through rituals and divination, the elders communicated with the ancestors. Thus, elders were in the best position to inform children of behavior that brings the wrath or pleasure of ancestors (Diallo and Hall, 1989; Kayongo-Male and Onyango, 1984; Herskovits, 1941). Ancestors interacted indirectly (through elders) and directly (through reincarnation). The coming and going between the visible and invisible worlds is vividly illustrated in a contemporary African drummer's account of his own birth: "I was born in my paternal grandmother's house in Fienso. She was the midwife who assisted all the births in our village. . . . I was born so quickly there was no time . . . for the customary attendance of the older women. My grandmother looked at my newborn face and said, 'Oh no, not him!' She recognized me as an ancestor returned to earth. This does not disturb me. I accept this double role of being both myself and an ancestor at the same time" (Diallo and Hall, 1989, p. 15). Despite this duality of being, children considered to be the reincarnation of an ancestor were still treated as unique individuals.

The Circle of African Children

Further expanding the family were same-gender/same-age peer groups. Although they had a weaker authority than the elders over socialization, they had powerful control over the behavior of youth. Their influence extended into adulthood for males and ended at marriage for those women in patrilineal societies. Unlike males, the women would marry in their teens and move to the homes of their husbands, becoming integrated into the women's group of their husbands' community.

Peer groups had no leader, and all decisions were made by consensus. Many practices facilitated the feeling that children were equal. They ate from the same plate and dressed in similar clothing. While it is true that the eldest had more authority, there was no exclusivity in possessions. Any child could take the eldest's possession without permission. During meals, the eldest ate only after the younger ones had satisfied their hunger.

Unlike mainstream American peer groups, traditional African peer groups were "pro-parents," working in conjunction with parental and kin values and goals. Discipline primarily took the form of social ostracism. Also, unmerciful teasing was used to help children accept or change the reality of their condition (being overweight or timid). Age-peer groups stayed together through the best and worst of times, kept secrets, and swore to come to the aid of any member in trouble. Making oneself available for the needs of the group was one of the most valued lessons learned within peer groups. The elders watched these groups closely, since the future of the village belonged to them (Diallo and Hall, 1989; Kayongo-Male and Onyango, 1984).

Fostering Children in African Societies

Because all adults were considered teachers and parents, African cultures such as the Minianka had no word for teacher or uncle and aunt. All adult males were considered fathers and all adult females mothers. As such, they were responsible for the teaching of all children. It was not unusual for children to spend the greater part of their childhood being raised not by their parents but their "uncles" or "aunts," particularly if such kin were childless. At times, adults would foster even nonrelatives' children.

In addition, fostering children took the form of children exchange and "sister/brother-in-law parenting." Among married brothers, each would take one or more children from the other. These children knew who their biological parents were, although they spent most of their time away from them. Both their parents and uncles or aunts were called "father" or "mother." The practice of *levirate* or "in-law" parenting protected children and the family line. According to this practice, when a married man died his brother inherited both his widow and children. If there were no surviving children, then children born of the widow's second marriage were referred to as if they had been fathered by the deceased—a type of "ghost marriage." A parallel arrangement, *sororate,* occurred in the case of the death of a child's mother. Rather than being disruptive, such arrangements served as a reaffirmation of trust among the kin members involved and reemphasized the belief that each child is not only a child of the parent, but also of the larger kin group. Children are so highly valued for their role in maintaining the family line and a sense of immortality that even today, an African marriage is seen as meaningless without them (Mbiti, 1973; Kayongo-Male and Onyango, 1984).

The African kinship ties provided self-identity by absorbing all children and adults into existing kin networks. These ties were so strong that banishment, not death, was considered the supreme punishment. In marriage and divorce, kin had obligations for maintaining family continuity. The concept of neolocality—that is, where a couple or an unmarried woman with or without children sets up an independent household—was not a typical structure within African culture.

When couples married, they joined a family village or compound of either the bride or the groom, depending on whether the society was patrilineal or matrilineal. The couples' children became the children of the compound. When couples divorced, the "out-marrying" spouse returned to his or her blood kin and the children remained with the compound. Thus, children continued their lives with their father in patrilineal societies and their mother in matrilineal societies. Such a system ensured that children and adults would always be part of a familiar family circle (Diallo and Hall, 1989; Sudarkasa, 1988; Stephens, 1963). In essence, the concept of being one step removed from belonging to a family, such as in the case of step-families, had little meaning.

Slavery's Namesakes and Postslavery Adoptions

Initial enslavement shattered consanguineal ties for all but a few slaves. However, during the inner passage, slaves converted kin relationships into symbolic (or fictive) kin ties. African children called their parents' shipmates "aunt" and "uncle." On the slave plantation, slave children were taught to call all adult slaves (kin and nonkin) "aunt" and "uncle." Such names converted nonkin into quasi-kin networks of mutual obligations. Throughout slavery, the strength of kinship relationships was revealed in three major ways: naming children, fostering children, and the community welfare system (Miller and Smith, 1988; Gutman, 1976).

As a way of spiritually linking dead and living generations, slave children were often named for living and dead blood relatives—grandparents, parents, aunts and uncles. Surprisingly, slave daughters seldom carried their mothers' names, while sons often had their fathers' names. This is particularly noteworthy since the mother-child relationship was most likely to be maintained in the event of family breakup, and slave owners rarely recorded the names of slave fathers in plantation birth registries. This distinct naming practice in effect protected the loss of lineage when slave fathers were sold away from their families. This further underscored the importance of family ties in the slave community (Gutman, 1976).

A vivid sense of the slaves' connection with the dead is revealed in the frequent naming of children after deceased siblings. Slaves suffered from extraordinary rates of infant mortality (twice that of Whites) prior to and just after birth. The low priority White masters gave to family well-being of slaves meant that new mothers with infants often had to walk long distances from field to nursery to feed and care for their infants. Poor nourishment and inattentiveness contributed to the rate of only two out of three Black children surviving to the age of ten during the 1850–1860 period. Mothers' emotional suffering was partially relieved by their faith in the West African tenet that held that if you remember the deceased, they will never die. Remembrance took the form of naming surviving children after their dead siblings. Others who had suffered the loss of an infant gave a subsequent surviving child the name of the deceased sibling, because he or she was believed—in line with West African tradition—to be the deceased reincarnated (Diallo and Hall, 1989; Jones, 1985; Kayongo-Male and Onyango, 1984; Gutman, 1976).

Obligation toward nonslave kin was compassionately expressed during and immediately after the Civil War. Although the exact numbers are unknown, numerous children were orphaned by the sale, death, desertion, and wartime dislocation of their parents. Many were absorbed into extended kin groups, and others found homes with nonkin. These "motherless children" were adopted by ex-slaves who could hardly care for their own families. With superstitious care, some families would feed and care for as many as half a dozen nephews and nieces as well as additional non–blood kin children. When family absorption was virtually impossible, church and community funds were raised to build orphanages (Gutman, 1976).

In contemporary Black culture, fostering and informally adopting children continues to be a striking feature of the Black kinship experience. One reason for this is the historical bias against Black families in the policies and practices of formal adoption agencies. The fact that child services began and developed in the North in the nineteenth century made it unlikely that poor Southern Black children were of serious concern. Further, child welfare systems were governed by two major philosophical orientations: individual responsibility for poverty and the Darwinian doctrine of the survival of the fittest. These two perspectives, coupled with racism, did not provide an appreciation of the breadth, depth, and causes of poverty following emancipation (Billingsley and Giovannoni, 1972).

Further, the current screening criteria used by most agencies are designed to ensure that adopted children have economic security and a middle-class life-style; thus, preference is given to families that have the potential income of two middle-class parents. Too frequently, stable Black families with low incomes are disqualified. Fortunately, Black children have never had to solely depend on institutions in the broader society.

The old tribal view that "everyone belongs to someone" and that Black children are a "gift from God" is evident in the efforts of Black adopting families and in the numerous community-help programs offered by Black churches. It is a well-documented fact that in contemporary U.S. society, Black children are more likely than White children to be adopted by relatives. Current data show 13 percent of Black children living with their grandparents, as compared to 5 percent for Hispanics and 3 percent for Whites (Lewin, 1990). Black families adopt children from public welfare agencies at four and a half times the rate of Whites and Latinos (Jones, 1989). This practice is not recent. In the 1960s, Black families informally adopted children with a placement rate more than ten times that of formal adoption agencies and formally adopted at a higher rate than White families of similar means (Hill, 1972). In the early 1980s, Blacks were over twice as likely as Whites to adopt related children or noninfants (65 versus 24 percent), twice as likely to absorb the first premarital live births into the homes of relatives or friends, and seven times less likely to put out-of-wedlock children up for adoption (Bachrach, 1986).

In line with West African tradition, adopted Black American children are treated no differently from other children within the extended family network. Cousins living in the same house are taught to regard each other as brothers and sisters. Seldom is a child labeled "illegitimate" as a result of the conditions of his or her birth. In clothes, food, and shelter, parents strive to treat each child fairly. However, informally adopted children often make a distinction between their adoptive mother or age-dominant figure (usually their grandmother) and their biological mother. They may even call their grandmother "Big Mom" or "Momma" and the biological mother "Little Mom" or by her first name ("Momma Nellie"). Parallel names may be given to fathers and grandfathers. Even aunts and uncles may be called "Mom" or "Dad." This practice is also common among Blacks in the Caribbean, suggesting a common African source.

Many of the rationales used for informal adoptions by Black families resemble those of traditional West African families. In their eight-year study of Black extended families, Martin and Martin (1978) describe families who gave their children up to kin who needed companionship after the death of a spouse. The sense that children belong to the community is evident in the authors' description of family members who, without permission, simply took children who they felt were neglected by their parents. Some refused to give the children back, even when the parents demanded that they do so.

Other families who needed financial relief sent their children to live with a favorite aunt or uncle. During the period of Martin and Martin's study, 20 percent of children under eighteen lived with their aunts or uncles (Hill and Shackleford, 1986). Kin who step in on behalf of children gain family and community respect and gratitude. On the death of an adopting parent, it is not unusual for fostered nonkin children and blood kin to appear on the list of surviving relatives. Further, the deceased is heralded as an earthly saint for taking in needy children. The old Southern proverb "If you knock de nose, de eye cry" (one hurts; all hurt) simply illustrates the importance placed on the interdependence of the Black community. As in African societies, a high value is attached to those who can relieve human suffering.

Despite this impressive record of Black compassion and self-reliance, in the last decade the number of children in out-of-home care has increased. A primary culprit is the surge in drug addiction among young Black women. In California, foster care for Blacks increased from 47,700 in 1985 to 78,900 in 1989 (Hinds, 1990). Nationally, Black children constituted 40 percent of children awaiting adoption in 1990 (DelVecchio, 1990). Although recent statistics show the willingness of many Black families to formally adopt, the number of drug-exposed children has outstripped the capacity of the Black community to absorb them (Jones, 1989).

This situation has provided an additional rationale for transracial adoption, further fanning the fiery controversy over the development of Black identity and social coping skills of Black children raised in White families (Johnson, Shireman, and Watson, 1987). Yet organizations such as the National Association of Black Social Workers contend that potential Black adopting families are still available. Using nontraditional criteria, innovative Black adoption programs have flourished and have had unprecedented success in recruiting and placing Black children in Black homes (Lincoln and Mamiya, 1990; Washington, 1987).

The question remains as to whether these new approaches can outpace the drug epidemic, which is sending a rising number of Black parents to prison. When fathers go to prison, any childrearing responsibilities they had are quickly assumed by the mothers of their children with the help of kin. Although most families are hurt by the arrest and detention of the father, some families and marital relationships appear strengthened. This usually occurs when the offending parent's drug and alcohol addiction has created havoc within the family. Imprisonment allows the family to regain a new sense of self-reliance and to reorganize and pursue desired goals (Davis, 1990).

As tragic as fathers' incarceration can be, the imprisonment of Black mothers in American jails and prisons is even more crushing to children. The number of women in state and federal prisons increased from 13,420 to 30,834 during an eight-year period (Bohlen, 1989). In states with sizable Black populations, Black women represent the majority of such prisoners. This is partially due to the heavy police presence in Black neighborhoods and the public nature of Black women's drug transactions.

Their imprisonment is even more tragic today than in the past, since many more are incarcerated because of felony drug charges rather than misdemeanors, which carry shorter jail sentences. For married mothers with addictions, a prison term often means the termination of their marriage. According to one prison official, "You see that with the visits. You rarely see the boyfriends coming out here. With men, the women take care of them. But the men don't take care of the women. They abandon them. It's pitiful" (Bohlen, 1989, p. A-1).

Some children are unable to visit their mothers when prisons are located in remote rural areas. Often public transportation ceases running on weekends and holidays, when children are most able to visit. These women not only lose their partners, but also predictable physical contact with their children. While in prison, the children of female inmates are frequently cared for by grandmothers, aunts, and sisters, who have the awesome job of protecting them from drug-infested neighborhoods. Social agencies estimate that as many as 70 percent of the children in crack-ruled neighborhoods are being reared by older relatives, usually the grandmother.

Unfortunately, Black grandmothers take up the slack at a real sacrifice. Because they are related to the children, they may get only a third of the amount allotted to children who are in licensed group homes (Gross, 1989). Many were already helping their working daughter in raising the children, but with the daughter's imprisonment, the grandmothers face the task alone. The psychological trauma of starting over again after raising their own children puts them out of phase with their peers, who are partaking of the leisure years.

Still, a number of these grandmothers are young, in their thirties and forties, reflecting their own early initiation into childbearing and the fact that their children are repeating the cycle. Many are psychologically unprepared, feeling they are too young to be associated with their grandchildren (Burton and Bengston, 1985). Finally settled into steady full-time jobs, most have no desire to resign, either because of job contentment or the difficulty they perceive in finding another job (Furstenberg, Brooks-Gunn, and Morgan, 1987). They must integrate the demands of employment with transporting children to day-care centers and doctors' appointments and attending PTA meetings, school performances, and Little League games. In sum, they find themselves balancing their job with the full range of parenting responsibilities. If their family demands also include a husband and other dependent relatives, the burden can be overwhelming.

In addition, some find themselves under siege from the violence and erratic behavior of the child's mother. One woman's daughter left her son with her, stole her car, and threatened to kill her when confronted (White, 1989). When parents have to get restraining orders to prevent their drug-addicted adult children from visiting them or their children, the extended family network is rendered ineffective. The risk that drugs and alcohol abuse places on children prompted former antidrug chief William Bennett to call for the removal of children from drug-infested neighborhoods and for placing them in orphanages.

This proposed national action wages war on drugs at the expense of the most economically vulnerable segment of the population—Black children and women. Yet drugs are not confined to the poor. In essence, lower-income Blacks are being penalized for their poverty, while millions of affluent American families escape relatively free (Lewis, 1990). With the parents in jail and the children in orphanages, the Bennett plan, if enacted, would set the stage for a vicious circle of Black family turmoil: an unthinkable situation in the supportive circles of traditional West African extended families.

Kinship and Upward Mobility

The greatest contribution of kin is their support in the upward mobility and self-esteem of family members. With substantially lower incomes and higher fertility than Whites,

Black families not only do not typically have wealth to pass on to succeeding generations but find the earnings of two parents essential for maintaining their present socioeconomic standing. For the large number of single mothers, upward mobility is exceedingly difficult to achieve, and for most, the passing of wealth is inconceivable. This situation is much the same for many working- and middle-class Blacks whose parents and grandparents escaped poverty. As noted in Chapter Three, technological advances, governmental foreign trade policies, and national economic deficits have threatened, halted, or reversed the upward mobility of many non-poor Black families.

Thus, each generation must depend on its own efforts and support from same-generation kin. Whether Black families are moving from poverty to the working class, from the working class to the middle class, or merely maintaining economic stability, it requires intensive efforts and perseverance by family members in order not to slip into a lower economic condition. As an example, typically it is only those single teenage mothers who receive help from kin who are able to complete high school or obtain college experience. The critical family support they receive in lodging, food, and child care frees them to acquire those skills necessary to secure and maintain a job and move out on their own (Furstenberg and Crawford, 1978; Furstenberg, Brooks-Gunn, and Morgan, 1987; McAdoo, 1988; Goldscheider and Goldscheider, 1991).

Even though Black children often receive financial help from parents, they are less likely than White children to receive educational assistance beyond high school. The younger the parent, the fewer the family financial resources for investing in college education for children. Available resources within extended families generally go to married adult children who are struggling to raise their own children (Goldscheider and Goldscheider, 1991; Taylor, 1986; Hill, 1972).

While evidence exists showing that parents' financial contribution to their children's educational expenses raises their children's educational expectations, nonmonetary resources are also important. One study of the supportive roles of relatives and community members showed that among postgraduate-educated Blacks, nearly a fifth received financial assistance from relatives other than their parents. However, over half claimed that their own achievement was inspired by the example and encouragement of relatives.

With few exceptions, parental encouragement comes from even those parents who have never set foot on a college campus prior to attending their child's baccalaureate. In reaching for their diploma, many graduates see their grandmother or some other supportive relative lose control with a shout of "Thank you, Jesus! Our prayers have been answered." This spiritual and emotional backing partially explains why so many of the Black students enrolled in elite Black colleges in the 1970s were unlikely candidates, in the sense that neither one of their parents had graduated from college and nearly 80 percent needed government financial assistance to remain in school (Goldscheider and Goldscheider, 1991; Manns, 1988; Hill, 1972). Apparently for many, emotional support, affirmation from others, and role modeling are essential motivating factors when parental economic support is lacking.

The old adage that "God helps those who help themselves" seems to be the guiding principle for Black parents assisting their upwardly mobile children. Black parents and children are more likely than Whites or Hispanics to be co-contributors to their children's educational expense. The more Black children contribute to their own expenses, the more parents help them. In fact, Black parents actually contribute more than comparable White parents when their children show extraordinary effort to work, sweat, and save for their education. In contrast, for White and Hispanic students, the more the parents contribute, the less they pay toward their educational expenses. White and Hispanic students appear not to have the same urgency about working as do Black students. Blacks as a group cannot have a lax attitude toward work as a means to upward mobility. Black students can expect to receive 50 percent less parental financial assistance than Whites just because they are more likely to come from lower-income families, mother-headed households, and mothers who started childbearing early (Goldscheider and Goldscheider, 1991).

If Black students fail to get adequate financial assistance from parents and other relatives, they either seek government financial aid or drop out to work. Tragically, since 1980, the Reagan administration and Congress have slashed $10 billion from health, day-care, and educational programs, making it exceedingly difficult for Black students, particularly if married with children, to remain in school (Edelman, 1986). Further, young Black men and women still find it difficult to secure a job. Thus, many Black students have no other choice but to drop out or join the army for its GI benefits.

While older Blacks are more likely to give than receive support, they are not forgotten by their children. In mapping their life course, youth look to both the future and the past. Many of those who temporarily drop out of school to work not only are saving for school, but are actively contributing to their parents' household expenses. The more they earn and the greater their parents' financial need, the more they contribute. Their sense of family obligation is not limited to their parents. These older children try to help out financially in meeting the needs of their younger siblings and other relatives who are in school or unemployed. Regardless of whether they come from one-parent or two-parent families, Blacks in general contribute substantially more to their parental family household than do Whites. Sons contribute slightly more than daughters, no doubt reflecting their higher wages and the male provider expectation (Goldscheider and Goldscheider, 1991; "The Black Male Shortage," 1986; Martin and Martin, 1978).

As children pass middle age, they rely less on their parents and the flow of support reverses. The obvious reason for this is that their parents' health and income begin to decline. The health and economic situations of elderly Blacks have generally been poorer than those of elderly Whites. Hypertension among Blacks sixty-five to seventy-four years old is higher than among Whites in this age group. Blacks are more likely to be sick and disabled and to see themselves as being in poor health than White elderly. More often than Whites, they are likely to depend on one or two sources of government income (social security and/or Supplemental Security Income) or to have no income. In these leisure years, many White elderly are pretty much able to buy anything they need, and a large minority actually save and invest. But the large majority of Blacks merely scrape by or find themselves in real financial difficulties. The bottom line is that years of economic depri- vation take their toll (Murray, Khatib, and Jackson, 1989).

If it were not for extended families, a larger number of elderly Blacks would be homeless on the American streets. While both Black and White elderly identify about the same proportion of adult children whom they can depend on for all types of help, the extended kin play a larger role for Black families. Black elderly are more likely to live in an extended household and less likely to be in a nursing home. Conse- quently, when physically or mentally impaired, their decision- making power is more likely to be usurped by an adult child or a competent spouse than by formal community agencies (Smerglia, Deimling, and Barresi, 1988; Hofferth, 1984).

Numerous arrangements for the support and respect of the elderly can be found in Black communities. It is not uncommon for elderly Blacks to be heavily supported by their own children and their grandchildren. For example, five adult siblings who grew up in poverty and experienced periodic welfare placed their mother in a comfortable middle-class retirement home. Each child was assessed a monthly fee according to his or her means. Their mother's social security check could then be used to her liking. Grandchildren were also instructed to continue this self-help if needed. Sometimes elderly parents are given the master bedroom in their chil- dren's home. This gesture is one way of making the grand- parents more comfortable in their later years, while sym- bolically honoring their position in the family.

While in their children's home, grandmothers are more likely than grandfathers to become heavily involved in their

grandchildren's lives. Those grandmothers who live with
their single-parent daughters or daughters-in-law see themselves and are seen by their grandchildren as being more
active in supporting, disciplining, and controlling their grandchildren than grandmothers who have separate households.
This relatively active participation of grandmothers is also
true in two-parent multigenerational households. Grandchildren seem to benefit from having grandma in the home. They
are better adjusted, and the quality of the emotional support
they receive from their mother is greatly improved. However,
many young grandparents prefer their grandchildren to live
near but not with them (Wilson, 1986; Jackson, 1986). When
these grandparents become ill, it presents a big emotional
crisis in terms of lost support and their contribution to the
family well-being. Given the fact that the typical Black family
has limited economic resources, it becomes necessary to
arrange creative home care. Children are often assisted by
other members within their kinship circle. The greatest community assistance they receive is from the Black church,
which is second only to families in its response to the needs
of Black people.

The Black Church

Most churches cannot avoid becoming intimately involved in
fulfilling the needs of Black family networks. Families constitute the building blocks for the church congregations.
Some churches are dominated by generations of kinship
groups, so that the concept of the "family or kin church" is
more reality than ideology. Through preaching, teaching,
cooperative benevolence, symbols, belief systems, morality,
and rituals, the church welds community and unrelated families to each other. Within this context, the church is the
modern-day tribe. Each member is literally referred to as "sister" or "brother," elders receive high respect, the minister is
venerated as the earthly spiritual chief, and a host of unseen
heavenly angels and a supreme Father are believed to be
governing the living and the dead. With varying degrees of

intensity, the church has historically served as the ordained leader of Black families.

After the Civil War, Black churches legitimized the informal marriages of many former slaves, demanded marital fidelity, designed programs to foster male leadership in the family, encouraged honest hard work, affirmed individual self-worth, and urged the family to function as an "extended church" by conducting family worship within the home. Most of these efforts have not been seriously challenged. Contemporary parents often bring their children to church, and sometimes older children are forced to attend, because these parents believe that only within the religious extended family can their children get a dose of moral education, positive group identity, and personal self-worth (Lincoln and Mamiya, 1990; Poole, 1990).

Yet there have been questions as to whether the church has provided the environment necessary to overcome the psychological stigma of living in a racist society. This concern was prevalent during the time that the Clark and Clark "doll test" experiments were popularized (see Chapter Eight). If children's preference for White dolls is indicative of self-hatred, this challenges the message of the Black church. Without self-acceptance, the Christian command to love your neighbor as yourself is problematic. Likewise, minimum credence could be given to the claim that salvation brings wholeness to human personalities if Black children detest themselves and their people (Lincoln and Mamiya, 1990; Baldwin, 1979).

Today, many scholars do not believe that Black children's rejection of Black dolls reflects their hatred for themselves and their race. However, preferences for White dolls may still imply that children perceive that it is preferable to be of another race. Black parents and churches must still struggle with the meaning of race, particularly when socializing children (Lincoln and Mamiya, 1990).

In this struggle, how much importance should be placed on Whites' evaluation of Blacks is of concern. It is doubtful whether the most significant others in Black people's lives are Whites. Recent research shows that negative feedback from Whites may not represent a salient source of influence on Black self-concept. This research suggests that because most Black people associate racism with White people, they tend to discredit Whites' negative evaluations of them (Baldwin, 1979). Thus, it is unlikely that the soul of Black folks is based primarily on the opinions of Whites.

As with Whites, the significant others in the early experiences of Black children are others of similar color. The limited use of television and the pervasive racial segregation from the 1930s to the early 1950s meant that this was even more true then than in today's less segregated society. Lending support to this is the Clarks' finding (Clark and Clark, 1950) that children from segregated settings (the South) made more choices favoring brown dolls than children in interracial nursery schools.

Martin Luther King once stated that the most segregated hour in America is Sunday morning. He obviously was referring to the historical racial segregation of America's religious institutions. Apart from the negative implication of this fact, this situation has worked to the benefit of Black people, particularly children. For the majority of Blacks, the church has served as a buffer against the negative feedback of the White community. It is the only institution that has historically operated independently of the White power structure. As such, it has been in a position to chart its own missions (Harris, 1987; Baldwin, 1979).

One of the powerful missions of the Black church is affirming the worth of every human being. The doctrine that every human being is made in the image of God and the promise that God will punish the sinful violators of human dignity not only serves to discredit Whites' evaluation of Blacks but has prevented the complete dehumanization of Blacks through the ages. Further, for some Blacks, the message that the meek will inherit the Kingdom of God subtly elevated the humanity of Blacks over Whites and provided additional strength during the difficult period of bondage (Baldwin, 1979; Fordham, 1975). The church has not only provided a refuge in times of severe trouble, but it continues to give members weekly reinforcement in resisting personal and social stressors. Within the church family, children as well as adults find their self-esteem affirmed in many ways.

For many Black children, it is within the church that they first learn to read and give public speeches. Children who falter when giving an oral or musical presentation hear the pews and walls resonate with the encouraging "Amens" and "Go on, child; it's all right." Whether the presentation is perfect or imperfect, there are always adults waiting in the foyer to applaud a young child's efforts. Such responses allow children to be affirmed as they are and to continue practicing and performing without the fear of rejection. This message of affirmation is presented to children in still another way. One of the major strengths of the church has been its willingness to provide status that is not available in the White society. Children see the dignity of even the lowliest person confirmed. The head deacon can be a janitor, the head usher a domestic worker, and the young people's association leader a medical doctor. Regardless of their station in the larger society, all receive recognition and status in the church.

Perhaps one of the most important functions the church performs is creating a forum in which children can emulate adult role models. In Scanzoni's 1978 study of Black working- and middle-class families, ministers ranked second only to schoolteachers and Sunday school teachers ranked third among the adult role models who showed an interest in the youth. In his book on the life of Martin Luther King, Keith Miller (1991) gives credit to King's Sunday school teacher for helping shape the thought and character of the most important American in this century. If affirmation and value setting were the only contribution of Black churches, this would be enough to applaud. Their contribution does not stop here. Serving as concert hall, art gallery, and public forum, the church has trained singers, artists, mayors, Congressional representatives, and thousands of youth for public leadership.

Although church services are oriented toward the adult, every major Black denomination in the United States offers a

wide range of programs for the youth. There are special Sab-
baths such as "Children's Day" or "Youth Church" that allow
children to take leadership. Youth are inspired by programs
that honor members who have distinguished themselves in
their chosen profession. Evening socials, banquets, picnics,
sports teams, and church outings are designed for both youth
and adult fellowship. For many children, the first trip out of
their local community was made possible by a church-spon-
sored event. At least one Black denomination has a travel
agency and owns a bus company to provide affordable transportation for its members. Others own elementary schools
and colleges. Most of these schools were originally founded as
a reaction to segregation in the public school system. Today,
86 percent of Black churches support these schools, believing
that they continue to provide a nonracist environment in
which a healthy Black self-identity can be realized (Lincoln
and Mamiya, 1990).

The Black church continues its focus on needy children. Apart from raising money for orphanages, church societies have organized adoption programs. A noted example is
the successful Black-adoption program inspired by the Black
Catholic priest George Clements. Against strong opposition
from his superiors, this priest adopted a child for himself
before beginning a nationwide campaign urging each Black
church to adopt at least one Black child. Within the state of
Illinois, the One Church, One Child program is cosponsored
by the Interdenominational Coalition of Black Churches/Pas-
tors and the Illinois Department of Social Services. With each
pastor encouraging families to adopt at least one child, the
number of Black children of all ages awaiting adoption has
dropped from 700 to about 60.

Among the most pressing needs is to respond to the
one in two Black children who are mired in poverty. To attack
the myriad problems these children face, some of the larger
urban churches maintain day-care centers for working parents, job training for the unemployed, food and clothing
banks, emergency funds, drug abuse centers, and tutorial programs for parents and children within the community and in

prisons. In sum, these churches are providing for what amounts to the whole gamut of unattended needs associated with being poor in Black America (Lincoln and Mamiya, 1990; Harris, 1987; Frazier, 1964).

Whether people are old or young, the church is compelled to respond. Those fifty years and older are particularly important since they are the preservers of church tradition. They, especially the females, are more likely than the young to support the church with their tithes, offerings, attendance, and loyalty. They are also more likely to internalize the teachings of the church and to engage in church activities outside of weekend services (Taylor and Chatters, 1989). To encourage the prayers and visitations by mobile members, many Black churches publish weekly lists of those who are shut in because of illness or old-age impairments.

While it is to be expected that church members receive spiritual and moral support, one study showed that one out of five members also receive either financial assistance, goods and services, or total support (Lincoln and Mamiya, 1990; Taylor and Chatters, 1989). At times, the collection plate is passed in order to turn the heat on in Sister Mills's home or to pay for Brother Monroe's operation. Sometimes minivans are purchased for providing church and shopping transportation for the elderly. Using HUD grants or congregational funds, a few churches have purchased real estate to provide safe and convenient public housing for their elderly and disabled members. Some wealthy entrepreneurs and entertainers have challenged churches to match them in buying abandoned houses not only to house low-income members, but to purge the community of crack houses.

There is general agreement that the church is a prominent institution in the Black community. Yet it has not been without its critics. The emphasis placed on family values and moral integrity after emancipation was motivated by political as much as scriptural concerns. It was hoped that conformity to White family norms of morality would advance the Black race into full acceptance into the White world. When Blacks migrated to urban areas, their hopes were shattered. They found low wages and the dehumanization of racism and other forms of oppression. Black troops sent to defend democracy in Europe were segregated from White troops and returned to encounter racism at home. The persistence of these conditions has led Blacks to question the significance of the Black churches' formula for uplifting the race. Disenchantment has given rise to Black sects, cults, storefront churches, and nationalist movements, such as the Nation of Islam and the Universal Negro Improvement Association of Marcus Garvey. The rapid growth of more secular organizations, such as the National Urban League and the NAACP, indicates that an increasing number no longer see the church as the only vehicle for advancing the race (Poole, 1990; Lincoln and Mamiya, 1990).

Despite this disenchantment, fewer than 15 percent of Blacks believe that Black churches are not a force that continues to integrate and support the physical, social, and spiritual needs of the Black community. Seventy-eight percent of the Black population claim church membership, and slightly fewer than half (44 percent) attend church weekly. Rather than give up on the church, the laity is doing what it has done in the past—adapting its theology to the unique conditions of the times.

The majority of Black laity still believe that part of the church's mission is to liberate individuals from economic, political, and physical suffering. They expect pastors to embrace the spirit of ministers such as Nat Turner, Denmark Vessey, and Martin Luther King, whose religious convictions moved Blacks toward greater freedom for themselves and their families. But some question whether churches or the existing family social support network can adapt in time to meet the needs of vast numbers of Black youth.

An entire generation of teenagers and young adults, particularly Black males, are slipping from the reach of their families and traditional help systems. For the first time in Black history, a generation of unchurched youth are emerging from Northern and Western urban areas and to a lesser extent Southern cities. The high unemployment (40 to 80 percent) among Black teenagers during the 1980s forced many into the streets. In their need for survival and their search for meaning, a significant minority are finding formal and informal employment in gangs and illegal activities. For some, gangs have replaced their loyalty to their parents, siblings, and the church. In its worst manifestation, gang warfare has resulted in the undeserved massacre of entire families.

Imprisonment is a natural outcome of illicit street life. In some prisons, Black males constitute nearly the entire prison population. While women represent only 4 percent of the prison population, Black women constitute about 51 percent of all women prisoners. Nationally, about a quarter of all Black American males between twenty and twenty-nine are in jail, on parole, or on probation. A substantial number of those aged twenty-five to thirty-four who have felony records are high school dropouts. In speeches over the last decade, Jesse Jackson has clearly and solemnly indicated the magnitude of the problem when he has noted that there are as many Black men in prison as there are in college. Ironically, the annual cost of supporting each inmate is higher than tuition, room, and board at Harvard or Yale (Thomas, 1992; Morganthau, 1992). Tragically, few Black congregations are involved in prison ministries, and over half of prison inmates in many prisons do not receive visits from families or friends (Lincoln and Mamiya, 1990).

Of course, 75 percent of all Black male youth have selected legitimate survival strategies, and the vast majority of all Black families are law-abiding. Yet, regardless of their adaptation choice, many of the pressing issues for the Black community stem from those mired in poverty, the unskilled and skilled unemployed, and the millions of Black children born within a sociopolitical structure that makes it difficult for them to thrive.

Summary

It is unclear which specific features of the African family circles of ancestors, elders, and children are directly linked to present-day Afro-American families. There is no doubt, however, that Afro-American patterns of naming and fostering children reflect their high regard for kinship ties. Through these ties and the self-help gospel practiced by families and churches, Black Americans weathered the hardships of the transatlantic slave ship voyage, enslavement, emancipation, and the post-Reconstruction era. Further, without the support of kin, upward socioeconomic mobility would be an elusive dream for many.

Despite the effectiveness of Black kinship ties and self-reliance, the unique conditions of postindustrial society demand concerted efforts on the part of all individuals and support groups within the Black community. Urban problems have become so severe that ordinary citizens are seeking grass-roots solutions. In one city, Black middle-class professionals "adopted" thirty-six members of an eighth-grade class, providing counseling to the fatherless, academic tutoring, and college tuition money for the twenty women and thirteen men who made it through high school. In the late 1970s Edmond Burton, a dentist, armed with his Radio Shack Model One computer, began giving neighborhood kids job training after school and Saturdays. Today he teaches them Basic Lotus and WordPerfect on twenty computers and trains them in the techniques of job interviewing—and they get hired. In Cleveland, Charles Ballard of the National Institute of Fatherhood and Family Development coaches unwed fathers to behave like responsible men. Soft Sheen Products Incorporated has begun a learning center in Chicago's worst housing project. Gregory Boyle, a Jesuit priest, heads the Jobs for the Future program that finds work for gang members in East Los Angeles. He offers crack-dealing youth $5 an hour to go straight—and most do. The Crown Heights Youth Collective in New York has 5,000 kids involved in its program that provides help with job development, counseling, and interview self-presentation. Seventy-five percent of the youth who complete this program are placed in entry-level positions. A central motto for all these groups is Nothing Works to Build Sound Families like Work (Mathews and others, 1992).

These grassroots efforts are praiseworthy. Yet they are insufficient for fighting job discrimination, political logjams over urban anticrime bills, and reforms in the health care and school systems. As the resources of these individuals and grass-roots organizations thin in the face of severe urban problems, heavy pressure is being placed on the most powerful groups in the Black community, particularly Black churches. Church leaders in turn realize the need for an astute knowledge of the political process. Along with social scientists they have specific recommendations for political strategies.

Among many strategies, churches are urging public officials to provide financial incentives for preventive and intervention help systems already in place in the Black community. Using their influence, Black Protestant churches and the National Black Catholic Congress are pushing for reform in many directions—accurate treatment of Black family life in textbooks and the media, elimination of racial bias in the criminal justice system, employment for Black youth, full compensation for grandmothers supporting grandchildren left without their parents, on-the-job training for young parents on AFDC, extension of Medicaid to young parents living in extended households, and adequate medical and nutrition services for those families without financial resources.

Black churches historically have had a liberation theology dictated by the deprived position of the Black population. They have traditionally provided programs designed for the social, political, physical, and spiritual needs of Black families and their communities. It is Black churches, with their circle of intersecting families and spiritual leaders, who are in the best position to foster the strong tradition of intergenerational kin support. They, more than any other organized group, are the trustees of future Black generations.

10

Social Change,
Problems,
and Prospects

As scholars and practitioners involved with families, we are all
aware of and concerned about the alleged deterioration of the
Black family. The rising tide of female-headed households and
out-of-wedlock births has reached dramatic proportions and
taken a deadly toll on the society in terms of high school dropouts, increased crime rates, and spiraling welfare loads. While
the effects are known, the causes are generally reduced to those
of promiscuous sex and Black family values—or the lack of
such values as a strong work ethic and a belief in the monogamous nuclear family (Gilder, 1981). Those who subscribe to
these cultural generalities tend to ignore the fact that the statistics on Black family "pathology" reflect economics more than
race-bound promiscuity and other values. Whereas the Black
middle class has an above-average divorce rate and may be sexually active prior to marriage, they are not a cause for concern.
Like Euro-Americans, they remarry or are self-supporting in
the event of a divorce. If their nonmarital sexual activity culmi-
nates in a pregnancy, middle-class Black women follow the
mainstream model and get an abortion or marry the father.

The State and Public Policy

According to Bell and Vogel (1968), the family contributes its
loyalty to the government in exchange for leadership that

will provide direct and indirect benefits for the nuclear family. While there is little doubt that Black families have been loyal to the political state in America, it appears that they have derived few benefits in return. Although the political system has the power to affect many of the conditions influencing Black family life, it has failed to intervene in the service of the Black population and, in fact, has been more of a negative force in shaping the conditions under which Black families must live. As Billingsley (1968, p. 177) has stated, "No sub-system has been more oppressive of the Negro people or holds greater promise for their development."

Historically, we find that state, local, and federal governmental bodies have been willing collaborators in the victimization of Black families. Under slavery, marriages between slaves were not legal since the slave could make no contract. The government did nothing to ensure stable marriages among the slave population or to prevent the arbitrary separation of slave couples by their owners. Moreover, the national government was committed to the institution of slavery, a practice that was most inimical to Black family life (J. H. Franklin, 1987).

For reasons that may be related to the sacrosanct nature of the family in America, this country has rarely had any clearly defined plans or policies concerning the family. The closest thing has been the welfare system, which has actually done more to disrupt families than to keep them together (Jewell, 1988). In light of the continuing decline of the extended family, which once provided valuable back-up services to the nuclear family, some sort of family support system seems necessary. While the Black family has an extended character to it, it is no longer as viable a support force as it once was. The central problems facing Black families require much greater attention than they have received so far; a well-formulated public policy as well as appropriate action programs that address these problems are called for.

We have just reviewed the past relationship of government to the structure of Black family life. In general, the government's efforts have been sporadic, misguided, and ineffective. Since future trends are in the direction of increasing numbers of female-headed households, which are characterized by a below-average income and above-average number of children, a public policy relevant to Black families has been proposed. It includes a universal family allowance, elimination of gender discrimination in employment, community-controlled day-care centers, a child development program, and expanded government employment. Only through a combination of these measures will Blacks have a choice of family arrangements (Dewart, 1991).

Supporting the need for that public policy are the findings of the Commission on Civil Rights (1991). The commission found poverty endemic among fully employed Black women. Their wages are so low, in comparison to fully employed men, that an employed status is not sufficient to remove them from poverty. American society continues to pay women salaries that are often only adequate when they supplement a male breadwinner's income. Since a majority of Black families with children under the age of eighteen are headed by a woman, who is generally the sole wage earner, these families are consigned to poverty and all its ramifications. Because the educational level of Black women is above that of Black men, the method of comparable worth is one mechanism for attaining income parity with their male counterparts.

However, Leashore (1991) documents that Black males have a different set of problems. Many of them are unable to secure full-time employment and have a variety of health and educational problems. While it may be futile to argue who is worse off, it must be noted that childless Black males are seldom eligible for any welfare benefits in many states. Other than a life of crime or enlisting in the military, most of them are left without any options for survival in this society. Leashore has called for a national effort to provide job training, full employment, health care, and so on.

It will be necessary to advance a public policy to reverse the trend toward an upward redistribution of wealth. Yet, when asked whether the federal government should see to it that every person has a job and a good standard of living, 65 percent of Blacks but only 24 percent of Whites thought so. Whites were inclined to give more support to the idea of individuals "getting ahead on their own" versus government intervention (Harris and Williams, 1986). Again, there is an assumption in the White consciousness that government programs only encourage indolent minorities. In the more racially homogeneous countries of Europe, public policy has long been used to support an equalization of wealth. In contrast, the American body politic has elected a political administration that has spent a trillion dollars between 1980 and 1986 on a military buildup. The victims of that policy were largely families with children. Between 1977 and 1988, the poorest families' income decreased more than 10 percent, while the top 1 percent more than doubled their income in the same period (McLeod, 1991).

Finally, it would be instructive to note that the direction of change is the same for all families in the United States. Where Black families were in 1960, White families are in 1990. The trend toward out-of-wedlock births, female-headed households, and other changes in family structure are an artifact of the changing economic base of family life (Moynihan, 1987). Instead of relying on racial stereotypes as an explanation for a group's family structure, we need to understand that they are only further down a road all families are traveling.

The Economic Factor

In any discussion of the changes that have occurred in the Black family over the last thirty-five years, a common assumption is that Black family problems are a function of the decline of familial values and the triumph of hedonism over the discipline and perseverance necessary for marital stability. In some quarters, the old canard is that slavery and its concomitants destroyed the value of family life for many Afro-Americans. Any objective analysis of marital and family patterns in the United States would reveal a weakening of the patriarchal, monogamous, and nuclear family for all racial groups during the past third of a century (Skolnick, 1992). One remarkable and understated fact is that the statistics used as an indicator of Black family deterioration thirty years ago are almost the same for White families in the decade of the nineties. The direction of change, although not necessarily the causes, has been the same for all racial groups in American society. However, the definition and interpretation of those phenomena tend to be negative when applied to Black Americans. As Peters (1985, p. 160) once noted, "When Blacks are studied, so-called problem populations are often the focus of research—single parents, parents of emotionally disturbed, mentally retarded, or academically nonachieving or delinquent children and youths, or low income families."

A combination of etiological forces have contributed to the decline of the nuclear family, among them the weakening of the patriarchy by the increasing economic and psychological independence of women, the sexual revolution, greater mobility and urbanization patterns, and the liberalization of divorce laws. Many of those same causes impact on Black family instability; however, a more central source appears to be the declining participation of Black males in the labor force. While we have addressed how the shortage of Black males has led to the increase in single-parent households, marital dissolutions, and out-of-wedlock births earlier, we also need to understand the reasons behind the growing unemployment and underemployment rates of Black males.

One reason was that employment in government service, an important source of jobs for Blacks, declined when governments used tax monies to subcontract services to private businesses. This was particularly true of defense work, which was generally contracted out to private firms whose work force was largely White and male. Besides these unemployment trends, other forces were at work. One of them was the shift of jobs from the racially diverse inner cities to the largely White suburbs. Almost two-thirds of all new office construction now takes place in the suburbs. Consequently, many jobs are moving away from poorly skilled and displaced racial minorities. Along with the shift of jobs from cities to suburbs has been the fact that the greatest increase in jobs has occurred in small businesses, another factor that works against Blacks. Small businesses often recruit workers through informal means and look for a "personality fit" in workers. This frequently means that currently entrenched Euro-American workers bring in their friends and relatives to work for the same firm, a process that largely excludes Afro-Americans. The advantage of huge, bureaucratically organized, strongly led organizations for Blacks is that it is easier to change racial employment patterns in them than in small ones that hire friends and relatives or people of the same ethnic background and where the personal prejudices of the employer can be decisive.

A critical factor in Black unemployment trends has been the decline of industrial manufacturing jobs and the proliferative growth of jobs in the service and information processing spheres. In 1986, only 25.2 million Americans were employed in goods-producing industries, a net loss of 700,000 since their peak in 1979, compared to 74.5 million now earning their living in services, an all-time high and a net increase of 10.1 million since 1979 (Shinoff, 1986).

These service jobs often require no specific skills beyond literacy and tend to be nonunionized, meaning that they lend themselves to subjective and hence arbitrary recruitment and employment practices. Industrial manufacturing jobs had the distinction of being highly unionized, with retention being determined by seniority, not employer discretion. They rarely required standardized tests for entry-level jobs, and the demonstration of job proficiency was fairly precise.

Of course, it is alleged that large numbers of Black males lack the minimal literacy skills necessary for employment in the service and information processing industries. A shocking 44 percent of Black males are estimated to be functional illiterates, a considerably higher number than thirty years ago (Kozol, 1985). Certainly, the responsibility for these high rates lies with the public school system, which promotes these males without their having obtained reading and writing skills. In the South, the causes of Black male illiteracy might be attributed to the fact that the increasingly Black public schools are now controlled by Euro-Americans. For example, in Georgia—where 52 of the state's 187 school districts have a majority Black student population—only four school superintendents are Black, and only one school board outside Atlanta is Black controlled (Chendinen, 1986). It might be also noted that the federal government has decreased its funding of public education during the 1980s.

A constellation of interlocking factors has pushed Black males out of the labor force and into the shadow economy of drug sales and petty theft, a fact that has increased their percentage of the American jail population to 49 percent (Beck, 1991). The malfunctioning of America's free market economy has created a million millionaires and forced several millions into a new kind of poverty. America's constant emphasis on competition, reflected in the loss of millions of jobs to foreign nations using cheap labor to provide inexpensive imports, has propelled many high school graduates to seek college degrees as an entry into the white-collar sphere of the private sector. Black males face a double dilemma in this evolving economy: they are not competitive with the White and Black women whose literacy and interpersonal skills are better, and the menial jobs that once were their monopoly must now be fought over with the newly arrived Third World immigrants. All three groups—women, Black men, and Third World immigrants—are exploited by this situation (Stewart and Hyclak, 1986). Of the white-collar jobs added since 1980 and mostly occupied by women, a third are in retail, where the average annual salary in 1984 was $9,521 below the government's poverty level for a family of four (Jaynes, 1990).

Meanwhile, the electorate continues to elect to political office administrations widely perceived as representing the interests of the wealthy. The small benefits that have trickled down have gone largely to middle-class White males. Between 1980 and 1986, government expenditures on the military have increased by 100 percent, and the major beneficiaries have

been White males (Brown, Wolf, Starke, and Jacobson, 1986).
The trillion dollars this country has spent on its military
buildup has diverted capital away from the improvement of
basic industries in such vital areas as steel, automobiles, and
machine tools, the very sector of the economy where most
Black men are located. The concentration of joblessness in
the Black community has resulted in unemployment receiving
a low priority among mainstream Americans. As Reeves
(1986, p. 85) has observed, "One of the secrets of the acceptance of the doubled crisis level in Black unemployment is
the fact that unemployment among adult white males is still
in the old range, below 6 percent." Certainly, the captains of
industry would not want full employment, which would
create a situation where employers would have to bid for
workers rather than the reverse.

Problems and Prospects

Almost thirty years since the publication of the Moynihan
report (1965), the figures Moynihan cited as evidence that the
Black family was deteriorating have doubled, almost tripled
in some areas. How is it that a group that regards family life
as its most important source of satisfaction finds a majority
of its women unmarried? Why does a group with more traditional sexual values than its White peers have a majority of
its children born out of wedlock? How is it that a group that
places such emphasis on the traditional nuclear family finds
a near majority of its members living in single-parent households? While theorists have offered a number of answers, we
suggest the major explanation has to do with the structural
conditions of the Black population.

The basis of a stable family rests on the willingness and
ability of men and women to marry, have children, and fulfill
socially prescribed familial roles. In the case of women, those
roles have traditionally been defined as giving birth to children and socializing them; providing sexual gratification,
companionship, and emotional support to their husbands;
and carrying out domestic functions such as cooking and

cleaning. There is abundant evidence that Black women are willing and able to fulfill those roles (Collins, 1986). The roles of men in the family are more narrowly confined to economic provider and family leader. There are indications that close to a majority of Black American males cannot implement those roles (Bowman, 1985). When it comes to a choice between remaining single or getting married, individuals often do a cost-benefit analysis. Marriage is frequently a quid pro quo arrangement. The desire to enter and maintain a conjugal relationship is contingent on people's perception of the benefits, as well as the anticipated costs, of such a relationship (Jewell, 1988).

As much as family and nonfamily male-female disruptions impact negatively on the psychology of males and females, the reality is that even when the rationale for the behavior of the male is understood, it does not negate the fact that the female is still forced to view male-female relations in terms of the cost-reward dichotomy. This approach may signal the fact that Black women, when confronted with eligible Black men who cannot give them financial security, willingly opt for a rational exchangist view that says that poverty in singlehood may be preferable to poverty in marriage, with all the accompanying stresses and tensions of marital discord. Even when the attraction of emotional attachment or sexual satisfaction is present, it loses its force eventually if financial security is not forthcoming. Hence, the economic exchange becomes the most potent and the most useful model of exchange relations.

There is no great mystery as to what has happened to the Black family in the last twenty-five years: it has experienced an acceleration of trends set in motion during the 1960s. A highly sexualized culture—via media, clothing, and example—has conveyed to American youth the notion that nonmarital sexual relations are not only acceptable but required for individual fulfillment. Furthermore, the consequences of teenage sexual behavior are counteracted somewhat by easier access to effective contraceptives and abortion, and the number of pregnant teenagers has not really increased—

only the proportion of births to that group of women as a result of the rapid decline in births to older married women. While the nonmarital sexual activity rates of Black and White teenage women are converging, the Black female is more likely to be engaging in unprotected intercourse and less likely to marry or have an abortion if she becomes pregnant (Jones and Battle, 1990).

While it is reasonable to question the wisdom of young Black women attaining motherhood at such an early age, their decision to bear the children and raise them alone reflects their traditional values and limited options. Among Black males under age twenty-one, the official unemployment rate is 27 percent, and as many as 60 percent of young Black men remain outside the work force (Larson, 1988). While employment may be easier for Black women to obtain, it often will be in dead-end jobs that pay only half the wages earned by White males. Rather than remain childless and husband-less, these women choose to have children and raise them alone. A good explanation of these life choices is given by Hortense Canady (1984, p. 40), president of Delta Sigma Theta Sorority: "Having a child is probably the best thing that's ever going to happen to them in their whole lifetime and the only thing they can contribute—this is not true in most other countries in the world. . . . If you belong to a class or a group of people who have no educational opportunities stretching out before them, no other goals, that's probably the single, best thing that's ever going to happen to you in your life."

Having limited educational and career options to set against bearing a child is not the only reason for the increase in female-headed households. A welfare system that often requires men to be absent from the home is part of the problem, and Black women realize that the meager welfare payments are more reliable than a class of men who may never know gainful employment in their entire lives (Rein, 1982). In general, unemployed men do not make good husbands and fathers. Since employment and income are the measure of a man's masculinity in this society, men who have neither do not tend to feel good about themselves or act positively toward their wives and children. In the Hampton study (1980), for example, husbands who were not satisfied with themselves had a fairly high level of marital disruption.

However, the major reason for the increase in Black female-headed households is the lack of "desirable" men with whom to form monogamous marriages. According to Joe and Yu (1991), between 1976 and 1983 the number of Black families headed by women rose by 700,000, and the ranks of Black men out of the labor force or unemployed increased by the same number. The same trend has existed for the last twenty-five years: almost 75 percent of Black men were working in 1960, and Black families headed by women accounted for 21 percent of all Black families in the same year, but by 1982, only 54 percent of all Black men were in the labor force, and 42 percent of all Black families were headed by women (Joe and Yu, 1991).

Having a child out of wedlock and failing to marry account for 51 percent of all Black households headed by women. Another 41 percent of Black women are divorced or separated from their spouses (Bureau of the Census, 1991a). These marriage disruptions are generally susceptible to the same structural conditions that plague never-married Black women. Unemployment and underemployment, the public assistance complex, the educational system, and the health care system all produce economic and psychological alienation in the Black male. As Hampton (1980) found, the pressures that push many Black males out of other social institutions within society also work to push them out of marital relationships.

A number of social characteristics place Blacks at risk for divorce. They have a higher rate of urbanization, greater independence of women, earlier age at marriage, earlier fertility, higher education and income levels for the wife, and lower income status for the husband. Most Black marriages involve a wife who is better educated than her husband (Glick, 1988). In one out of five Black marriages, the wife earns a higher income than her husband (Bureau of the Census, 1983). This incongruity between the socially assigned roles of the male as the primary provider and the wife as a subordinate member of the marital dyad may undermine the husband's self-esteem, frustrate the wife, and create marital dissatisfaction for both partners. In Hampton's study (1980), the highest percentage of disrupted marriages (27.4 percent) was observed among wives with incomes accounting for 40 percent or more of the family's income. His explanation was that when women have other means of support in the form of welfare or their own earnings, they may be less constrained to remain in a personally unsatisfying relationship. Alternatively, the wife may be satisfied with the husband's role, but her high income may threaten the husband's authority and status, undermining his self-concept.

These problems of the Black family are only variations of the general problems of American families. Guttentag and Secord (1983) demonstrate that unbalanced sex ratios have certain predictable consequences for relationships between men and women. They give rise to higher rates of singlehood, divorce, out-of-wedlock births, and female-headed households in different historical epochs and across different societies. According to Ehrenreich (1983), the breakdown of the family began in the 1950s, when men began a flight from commitment to the husband and father role. In the case of the Black family, it stems from the institutional decimation of Black males.

Our basic thesis here is that the dissonance between Black family ideology and actual family arrangements is caused by the intervention of structural conditions that impede the actualization of Black aspirations for traditional family life and roles. The central factor in this situation is the inability of Black males to meet the normative responsibilities of husband and father. Questions may be raised as to how the problem has reached its present magnitude and why it is so pronounced among the Black population. The answer appears to involve a combination of cultural and economic forces that have been ascendant in the last thirty years.

As detailed earlier, a basic cause of Black male unemployment has been the change in the economy and composition of the work force: automation and foreign competition have eliminated large numbers of jobs in manufacturing industries in the United States over the last couple of decades. The expansion of the economy was in the private sector's high-technology and service industries, which brought Black males into competition (or noncompetition) with the burgeoning numbers of White women entering and reentering the labor force (Billingsley, 1988).

Women, both Black and White, are better prepared to deal with the educational qualifications of an economy based on high-technology and service industries. Jobs in these fields require good reading and writing skills at precisely the time when the ability of the public school system to produce students with the necessary attributes has begun to decline. Black and Hispanic males have the highest rates of functional illiteracy among the twenty-three million Americans so classified (Kozol, 1985). One explanation is that when a Black male perceives the opportunity structure as not allowing for his upward mobility through education, he is more likely to divert his energy into sports, music, or hustling. On the other hand, Black females—with fewer opportunities—continue to progress in the same educational system (Hale, 1982).

The same general trends also occur to varying degrees among Whites, but they affect their family structure differently. White male teenagers have an unemployment rate half that of the officially recorded rate for similar Black males. Moreover, the White male teenager ultimately uses his kinship and friend-of-the-family networks more effectively to secure employment, while many Black male teenagers who lack such networks drop out or never join the work force. The poor employment prospects for young Black males are illustrated by the fact that some employers refuse to hire them for jobs that were totally subsidized by federal funds. Lack of steady employment largely accounts for the Black male's high enlistment rate in the military, drug and alcohol abuse, and participation in criminal activities, ultimately leaving less than half the Black male population as feasible husband and father candidates (Gibbs, 1988b).

Under positive conditions, there are good indications that the Black family is strong. College-educated Black women, for example, have their children later and in smaller numbers than any other socioeconomic or racial group in the United States. While probably as sexually active as lower-income Black women, they use birth control more effectively and are more likely to resort to abortion if pregnancy occurs. Although college-educated Black males earn less than White male high school dropouts, approximately 90 percent of them are married and living with their spouses (Glick, 1988). Where negative social conditions are absent, family ideology prevails.

A central question that remains is why Black family ideology has not changed or adjusted to changing conditions. One answer is that it has changed among one stratum of the Black population: the middle class. Within that segment of the Black community, mainstream values—even changing ones—are stronger because they have a higher level of acculturation into those norms due to their greater participation in the majority group's institutions (Staples, 1981). Even among this group, however, traditional values are still strong and exert an influence on their ideological posture toward the family. In part, that is a function of their recent entry into the middle class and the retention of values from their class of origin. Another factor, however, is that their participation in mainstream institutions and embrace of normative ideologies are still marginal, keeping traditional values attractive to many. Gary, Beatty, and Price (1983) found that their middle-class Black subjects cited their family life as the source of most satisfaction, while the source of least satisfaction was their jobs. Hence, traditional family life remains the one viable option for Black Americans of all socioeconomic strata because it is less subject to the vagaries of race than any other institution in American life.

Similarly, lower-income Blacks sustain traditional beliefs about marriage and the family because the many traumas experienced by this group have led to a stronger belief in the value of the family as a resource for their survival in a society not always hospitable to their aspirations. Other than the church, the family has been the only institution to serve as a vehicle for resisting racial discrimination and facilitating the movement toward social and economic equality. Another factor may be the continued physical and social isolation of Blacks—especially lower-income Blacks—from members of the majority group who are in the forefront of social and cultural change. In any context of social change, there is a gap between the ideal statements of a culture and the reality in which people live out their lives—a time lag between the emergence of new cultural forms and their internalization by the individuals who must act on them. Thus, it would appear that Black family ideologies will change only as the social and economic isolation of Blacks diminishes.

In many ways, this situation is nothing new for the Black population. Social scientists continue to view the deterioration of the family as the problem when, in reality, the underpinnings of Black family structure are the structural conditions that prevent the fulfillment of Black family ideology. Given the present political and economic trends, there is little reason to expect an abatement of these trends in the Black family. The problem of the Black family cannot be solved without resolving the economic predicament of Black men. They are one and the same.

The Best- and Worst-Case Scenarios

As we have seen at many points in the book, the future of the Black family is inextricably tied up with the current and future status of the Black male. Current figures indicate that 46 percent of Black males between the ages of sixteen and sixty-two are not active participants in the American labor force, a figure closely associated with the 48 percent of Black families headed by women and the 62 percent of Black children born out of wedlock (Joe and Yu, 1991). If the employment rate of Black men does not improve, demographic

projections are that 59 percent of Black families will be
headed by women by the year 2000 and that only 8 percent of
Black children born in the year 1980 will spend their entire
childhood with two parents (Espenshade and Braun, 1982).

Unless unforeseen social forces reverse current trends,
women are likely to achieve superiority over men in the vital
areas of education, occupation, and income. Already, Black
women are more educated than Black men at every level,
including the doctorate. The 1990 figures reveal that 20.7 percent of Black women are managers and professionals, compared to 15.9 percent of Black men. College-educated Black
women currently earn 85 percent of the income of college-
educated Black men (Department of Labor, 1990). As Black
women gradually move ahead of Black men, it is possible
that a role reversal may take place. Since Black women will
not need to marry a man to attain a decent standard of living,
many of them may begin to select dating partners and husbands on the basis of sex appeal rather than the traditional
criterion of socioeconomic status. Conversely, Black men may
become the gender bartering their sexuality for a "good marriage" with a successful woman.

The shortage of Black men who are desirable and available for marriage will continue into the twenty-first century.
Black women may adapt to their situation by a variety of
means. Lesbianism may increasingly be viewed as a viable
option by women who want their affection and companionship needs met. Among the women who experience the greatest shortage of men, those over the age of sixty, a kind of gray
lesbianism may emerge in response to the unavailability of
men. In the college-educated segment of the Black female
population, out-marriages to men of different races may
become one of their adaptive responses to the male shortage.
Some of them may seriously consider a more formalized participation in polygamous relationships or liaisons with married men, instead of remaining celibate and childless their
entire lives.

For the vast majority of Black women, there will continue to be some involvement with Black men. Chances are

that many will continue to be sexually active at an early age, to bear children out of wedlock, and to rear them with the assistance of a female-based kin network. They will likely have varying periods of cohabitation with a man, but legal marriage rates will continue to decline except in the case of college-educated Black males, the one subgroup in the Black community not plagued by low income, high rates of unemployment, and a shortage of compatible mates.

As for Black men, their employment chances will rise or fall with changes in the economy and other demographic changes in American society. If the economy continues its transformation from a goods-production to a service-dominated economy, Black men's participation rate in the labor force may decline, since the latter type of economy favors female workers. That will mean their continued dependence on the underground economy, cohabitation with a woman of some means, or living at home with their parents. One countervailing force could be the shortage of young workers predicted by the year 2000, when large numbers of the baby boom generation reach retirement age. Demographic projections are that by the year 2000, 40 percent of the school population graduating into the work force will be Black (Ferleger and Mandle, 1991). Given a substantial improvement in their employment situation, it is likely to result in an increase in marriage rates and a decline in out-of-wedlock birth rates.

However, these demographic changes are already being manifested in many parts of the United States, with no discernible improvement in the employment prospects for young Black males. While employers in low-wage industries, such as fast food outlets, are complaining of an inability to fill job vacancies in the affluent suburbs, there are still more young workers than jobs in the central cities. Young White workers are often obtaining part-time and summer work at wages of $9 or $10 an hour, while Black high school graduates in Los Angeles found average entry-level jobs at $4.75 an hour in 1991 (Rutten, 1991). Even when available, many Black teenagers rightfully perceive fast food and other minimum wage jobs as dead-end positions that have no long-term payoff.

Other barriers to employment remain. A director of a youth employment program states that "minorities have a 30 percent chance of being hired when dispatched to an interview. But, when we send someone who is not a minority they get hired" ("Summer Vacation Travails," 1986, p. D-1). Sadly, these teen-agers often find themselves competing with their older neighbors for such jobs. This sharp distinction between summer job prospects in central cities and the suburbs belies the rosy projections for young workers in the 1990s ("Employers Prefer Whites, Study Says," 1991, p. A-2).

A best-case scenario for Black families would be the election of an enlightened government that would provide the conditions for the strengthening of Black family life. First and foremost would be the implementation of a full-employment policy. This would require a substantial redistribution of income from the relatively affluent to the poor through a rigidly enforced system of progressive income taxation and the reduction of military expenditures to the bare minimum necessary to defend the country from an attack by foreign nations. This would not mean the creation of a huge federal bureaucracy, since it would only be necessary to fund already-existing projects and agencies such as highway construction, housing, education, the postal service, water conservation, public parks, child care, and the like. There is no reason to make it racially based, since Blacks would automatically share in the benefits of a full-employment economy. Some government-financed training programs, in community-based institutions, would be necessary to develop and improve skills of some undereducated workers.

Another governmental act suggested would be the formulation of a family allowance plan, already in effect in most Western nations (Kahn and Kamerman, 1983–84). This family allowance should be set at the level most economists agree is a "good" standard of living, not the poverty level, which only permits families to exist at the lowest standard of misery. The family allowance would be provided to all American families, reducing the stigma of current welfare programs, and the rigid system of progressive income tax rates would retrieve it from more affluent families. A family allowance plan would permit all families to have a decent income and to work out other difficulties in their relationships as best they can. While it will work to the advantage of most American families, it should benefit Black families most by lifting their ability to create and maintain a family from under the scourge of economic pressures.

Summary

The problems Black people face are essentially the same now as for the past century. Those problems are not related to family stability, but to the socioeconomic conditions that tear families asunder. In general, the problems are poverty and racism. While the past decade has produced a slight reduction in racial segregation and White stereotypes of Black inferiority, Blacks are still singled out for discriminatory treatment in every sphere of American life. Moreover, while Whites are in agreement about the racial discrimination Blacks are subjected to, any national effort to further remedy these practices has a low priority among White Americans.

A low socioeconomic status continues to plague many Black families. Whereas some Blacks have achieved a higher standard of living as a result of the civil rights movement, large numbers of Blacks continue to live below the poverty level. A disproportionate number of these Blacks are female heads of families. They have more responsibilities and less income than any other group in American society. Yet no effective programs are being proposed to meet the needs of one-half of all Black families.

Making futuristic predictions about the nature of any group's family life is a risky endeavor. Few, for instance, could have projected what has happened to the American family as a whole in the last thirty years. Of course there were trends leading us in certain directions, but it was the acceleration of those trends that caught many of us by surprise. In the case of the Black family, the research literature is still so sparse and biased that we have practically no attempts to analyze Black families of the future or alternative family life-styles. But certain barometers of the future can be seen in light of the existing social conditions for Blacks as well as in terms of the trends in sexual behavior, fertility patterns, gender-role changes, and marital adjustments.

Some adaptations to alternative life-styles will occur because large numbers of Blacks, especially the middle class, are taking on the values of the majority culture. However, Blacks as a group will continue to face certain problems that may not be unique to them except to the extent of their prevalence. The continuing high unemployment rate among Black men and women will still have serious ramifications for the kind of family life they will have. That will primarily be a problem of the lower-income group, but all classes will have to adapt to the increasingly critical problem of a male shortage and the consequences thereof.

So far, the problem of the male shortage has been handled by a type of serial polygyny, where Black men have more than one wife in a lifetime but not at the same time. Some men remain married but are free floating in their relations with other women. Sharing of males may be necessary for a group with such an imbalanced sex ratio. However, it gives rise to many conflicts between men and women who are strongly socialized into monogamous values. The instability of many Black marriages can be accounted for by this factor, as well as by the general range of forces that cause marital disruption. In the future, alternative family life-styles should be well thought out and implemented in a way conducive to individual and group harmony.

It is difficult to project the future of Black families, because there are several parallel trends occurring at the same time. Many Blacks are entering the middle class as a result of higher education and increased opportunities. At the same time, the future is dim for those Blacks in the underclass. Automation is rendering obsolete the labor of unskilled Black men, who are in danger of becoming a permanent army of the unemployed. The status of Black women is in a state of flux. Some welcome the liberation from male control, while others urge a regeneration of Black male leadership. Whatever the future of Black families, it is time to put to rest all the theories about Black family instability and give recognition to the crucial role of this institution in the Black struggle for survival.

References

Absug, R. H. "The Black Family During Reconstruction."
In N. I. Huggins, M., Kilson, and D. M. Fox (eds.), *Key
Issues in the Afro-American Experience.* Orlando, Fla.: Har-
court Brace Jovanovich, 1971.

Adams, P. L., Milner, J. R., and Schrepf, N. A. *Fatherless Children.* New York: Wiley, 1984.

Addison, D. P. "Black Wives: Perspectives About Their Husbands and Themselves." In C. E. Obudho (ed.), *Black Marriage and Family Therapy.* Westport, Conn.: Greenwood
Press, 1983.

Aldous, J. "Wives' Employment Status and Lower-Class Men
as Husband-Fathers: Support for the Moynihan Thesis."
Journal of Marriage and the Family, 1969, *31,* 469–476.

Aldridge, D. "Interracial Marriages: Empirical and Theoretical Considerations." *Journal of Black Studies,* 1978, *3*(3),
355–367.

Ali, S. *The Blackman's Guide to Understanding the Blackwoman.* Philadelphia: Civilized Publications, 1989.

Allen, W. R. "The Search for Applicable Theories of Black
Family Life." *Journal of Marriage and the Family,* 1978, *1,*
117–130.

Allen, W. R. "Moms, Dads, and Boys: Race and Sex Differences in the Socialization of Male Children." In L. E. Gary
(ed.), *Black Men.* Newbury Park, Calif.: Sage, 1981.

Anderson, E. "Sex Codes and Family Life Among Poor Inner City Youths." *Annals of the American Academy of Political and Social Science,* 1989, *501,* 59–78.

Asante, M. *The Afrocentric Idea.* Philadelphia: Temple University Press, 1987.

Atkins, E. "For Many Mixed-Race Americans Life Isn't Simply Black or White." *New York Times,* June 5, 1991, p. B-8.

Azibo, D.A.Y. "Perceived Attractiveness and the Black Personality." *Western Journal of Black Studies,* 1983, *7,* 229–238.

Bachrach, C. A. "Adoption Plans, Adopted Children, and Adoptive Mothers." *Journal of Marriage and the Family,* 1986, *48,* 243–253.

Baldwin, J. A. "Theory and Research Concerning the Notion of Black Self-Hatred: A Review and Reinterpretation." *Journal of Black Psychology,* 1979, *5*(2), 51–77.

Baldwin, R. O. "Femininity-Masculinity of Blacks and Whites over a Fourteen-Year Period." *Psychological Reports,* 1987, *60,* 455–458.

Ball, R. E., and Robbins, L. R. "Marital Status and Life Satisfaction Among Black Americans." *Journal of Marriage and the Family,* 1986, *48,* 389–394.

Bane, M. J., and Jargowsky, P. "The Links Between Government Policy and Family Structure: What Matters and What Doesn't." In A. Cheslin (ed.), *The Changing American Family and Public Policy.* Washington, D.C.: Urban Institute, 1988.

Baratz, S. S., and Baratz, J. C. "Early Childhood Intervention: The Social Science Base of Institutional Racism." *Harvard Educational Review,* 1970, *40,* 29–50.

Bass, B. A. "Interracial Dating and Marital Relationships: A Lecture." In B. A. Bass, G. E. Wyatt, and G. J. Powell (eds.), *The Afro-American Family: Assessment, Treatment, and Research Issues.* Philadelphia: Grune & Stratton, 1982.

Bauman, C. D. "Relationship Between Age at First Marriage, School Dropout, and Marital Instability: An Analysis of the Glick Effect." *Journal of Marriage and the Family,* 1967, *29*(4), 672–680.

Beck, A. J. *Profile of Jail Inmates, 1989.* Washington, D.C.: U.S. Department of Justice, 1991.

Beckett, J. O., and Smith, A. D. "Work and Family Roles: Egalitarian Marriage in Black and White Families." *Social Service Review*, 1981, *55*, 314–325.

Belcastro, P. A. "Sexual Behavior Differences Between Black and White Students." *Journal of Sex Research*, 1985, *21*, 56–67.

Bell, A. P. "Black Sexuality: Fact and Fantasy." In R. Staples (ed.), *The Black Family: Essays and Studies*. (2nd ed.) Belmont, Calif.: Wadsworth, 1978.

Bell, A. P., and Weinberg, M. *Homosexualities*. New York: Simon & Schuster, 1978.

Bell, N., and Vogel, E. *A Modern Introduction to the Family*. New York: Free Press, 1968.

Bell, R. "Comparative Attitudes About Marital Sex Among Negro Women in the U.S., Great Britain, and Trinidad." *Journal of Comparative Family Studies*, 1970, *1*, 71–81.

Bell, R. "The Related Importance of Mother-Wife Roles Among Lower-Class Women." In R. Staples (ed.), *The Black Family: Essays and Studies*. (1st ed.) Belmont, Calif.: Wadsworth, 1971.

Bell-Scott, P., and others. *Double Stitch: Black Women Write About Mothers and Daughters*. Boston: Beacon Press, 1991.

Benjamin, L. "The Dog Theory: Black Male/Female Conflict." *Western Journal of Black Studies*, 1983, 7, 49–55.

Bennett, L. "Roots of Black Love." *Ebony*, Aug. 1981, pp. 31–36.

Bernard, J. *Marriage and Family Among Negroes*. Englewood Cliffs, N.J.: Prentice-Hall, 1966.

Berry, M. F., and Blassingame, J. *Long Memory: The Black Experience in America*. New York: Oxford University Press, 1982.

Bibb, H. *Narrative of the Life & Adventures of Henry Bibb, an American Slave*. Salem, N.H.: Ayer, 1849.

Billingsley, A. *Black Families in White America*. Englewood Cliffs, N.J.: Prentice-Hall, 1968.

Billingsley, A. "The Impact of Technology on Afro-American Families." *Family Relations*, 1988, *37*, 420–425.

Billingsley, A. "Understanding African-American Family Diversity." In J. Dewart (ed.), *The State of Black America 1990*. New York: National Urban League, 1990.

Billingsley, A., and Giovannoni, J. M. *Children of the Storm: Black Children and American Child Welfare.* Orlando, Fla.: Harcourt Brace Jovanovich, 1972.

Billy, J.O.G., and Udry, J. R. "The Influence of Male and Female Friends on Adolescent Sexual Behavior." *Adolescence,* 1985, *20,* 21–32.

Binion, V. J. "Psychological Androgyny: A Black Female Perspective." *Sex Roles,* 1990, *22*(7/8), 487–507.

"The Black Male Shortage." *Ebony,* Aug. 1986, pp. 22–25 (special issue on "The Crises of the Black Family").

"The Black Sexism Debate." *Black Scholar,* 1979, *10,* 1–96.

"Blacks Fresh Trials." *Newsweek,* May 15, 1978, p. 77.

Blassingame, J. *The Slave Community.* New York: Oxford University Press, 1972.

Blau, P. *Exchange and Power in Social Life.* New York: Wiley, 1964.

Blauner, R. *Racial Oppression in America.* New York: HarperCollins, 1972.

Blood, R. O., and Wolfe, D. M. *Husbands and Wives: The Dynamics of Married Living.* New York: Free Press, 1960.

Bohlen, C. "Number of Women in Jail Surges with Drug Sales." *New York Times,* Apr. 9, 1989, p. A-1.

Booth, A. (ed.). *Contemporary Families: Looking Forward, Looking Back.* Minneapolis, Minn.: National Council on Family Relations, 1991.

Bowman, P. J. "Black Fathers and the Provider Role: Role Strain, Informal Coping Resources, and Life Happiness." In W. Boykin (ed.), *The Seventh Conference on Empirical Research on Black Psychology.* Rockville, Md.: National Institute of Mental Health, 1985.

Bowman, P. J. "Research Perspectives on Black Men: Role Strain and Adaptation Across the Adult Life Cycle." In R. L. Jones (ed.), *Black Adult Development and Aging.* Berkeley, Calif.: Cobb & Henry, 1989.

Brock, R. "Future of Mom and Pop Businesses in the Black Community." *The Crisis,* 1991, *98*(5), 10–12, 14.

Broman, C. L. "Household Work and Family Life Satisfaction of Blacks." *Journal of Marriage and the Family,* 1988, *50,* 743–748.

Broman, C. L. "Gender, Work-Family Roles, and Psychological Well-Being of Blacks." *Journal of Marriage and the Family,* 1991, *53,* 509–519.

Brouwer, M. G. "Marriage and Family Life Among Blacks in Colonial Pennsylvania." *Pennsylvania Magazine of History and Biography,* July 1975, pp. 368–372.

Brown, I. C. *Race Relations in a Democracy.* New York: HarperCollins, 1949.

Brown, L., Wolf, E. C., Starke, L., and Jacobson, J. *State of the World 1986.* Washington, D.C.: Worldwatch Institute, 1986.

Bullock, A., and Stallybrass, O. (eds.). *The Harper Dictionary of Modern Thought.* New York: HarperCollins, 1977.

Bumpass, L. L., Sweet, J. L., and Martin, T. C. "Changing Patterns of Remarriage." *Journal of Marriage and the Family,* 1990, *52,* 747–756.

Bureau of the Census. *Social and Economic Status of the Black Population in the United States: 1971.* Current Population Reports, series P-23, no. 42. Washington, D.C.: U.S. Government Printing Office, 1972.

Bureau of the Census. *America's Black Population, 1970–1982: A Statistical View.* Current Population Reports, series P-20, no. 442. Washington, D.C.: U.S. Government Printing Office, 1983.

Bureau of the Census. *Marital Characteristics.* Washington, D.C.: U.S. Government Printing Office, 1985.

Bureau of the Census. *The Black Population in the United States: March 1988.* Current Population Reports, series P-20, no. 422. Washington, D.C.: U.S. Government Printing Office, 1989.

Bureau of the Census. *Statistical Abstract of the United States, 1990.* Washington, D.C.: U.S. Government Printing Office, 1990.

Bureau of the Census. *The Black Population in the United States: March 1990 and 1989.* Current Population Reports, series P-20, no. 448. Washington, D.C.: U.S. Government Printing Office, 1991a.

Bureau of the Census. *Educational Attainment in the United*

States: March 1989 and 1988. Current Population Reports, series P-20, no. 451. Washington, D.C.: U.S. Government Printing Office, 1991b.

Bureau of the Census. *Marital Status and Living Arrangements: March 1990.* Current Population Reports, series P-20, no. 450. Washington, D.C.: U.S. Government Printing Office, 1991c.

Bureau of the Census. *Marital Status and Living Arrangements: March 1991.* Washington, D.C.: U.S. Government Printing Office, 1992.

Bureau of Justice Statistics, Department of Justice. *National Corrections Reporting Program, 1985.* Washington, D.C.: U.S. Government Printing Office, 1990.

Bureau of Labor Statistics. *Marital and Family Patterns of Workers: An Update.* Washington, D.C.: U.S. Government Printing Office, May 1983.

Burgest, D. R. "Sexual Games in Black Male-Female Relationships." *Journal of Black Studies,* 1991, *22,* 645–656.

Burgest, D. R., and Goosby, M. "Games in Black Male/Female Relationships." *Journal of Black Studies,* 1985, *15,* 277–290.

Burkey, R. *Ethnic and Racial Groups: The Dynamics of Dominance.* Menlo Park, Calif.: Cummings, 1978.

Burton, L. M., and Bengtson, V. L. "Black Grandmothers: Issues of Timing and Continuity." In V. L. Bengtson and J. F. Robertson (eds.), *Grandparenthood: Research and Policy Perspectives.* Newbury Park, Calif.: Sage, 1985.

Cade, T. *The Black Woman: An Anthology.* New York: Signet, 1970.

Campolo, T., and Campolo, B. *Things We Wish We Had Said: Reflections of a Father and His Grown Son.* Dallas: World, 1989.

Canady, H. "Words of the Week." *Jet Magazine,* Mar. 19, 1984, p. 40.

Carnegie Council. *All Our Children.* New York: Harcourt Brace Jovanovich, 1977.

Carson, B. *Gifted Hands: The Ben Carson Story.* Washington, D.C.: Review and Herald, 1990.

Cash, T. F., and Duncan, N. C. "Physical Attractiveness

Stereotyping Among Black American College Students."
Journal of Social Psychology, 1984, *122,* 71–77.

Cazenave, N. "Middle Income Black Fathers: An Analysis of
the Provider's Role." *Family Coordinator,* 1979, *28,* 583–593.

Cazenave, N. "Black Men in America: The Quest for Manhood." In H. P. McAdoo (ed.), *Black Families.* (1st ed.) Newbury Park, Calif.: Sage, 1981.

Cazenave, N. "Black Male-Female Relationships: The Perceptions of 155 Middle-Class Black Men." *Family Relations,*
1983, *32,* 341–350.

Cazenave, N., and Smith, R. "Gender Differences in the Perception of Black Male-Female Relationships and Stereotypes." In H. E. Cheatham and J. B. Stewart (eds.), *Black
Families: Interdisciplinary Perspectives.* New Brunswick,
N.J.: Transaction, 1990.

Cazenave, N., and Straus, M. "Race, Class, Network
Embeddedness, and Family Violence: A Search for Potent
Support Systems." *Journal of Comparative Family Studies,*
1979, *10*(3), 281–299.

Centers for Disease Control. *HIV/AIDS Surveillance Report.*
Atlanta, Ga.: Centers for Disease Control, 1991.

Chavis, W. M., and Lyles, G. "Divorce Among Educated
Black Women." *Journal of the National Medical Association,*
1975, *67*(2), 128–134.

Chendinen, D. "Keeping Control: Southern Whites Keep
Their Grip on the Black Schools." *New York Times,* June
23, 1986, p. 11.

Clark, K. B., and Clark, M. P. "Emotional Factors in Racial
Identification and Preference in Negro Children." *Journal
of Negro Education,* 1950, *19,* 341–350.

Clark, K. B., and Clark, M. P. "Racial Identification and
Preference in Negro Children." In E. E. Maccoby, T. M.
Newcomb, and E. L. Hartley (eds.), *Readings in Social Psychology.* (3rd ed.) Troy, Mo.: Holt, Rinehart & Winston,
1958.

Clark, M. L. "Racial Group Concept and Self-Esteem in
Black Children." *Journal of Black Psychology,* 1982, *3*(2),
75–88.

Clark, R. M. *Family Life and School Achievement: Why Poor Black Children Succeed or Fail.* Chicago: University of Chicago Press, 1983.

Cleaver, E. *Soul on Ice.* New York: McGraw-Hall, 1968.

Coleman, L. M., Antonucci, T. C., Adelmann, P. K., and Crohan, S. E. "Social Roles in the Lives of Middle-Aged and Older Black Women." *Journal of Marriage and the Family,* 1987, *49,* 761–771.

Collins, P. H. "The Afro-American Work/Family Nexus: An Exploratory Analysis." *Western Journal of Black Studies,* 1986, *10,* 148–158.

Collins, P. H. *Black Feminist Thought: Knowledge, Consciousness, and the Politics of Empowerment.* Boston: Unwin Hyman, 1990.

Combahee River Collective. "A Black Feminist Statement." In G. T. Hull, P. B. Scott, and B. Smith (eds.), *But Some of Us Are Brave: Black Women's Studies.* Old Westbury, N.Y.: Feminist Press, 1982.

Commission on Civil Rights. *Unemployment and Underemployment Among Blacks, Hispanics, and Women.* Washington, D.C.: U.S. Government Printing Office, 1982.

Commission on Civil Rights. "Disadvantaged Women and Their Children." In R. Staples (ed.), *The Black Family: Essays and Studies.* (4th ed.) Belmont, Calif.: Wadsworth, 1991.

Cone, J. H. *Martin and Malcolm in America.* New York: Orbis, 1991.

Conner, M. E. "Teenage Fatherhood: Issues Confronting Young Black Males." In J. T. Gibbs (ed.), *Young, Black, and Male in America: An Endangered Species.* New York: Auburn House, 1988.

Coughlin, E. K. "Scholars Work to Refine Africa-Centered View of the Life and History of Black Americans." *Chronicle of Higher Education,* Oct. 28, 1987, p. A-10.

Crosby, J. F. *Illusion and Disillusion: The Self in Love and Marriage.* (4th ed.) Belmont, Calif.: Wadsworth, 1991.

Daley, S. "Girls' Self-Esteem Is Lost on Way to Adolescence: New Study Finds." *New York Times,* Jan. 9, 1991, p. B-1.

Daniel, J. H., Hampton, R. L., and Newberger, M. D. "Child Abuse and Accidents in Black Families: A Controlled Comparative Study." *American Journal of Orthopsychiatry*, 1983, *53*(4), 649–653.

Darity, W. A., Jr., and Myers, S. L., Jr. "Does Welfare Dependency Cause Female Headship? The Case of the Black Family." *Journal of Marriage and the Family*, 1984, *45*, 765–779.

Davidson, B. *The Lost Cities of Africa*. Boston: Little, Brown, 1959.

Davis, A. "Reflections on the Black Woman's Role in the Community of Slaves." *Black Scholar*, 1971, *2*, 2–16.

Davis, A. *Women, Race, and Class*. New York: Random House, 1983.

Davis, A. *Women, Culture, and Politics*. New York: Random House, 1989.

Davis, A., and Davis, F. "The Black Family and the Crisis of Capitalism." *Black Scholar*, 1986, *17*, 33–40.

Davis, L. G. "Trends in Themes of African American Family Research 1939–1989: A Synopsis." *Western Journal of Black Studies*, 1990, *14*(4), 191–195.

DeJarnett, S., and Raven, B. H. "The Balance, Bases, and Modes of Interpersonal Power in Black Couples: The Role of Sex and Socioeconomic Circumstances." *Journal of Black Psychology*, 1981, 7(2), 51–66.

Dollard, J. *Caste and Class in the Southern Town*. New York: Doubleday, 1957.

DelVecchio, R. "State Fails Foster Kids, Group Says." *San Francisco Chronicle*, Apr. 27, 1990, p. A-4.

D'Emilio, J., and Freedman, E. *Intimate Matters: A History of Sexuality in America*. New York: HarperCollins, 1988.

Demos, V. "Black Family Studies in the *Journal of Marriage and the Family* and the Issue of Distortion: A Trend Analysis." *Journal of Marriage and the Family*, 1990, *52*, 603–612.

Department of Health and Human Services. *Report of the Secretary's Task Force on Black and Minority Health*. Washington, D.C.: U.S. Government Printing Office, 1985.

Department of Labor. *Employment and Earnings, May 1990*. Washington, D.C.: U.S. Government Printing Office, 1990.

Dewart, J. (ed.). *The State of Black America 1991*. New York: National Urban League, 1991.

Diallo, Y. D., and Hall, M. *The Healing Drum: African Wisdom Teachings*. Rochester, Vt.: Destiny Books, 1989.

Dickinson, G. E. "Dating Behavior of Black and White Adolescents Before and After Desegregation." In R. Staples (ed.), *The Black Family: Essays and Studies*. (2nd ed.) Belmont, Calif.: Wadsworth, 1978.

Dilworth-Anderson, P., Johnson, L. B., and Burton, L. M. "Reframing Theories for Understanding Race, Ethnicity, and Families." In P. Boss and others (eds.), *Sourcebook of Family Theories and Methods: A Contextual Approach*. New York: Plenum, 1992.

Diop, C. A. *Precolonial Black Africa: A Comparative Study of the Political and Social Systems of Europe and Black Africa*. Trenton, N.J.: Africa World, 1987.

Donloe, D. C. "Interracial Center Fills a Need for Racially Mixed." *Los Angeles Sentinel*, Jan. 22, 1987, p. A-5.

Draughn, P. S. "Perceptions of Competence in Work and Marriage of Middle-Age Men." *Journal of Marriage and the Family*, 1984, *46*, 403–409.

Du Bois, W.E.B. *Some Efforts of the American Negroes for Their Own Betterment*. Atlanta, Ga.: Atlanta University Press, 1898.

Du Bois, W.E.B. *The Negro American Family*. Atlanta, Ga.: Atlanta University Press, 1908.

Ducille, A. "Othered Matters: Reconceptualizing Dominance and Difference in the History of Sexuality in America." *Journal of the History of Sexuality*, 1990, *1*, 102–127.

Edelman, M. W. "The Sea Is So Wide and My Boat Is So Small: Problems Facing Black Children Today." In H. P. McAdoo and J. L. McAdoo (eds.), *Black Children: Social, Educational, and Parental Environments*. Newbury Park, Calif.: Sage, 1985.

Edelman, M. W. "Save the Children." *Ebony*, Aug. 1986, pp. 53–54, 58–59.

Edelman, M. W. "An Advocacy Agenda for Black Families and Children." In H. P. McAdoo (ed.), *Black Families*. (2nd ed.) Newbury Park, Calif.: Sage, 1988.

Ehrenreich, B. *The Hearts of Men: American Dreams and the Flight from Commitment.* New York: Doubleday, 1983.

Elkins, S. *Slavery: A Problem in American Institutional and Intellectual Life.* Chicago: University of Chicago Press, 1968.

"Employers Prefer Whites, Study Says." *San Francisco Chronicle,* May 15, 1991, p. A-2.

Engels, F. *Conditions of the Working Class in England in 1944.* London: Oxford University Press, 1950.

Engram, E. *Science, Myth, Reality: The Black Family in One-Half Century of Research.* Westport, Conn.: Greenwood Press, 1982.

Escott, P. D. *Slavery Remembered: A Record of Twentieth-Century Slave Narratives.* Chapel Hill: University of North Carolina Press, 1979.

Espenshade, T., and Braun, R. "Life Course Analysis and Multistate Demography: An Application to Marriage, Divorce, and Remarriage." *Journal of Marriage and the Family,* 1982, *44,* 1025–1036.

Farber, B. *Family Organization and Interaction.* San Francisco: Chandler, 1964.

Ferleger, L., and Mandle, J. R. "African Americans and the Future of the U.S. Economy." *Trotter Institute Review,* 1991, *5,* 3–7.

Festinger, L. *A Theory of Cognitive Dissonance.* New York: HarperCollins, 1957.

Fogel, R. S., and Engerman, S. *Time on the Cross: The Economics of American Negro Slavery.* Boston: Little, Brown, 1974.

Foley, V. D. "Family Therapy with Black, Disadvantaged Families: Some Observations on Roles, Communication, and Technique." *Journal of Marriage and the Family,* 1975, *37,* 29–38.

Fordham, M. *Major Themes in Northern Black Religious Thought, 1800–1860.* Hicksville, N.Y.: Exposition Press, 1975.

Foster, H. "African Patterns in the Afro-American Family." *Journal of Black Studies,* 1983, *14,* 201–232.

Fox, G. L., and Inazu, J. K. "Mother-Daughter Communication About Sex." *Family Relations,* 1980, *29,* 347–352.

Franklin, C. W. "Black Male–Black Female Conflict: Individually Caused and Culturally Nurtured." *Journal of Black Studies*, 1984, *15*, 139–154.

Franklin, C. W. "Conceptual and Logical Issues in Theory and Research Related to Black Masculinity." *Western Journal of Black Studies*, 1986, *10*, 161–166.

Franklin, C. W. "Surviving the Institutional Decimation of Black Males: Causes, Consequences, and Intervention." In H. Brod (ed.), *The Making of Masculinities*. London: Allen & Unwin, 1987.

Franklin, D. "The Impact of Early Childbearing on Developmental Outcomes: The Case of Black Adolescent Parenting." *Family Relations*, 1988, *37*, 268–274.

Franklin, J. H. *From Slavery to Freedom: The History of Negro Americans*. (4th ed.) New York: Knopf, 1974.

Franklin, J. H. "A Historical Note on Black Families." In H. P. McAdoo (ed.), *Black Families*. (2nd ed.) Newbury Park, Calif.: Sage, 1988.

Frazier, E. F. *The Free Negro Family*. Nashville, Tenn.: Fisk University Press, 1932a.

Frazier, E. F. *The Negro Family in Chicago*. Chicago: University of Chicago Press, 1932b.

Frazier, E. F. *The Negro Family in the United States*. Chicago: University of Chicago Press, 1939.

Frazier, E. F. "The Negro Family in America." In R. Ashen (ed.), *The Family: Its Function and Destiny*. New York: HarperCollins, 1949.

Frazier, E. F. *The Black Bourgeoisie*. New York: Free Press, 1957.

Frazier, E. F. "Sex Life of the African American Negro." In A. Ellis and A. Abarbanel (eds.), *The Encyclopedia of Sexual Behavior*. New York: Hawthorn Books, 1961.

Frazier, E. F. *The Negro Church in America*. New York: Schocken Books, 1964.

Frederickson, G. M. "The Gutman Report." *New York Review of Books*, Sept. 30, 1976, pp. 18–22, 27.

Freud, S. *The Basic Writings of Sigmund Freud*. (A. A. Brill, trans.) New York: Modern Library, 1938.

Furstenberg, F. F. "As the Pendulum Swings: Teenage Childbearing and Social Concern." *Family Relations*, 1991, *40*, 127–138.

Furstenberg, F. F., Brooks-Gunn, J., and Morgan, S. P. "Adolescent Mothers and Their Children in Later Life." *Family Planning Perspectives,* 1987, *19*(4), 142–151.

Furstenberg, F. F., and Crawford, A. G. "Family Support: Helping Teenage Mothers to Cope." *Family Planning Perspectives,* 1978, *10*(6), 322–333.

Furstenberg, R., Hershberg, T., and Modell, J. "The Origins of the Female Headed Black Family: The Impact of the Urban Experience." *Journal of Interdisciplinary History,* 1975, *5*, 211–233.

Gallup, G., Jr. *American Families—1980: Summary of Findings.* Princeton, N.J.: Princeton University Press, 1980.

Gallup, G., Jr. "Women Want Babies and Jobs." *San Francisco Chronicle,* May 13, 1985, p. 2.

Garvey, M. *Philosophy and Opinions of Marcus Garvey.* London: Cass, 1967.

Gary, L. E., Beatty, L. A., and Price, M. *Stable Black Families: Final Report.* Washington, D.C.: Institute for Urban Affairs and Research, 1983.

Genovese, E. D. *Roll, Jordan, Roll.* New York: Pantheon, 1974.

Gibbs, J. T. "The New Morbidity: Homicide, Suicide, Accidents, and Life-Threatening Behaviors." In J. T. Gibbs (ed.), *Young, Black, and Male in America: An Endangered Species.* New York: Auburn House, 1988a.

Gibbs, J. T. "Young Black Males in America: Endangered, Embittered, and Embattled." In J. T. Gibbs (ed.), *Young, Black, and Male in America: An Endangered Species.* New York: Auburn House, 1988b.

Gibbs, J. T. "Developing Intervention Models for Black Families: Linking Theory and Research." In H. E. Cheatham and J. B. Stewart (eds.), *Black Families: Interdisciplinary Perspectives.* New Brunswick, N.J.: Transaction, 1990.

Giddings, P. *When and Where I Enter: The Impact of Black Women on Race and Sex in America.* New York: Morrow, 1984.

Gilder, G. *Wealth and Poverty.* New York: Basic Books, 1981.

Gilliam, D. "Sick, Distorted Thinking." *Washington Post,* Oct. 11, 1990, p. D-3.

Glenn, N., and Supancic, M. "Social and Demographic Correlates of Divorce and Separation in the United States: An

Update and Reconsideration." *Journal of Marriage and the Family*, 1984, *46*, 563–576.

Glick, P. "Demographic Pictures of Black Families." In H. P. McAdoo (ed.), *Black Families*. (2nd ed.) Newbury Park, Calif.: Sage, 1988.

Goldin, C. D. "Female Labor Force Participation: The Origin of Black and White Differences, 1870–1880." *Journal of Economic History*, 1983, 16–48.

Goldman, N., Westoff, C. F., and Hammerslough, C. "Demography of the Marriage Market in the United States." *Population Index*, 1984, *50*, 5–26.

Goldscheider, F. K., and Goldscheider, C. "The Intergenerational Flow of Income: Family Structure and the Status of Black Americans." *Journal of Marriage and the Family*, 1991, *53*, 499–508.

Goode, W. J. "The Sociology of the Family." In R. K. Merton (ed.), *Sociology Today*. New York: Basic Books, 1959.

Goode, W. "A Theory of Role Strain." *American Sociological Review*, 1960, *25*, 483–496.

Gooden, W. E. "Development of Black Men in Early Adulthood." In R. L. Jones (ed.), *Black Adult Development and Aging*. Berkeley, Calif.: Cobb & Henry, 1989.

Gordon, L. "The Politics and History of Family Violence." In A. S. Skolnick and J. H. Skolnick (eds.), *Family in Transition*. (6th ed.) Glenview, Ill.: Scott, Foresman, 1988.

Grier, W. H., and Cobbs, P. M. *Black Rage*. New York: Bantam Books, 1976.

Griffin, J. T. "West African and Black American Working Women: Historical and Contemporary Comparisons." *Journal of Black Psychology*, 1982, *8*(2), 55–73.

Gross, J. "Grandmothers Bear a Burden Sired by Drugs." *New York Times*, Apr. 9, 1989, p. A-1.

Gutman, H. *The Black Family in Slavery and Freedom, 1750–1925*. New York: Pantheon, 1976.

Guttentag, M., and Secord, P. *Too Many Women: The Sex Ratio Question*. Newbury Park, Calif.: Sage, 1983.

Hale, J. E. *Black Children: Their Roots, Culture, & Learning Styles*. Provo, Utah: Brigham Young University Press, 1982.

Haley, A. *The Autobiography of Malcolm X.* New York: Grove Press, 1965.

Haley, A. "We Must Honor Our Ancestors Who Helped Us Survive." *Ebony,* Aug. 1986, pp. 134, 138–140.

Hall, G. M. "The Myth of the Benevolent Spanish Slave Law." *Negro Digest,* 1970, *19,* 31–38.

Hampton, R. L. "Institutional Decimation, Marital Exchange, and Disruption in Black Families." *Western Journal of Black Studies,* 1980, *4,* 132–139.

Hampton, R. L. "Family Life Cycle, Economic Well Being, and Marital Disruption in Black Families." *California Sociologist,* 1982, *5,* 16–32.

Hampton, R. L. "Race, Class, and Child Maltreatment." *Journal of Comparative Family Studies,* 1987, *18*(1), 113–126.

Hare, B. R. "Re-Examining the Achievement Central Tendency: Sex Differences Within Race and Race Differences Within Sex." In H. P. McAdoo and J. L. McAdoo (eds.), *Black Children: Social, Educational, and Parental Environments.* Newbury Park, Calif.: Sage, 1985.

Hare, N., and Hare, J. *The Endangered Black Family: Coping with the Unisexualization and Coming Extinction of the Black Race.* San Francisco: Black Think Tank, 1984.

Harris, F., and Williams, L. "JCPS/Gallup Poll Reflects Changing Views on Political Issues." *Focus,* 1986, *14,* p. 4.

Harris, J. H. *Black Ministers and Laity in the Urban Church: An Analysis of Political and Social Expectations.* New York: University Presses of America, 1987.

Harris, W. "Work and the Family in Black Atlanta." *Journal of Social History,* 1976, *9,* 319–330.

Harrison, A. O. "The Black Family's Socializing Environment: Self-Esteem and Ethnic Attitude Among Black Children." In H. P. McAdoo and J. L. McAdoo (eds.), *Black Children: Social, Educational, and Parental Environments.* Newbury Park, Calif.: Sage, 1985.

Harrison, A. O. "Attitudes Toward Procreation Among Black Adults." In H. P. McAdoo (ed.), *Black Families.* (2nd ed.) Newbury Park, Calif.: Sage, 1988.

Harrison, A. O. "Black Working Women: Introduction to a

Life Span Perspective." In R. L. Jones (ed.), *Black Adult Development and Aging*. Berkeley, Calif.: Cobb & Henry, 1989.

Harrison, A. O., and Minor, J. H. "Interrole Conflict, Coping Strategies, and Satisfaction Among Black Working Wives." *Journal of Marriage and the Family*, 1978, *40*, 799–805.

Harvey, A. (ed.). *The Black Family: An Afro-Centric Perspective*. Washington, D.C.: Commission for Racial Justice, United Church of Christ, 1985.

Harwood, E., and Hodge, C. C. "Jobs and the Negro Family: A Reappraisal." *Public Interest*, 1971, *23*, 125–131.

Hatfield, E., and Sprecher, S. *Mirror, Mirror: The Importance of Looks in Everyday Life*. New York: State University of New York Press, 1986.

Hatfield, E., and Walster, G. W. *A New Look at Love*. Reading, Mass.: Addison-Wesley, 1981.

Heer, D. M. "The Prevalence of Black-White Marriage in the United States, 1960 and 1970." *Journal of Marriage and the Family*, 1974, *36*(2), 246–258.

Heiss, J. *The Case of the Black Family: A Sociological Inquiry*. New York: Columbia University Press, 1975.

Heiss, J. "Women's Values Regarding Marriage and the Family." In H. P. McAdoo (ed.), *Black Families*. (2nd ed.) Newbury Park, Calif.: Sage, 1988.

Hernton, C. *Sex and Racism in America*. New York: Doubleday, 1965.

Herskovits, M. *The Myth of the Negro Past*. Boston: Beacon Press, 1941.

Hill, R. "Contemporary Developments in Family Theory." *Marriage and the Family*, 1966, *28*, 10–26.

Hill, R., and Hansen, D. A. "The Identification of Conceptual Frameworks Utilized in Family Study." *Marriage and Family Living*, 1960, *22*, 299–311.

Hill, R. B. *The Strengths of Black Families*. New York: Emerson Hall, 1972.

Hill, R. B. "Critical Issues for Black Families by the Year 2000." In J. Dewart (ed.), *The State of Black America 1989*. New York: National Urban League, 1989.

Hill, R. B. "Economic Forces, Structural Discrimination, and Black Family Instability." In H. E. Cheatham and J. B. Stewart (eds.), *Black Families: Interdisciplinary Perspectives.* New Brunswick, N.J.: Transaction, 1990.

Hill, R. B., and Shackleford, L. "The Black Extended Family Revisited." In R. Staples (ed.), *The Black Family: Essays and Studies.* (3rd ed.) Belmont, Calif.: Wadsworth, 1986.

Hinds, M. D. "Addiction to Crack Can Kill Parental Instinct." *New York Times,* Mar. 17, 1990, p. A-1.

Hite, S. *The Hite Report.* New York: Macmillan, 1976.

Hobson, S. "The Black Family: Together in Every Sense." *Tuesday,* 1971, *1,* 28–32.

Hofferth, S. L. "Kin Network, Race, and Family Structure." *Journal of Marriage and the Family,* 1984, *46,* 791–805.

Hokanson, J. E., and Calder, G. "Negro-White Differences on the MMPI." *Journal of Clinical Psychology,* 1960, *16,* 32–33.

Homans, G. *Social Behavior: Its Elementary Forms.* Orlando, Fla.: Harcourt Brace Jovanovich, 1961.

Hooks, B. *Ain't I a Woman: Black Women and Feminism.* Boston: South End Press, 1981.

Hooks, B. *Feminist Theory: From Margin to Center.* Boston: South End Press, 1984.

Hooks, B. "Homophobia in Black Communities." *Zeta Magazine,* 1988, *1,* 35–38.

Howard, D. "A Structural Approach to Sexual Attitudes: Interracial Patterns in Adolescents' Judgments About Sexual Intimacy." *Sociological Perspectives,* 1988, *31,* 88–121.

Hull, G. T., Scott, P. B., and Smith, B. (eds.). *But Some of Us Are Brave: Black Women's Studies.* Old Westbury, N.Y.: Feminist Press, 1982.

Jackson, J. J. "Black Grandparents: Who Needs Them?" In R. Staples (ed.), *The Black Family: Essays and Studies.* (3rd ed.) Belmont, Calif.: Wadsworth, 1986.

Jackson, J. J. "Ordinary Husbands: The Truly Hidden Men." In R. Staples (ed.), *The Black Family: Essays and Studies.* (4th ed.) Belmont, Calif.: Wadsworth, 1991.

Jackson, J. S., McCullough, W. R., and Gurin, G. "Family, Socialization, Environment, and Identity Development in

Black Americans." In H. P. McAdoo (ed.), *Black Families*. (2nd ed.) Newbury Park, Calif.: Sage, 1988.

Jackson, R. H. "Some Aspirations of Lower Class Black Mothers." *Journal of Comparative Family Studies*, 1975, *6*(2), 172–181.

Jaynes, G. D. "The Labor Market Status of Black Americans: 1939–1985." *Journal of Economic Perspectives*, 1990, *4*, 34–42.

Jeffries, J., and Brock, R. E. "African-Americans in a Changing Economy: A Look at the 21st Century." *The Crisis*, 1991, *98*(6), 22–32.

Jensen, A. R. "How Much Can We Boost IQ and Scholastic Achievement?" *Harvard Educational Review*, 1969, *39*, 11–23.

Jewell, K. S. *Survival of the Black Family: The Institutional Impact of U.S. Social Policy*. New York: Praeger, 1988.

Jewell, L. N. *Psychology and Effective Behavior*. St. Paul, Minn.: West, 1989.

Joe, T., and Yu, P. "The Flip Side of Black Families Headed by Women: The Economic Status of Black Men." In R. Staples (ed.), *The Black Family: Essays and Studies*. (4th ed.) Belmont, Calif.: Wadsworth, 1991.

Johnson, C. S. *Shadow of the Plantation*. Chicago: University of Chicago Press, 1934.

Johnson, L. B. "Sexual Behavior of Southern Blacks." In R. Staples (ed.), *The Black Family: Essays and Studies*. (2nd ed.) Belmont, Calif.: Wadsworth, 1978.

Johnson, L. B. "Marital and Parental Roles: A Black Youth Perspective." Unpublished manuscript, Florida State University, 1980.

Johnson, L. B. "Perspectives on Black Family Empirical Research, 1965–1978." In H. P. McAdoo (ed.), *Black Families*. (2nd ed.) Newbury Park, Calif.: Sage, 1988.

Johnson, L. B. "The Employed Black: The Dynamics of Work-Family Tension." *Review of Black Political Economy*, 1989, *17*, 69–85. Also in H. E. Cheatham and J. B. Stewart (eds.), *Black Families: Interdisciplinary Perspectives*. New Brunswick, N.J.: Transaction, 1990.

Johnson, L. B., and Staples, R. "Family Planning and the Young Minority Male: A Pilot Project." *Urban League Review*, 1989, *12*, 159–169.

Johnson, P. R., Shireman, J. F., and Watson, K. W. "Transracial Adoption and the Development of Black Identity at Age Eight." *Child Welfare*, 1987, *1*, 45–55.

Jones, C. "Drugs Add to a Glut of Adoptable Black Children." *Los Angeles Times*, May 21, 1989, p. A-1.

Jones, D., and Battle, S. *Teenage Pregnancy: Developing Strategies for Change in the Twenty First Century.* New Brunswick, N.J.: Transaction, 1990.

Jones, J. " 'My Mother Was Much of a Woman': Black Women, Work, and the Family Under Slavery." *Feminist Studies*, 1982, *8*(2), 235–269.

Jones, J. *Labor of Love, Labor of Sorrow: Black Women, Work, and the Family from Slavery to the Present.* New York: Basic Books, 1985.

Joseph, G. I., and Lewis, J. *Common Differences: Conflicts in Black and White Feminist Perspectives.* Boston: South End Press, 1981.

Kahn, A. J., and Kamerman, S. B. "Social Assistance: An Eight County Overview." *Institute for Socio-Economic Studies*, 1983–84, *8*, 93–112.

Kayongo-Male, D., and Onyango, P. *The Sociology of the African Family.* London: Longman, 1984.

Keith, V. M., and Herring, C. "Skin Tone and Stratification in the Black Community." *American Journal of Sociology*, 1991, *97*(3), 760–778.

King, D. H. "Multiple Jeopardy, Multiple Consciousness: The Context of Black Feminist Ideology." In M. R. Malson, E. Mudimbe-Boyi, J. F. O'Barr, and M. Wyer (eds.), *Black Women in America: Social Science Perspectives.* Chicago: University of Chicago Press, 1990.

King, M. "The Politics of Sexual Stereotypes." *Black Scholar*, 1973, *4*, 12–23.

King, R.E.G., and Griffin, J. T. "The Loving Relationship: Impetus for Black Marriage." In C. E. Obudho (ed.), *Black Marriage and Family Therapy.* Westport, Conn.: Greenwood Press, 1983.

Kinsey, A. W., and others. *Sexual Behavior in the Human Female.* Philadelphia: Saunders, 1953.

Kitson, G. C. "Marital Discord and Marital Separation: A County Survey." *Journal of Marriage and the Family*, 1985, 693–700.

Komarovsky, M. "The New Feminist Scholarship: Some Precursors and Polemics." *Journal of Marriage and the Family,* 1988, *50,* 585–594.

Kozol, J. *Illiteracy in America.* New York: Morrow, 1985.

Krech, S. "Black Family Organization in the Nineteenth Century: An Ethnological Perspective." *Journal of Interdisciplinary History,* 1982, *12,* 429–452.

Ladner, J. *Tomorrow's Tomorrow: The Black Woman.* New York: Doubleday, 1971.

Landry, B. *The New Black Middle Class.* Berkeley: University of California Press, 1987.

Larson, T. E. "Employment and Unemployment of Young Black Males." In J. T. Gibbs (ed.), *Young, Black, and Male in America: An Endangered Species.* New York: Auburn House, 1988.

Leashore, B. "Social Policies, Black Males, and Black Families." In R. Staples (ed.), *The Black Family: Essays and Studies.* (4th ed.) Belmont, Calif.: Wadsworth, 1991.

Leffall, D. L. "Health Status of Black Americans." In J. Dewart (ed.), *The State of Black America 1990.* New York: National Urban League, 1990.

Lemann, N. *The Promised Land: The Great Black Migration and How It Changed America.* New York: Knopf, 1991.

Leslie, L. A., and Grady, K. "Changes in Mothers' Social Networks and Social Support Following Divorce." *Journal of Marriage and the Family,* 1985, *47,* 663–673.

Lewin, T. "Black Children Living with One Parent." *New York Times,* July 15, 1990, p. A-11.

Lewis, D. K. "The Black Family: Socialization and Sex Roles." *Phylon,* 1975, *36,* 221–237.

Lewis, G. "Bennett Idea on Children Draws Jeers." *San Francisco Examiner,* Apr. 28, 1990, p. A-1.

Liebow, E. *Tally's Corner.* Boston: Little, Brown, 1966.

Lincoln, E. C., and Mamiya, L. H. *The Black Church in the African American Experience.* Durham, N.C.: Duke University Press, 1990.

Linville, P. W. "Self-Complexity as a Cognitive Buffer Against Stress-Related Illness and Depression." *Journal of Personality and Social Psychology,* 1987, *52*(4), 663–676.

Litwack, L. *Been in the Storm So Long: The Aftermath of Slavery.* New York: Knopf, 1979.

Lloyd, S. A. "The Darkside of Courtship: Violence and Sexual Exploitation." *Family Relations,* 1991, *40,* 14–20.

Lockhart, L., and White, B. W. "Understanding Marital Violence in the Black Community." *Journal of Interpersonal Violence,* 1989, *4*(4), 421–436.

London, K. A. *Cohabitation, Marriage Dissolution, and Remarriage: United States, 1988.* Washington, D.C.: National Center for Health Statistics, 1991.

McAdoo, H. P. "Transgenerational Patterns of Upward Mobility in African-American Families." In H. P. McAdoo (ed.), *Black Families.* (2nd ed.) Newbury Park, Calif.: Sage, 1988.

McAdoo, J. L. "A Black Perspective on the Father's Role in Child Development." *Marriage and Family Review,* 1985–86, *9*(3/4), 117–133.

McCubbin, H. I., Patterson, J. M., and Lavee, Y. "Black Military Family Adaptation to Crises: Critical Strengths." Paper presented at the 46th annual meeting of the National Council on Family Relations, Ethnic Minorities Section, San Francisco, Oct. 1984.

McLeod, R. G. "Gulf Widening Between Rich and Poor in U.S." *San Francisco Chronicle,* July 29, 1991, p. A-4.

McMurray, G. L. "Those of Broader Vision: An African-American Perspective on Teenage Pregnancy and Parenting." In J. Dewart (ed.), *The State of Black America 1990.* New York: National Urban League, 1990.

Malson, M. R. "Black Women's Sex Roles: The Social Context for a New Ideology." *Journal of Social Issues,* 1983, *39*(3), 101–113.

Malveaux, J. "The Economic Statuses of Black Families." In H. P. McAdoo (ed.), *Black Families.* (2nd ed.) Newbury Park, Calif.: Sage, 1988.

Mannheim, K. *Ideology and Utopia.* Orlando, Fla.: Harcourt Brace Jovanovich, 1936.

Manns, M. "Supportive Roles of Significant Others in Black Families." In H. P. McAdoo (ed.), *Black Families.* (2nd ed.) Newbury Park, Calif.: Sage, 1988.

Marsiglio, W. "Adolescent Fathers in the United States: Their

Initial Living Arrangements, Marital Experience, and Educational Outcomes." *Family Planning Perspectives,* 1987, *19,* 240–251.

Martin, E. P., and Martin, J. M. *The Black Extended Family.* Chicago: University of Chicago Press, 1978.

Marx, K. *Capital.* New York: Modern Library, 1936.

Mathews, T., and others. "Help Begins in the 'Hood.' " *Newsweek,* May 18, 1992, 34–35.

Mays, V., and Cochran, S. "The Black Women's Relationship Project: A National Survey of Black Lesbians." In R. Staples (ed.), *The Black Family: Essays and Studies.* (4th ed.) Belmont, Calif.: Wadsworth, 1991.

Mbiti, J. S. *Love and Marriage in Africa.* London: Longman, 1973.

Meltzer, M. *In Their Own Words: A History of the American Negro, 1619–1865.* New York: Crowell, 1964.

Melville, K. *Marriage and Family Today.* New York: Random House, 1977.

Merton, R. K. "Insiders and Outsiders: A Chapter in the Sociology of Knowledge." *American Journal of Sociology,* 1972, *78,* 9–48.

Miller, K. D. "Scholar Keith Miller Gives Credit to King's Sunday School Teacher." *ASU Insight,* Jan. 14, 1991, p. 8.

Miller, R. M., and Smith, J. D. *Dictionary of Afro-American Slavery.* Westport, Conn.: Greenwood Press, 1988.

Millette, R. E. "West Indian Families in the United States." In H. E. Cheatham and J. B. Stewart (eds.), *Black Families: Interdisciplinary Perspectives.* New Brunswick, N.J.: Transaction, 1990.

Mitchell-Kernan, C. "Linguistic Diversity in the Service Delivery Setting: The Case of Black English." In B. A. Bass, G. E. Wyatt, and G. J. Powell (eds.), *The Afro-American Family: Assessment, Treatment, and Research Issues.* Philadelphia: Grune & Stratton, 1982.

Monahan, T. P. "Are Interracial Marriages Less Stable?" *Social Forces,* 1970, *48,* 461–473.

Moore, K. A., Simms, M. C., and Betsey, C. L. *Choice and Circumstance: Racial Differences in Adolescent Sexuality and Fertility.* New Brunswick, N.J.: Transaction, 1986.

Morganthau, T. "The Price of Neglect." *Newsweek*, May 11, 1992, p. 55.

Moynihan, D. P. *The Negro Family: The Case for National Action*. Washington, D.C.: Office of Policy Planning and Research, Department of Labor, 1965.

Moynihan, D. P. *Family and Nation*. Orlando, Fla.: Harcourt Brace Jovanovich, 1987.

Murray, C. B., Khatib, S., and Jackson, M. "Social Indices and the Black Elderly: A Comparative Life Cycle Approach to the Study of Double Jeopardy." In R. L. Jones (ed.), *Black Adult Development and Aging*. Berkeley, Calif.: Cobb & Henry, 1989.

Murstein, B. I., Merighi, J., and Malloy, T. E. "Physical Attractiveness and the Exchange Theory in Interracial Dating." *Journal of Social Psychology*, 1989, *52*, 325-333.

Mydans, S. "Homicide Rate for Young Blacks Rose by Two-Thirds in Five Years." *New York Times*, Dec. 7, 1990, p. A-1.

Myers, B. C. "Hypertension as a Manifestation of the Stress Experienced by Black Families." In H. E. Cheatham and J. B. Stewart (eds.), *Black Families: Interdisciplinary Perspectives*. New Brunswick, N.J.: Transaction, 1990.

Nathanson, C. A., and Becker, M. H. "Family and Peer Influence on Obtaining a Method of Contraception." *Journal of Marriage and the Family*, 1986, *48*, 513-525.

National Black Catholic Congress. "Public Policy Statements: Recommendations." Presented at 1992 Congress VII of the National Black Catholic Congress, New Orleans, La., July 1992.

National Center for Education Statistics, Department of Education. *Digest of Education Statistics 1990*. Washington, D.C.: U.S. Government Printing Office, 1991a.

National Center for Education Statistics, Department of Education. *Race/Ethnicity Trends in Degrees Conferred by Institutions of Higher Education: 1978-79 Through 1988-89*. Washington, D.C.: U.S. Government Printing Office, 1991b.

"New Study of Teenage Sex." *San Francisco Chronicle*, Jan. 2, 1991, p. A-3.

Noble, J. *Beautiful, Also, Are the Souls of My Black Sisters: A History of the Black Woman in America*. Englewood Cliffs, N.J.: Prentice Hall, 1978.

Nobles, W. W. "African-American Family Life: An Instrument of Culture." In H. P. McAdoo (ed.), *Black Families*. (2nd ed.) Newbury Park, Calif.: Sage, 1988.

Nobles, W. W., and Goddard, L. L. *Understanding the Black Family: A Guide for Scholarship and Research.* Oakland, Calif.: Institute for the Advanced Study of Black Family Life and Culture, 1986.

Norment, L. "Black Men, Black Women, and Sexual Harassment." *Ebony,* Jan. 1992, pp. 120–122.

Nye, I., and Berardo, F. (eds.). *Emerging Conceptual Frameworks in Family Analysis.* New York: Praeger, 1981.

Omari, T. P. "Role Expectations in the Courtship Situation in Ghana." In P. L. Van Berghe (ed.), *Africa: Social Problems of Change and Conflict.* San Francisco: Chandler, 1965.

Osmond, M. W. "Marital Organization in Low Income Families: A Cross-Race Comparison." *International Journal of Sociology of the Family,* 1977, 7, 143–156.

Ostrow, R. J. "U.S. Imprisons Black Men at 4 Times S. Africa's Rate." *Los Angeles Times,* Jan. 5, 1991, p. A-1.

Patterson, O. *Slavery and Social Death: A Comparative Study.* Cambridge, Mass.: Harvard University Press, 1982.

Peters, M. F. (ed.). "Black Families" [Special Issue]. *Journal of Marriage and the Family,* 1978, 40, 655–862.

Peters, M. F. "Racial Socialization of Young Black Children." In H. P. McAdoo and J. L. McAdoo (eds.), *Black Children: Social, Educational, and Parental Environments.* Newbury Park, Calif.: Sage, 1985.

Peters, M. F. "Parenting in Black Families with Young Children: A Historical Perspective." In H. P. McAdoo (ed.), *Black Families.* (2nd ed.) Newbury Park, Calif.: Sage, 1988.

Peterson, G. W., and Peters, D. F. "The Socialization Values of Low-Income Appalachian White and Rural Black Mothers: A Comparative Study." *Journal of Comparative Family Studies,* 1985, 16(1), 75–91.

Pietropinto, A., and Simenauer, J. *Beyond the Male Myth.* New York: Quadrangle, 1977.

Pinderhughes, D. M. "The Case of African Americans in the Persian Gulf: The Intersection of American Foreign and Military Policy with Domestic Employment Policy in the

United States." In J. Dewart (ed.), *The State of Black America 1991.* New York: National Urban League, 1991.

Platt, T. "E. Franklin Frazier and Daniel P. Moynihan: Setting the Record Straight." *Contemporary Crises,* 1987, *11,* 42–51.

Pleck, J. H. "Correlates of Black Adolescent Males' Condom Use." *Journal of Adolescent Research,* 1989, *4,* 247–253.

Poole, T. "Black Families and the Black Church: A Sociohistorical Perspective." In H. E. Cheatham and J. B. Stewart (eds.), *Black Families: Interdisciplinary Perspectives.* New Brunswick, N.J.: Transaction, 1990.

Porter, J. R. *Dating Habits of Young Black Americans: And Almost Everybody Else's Too.* Dubuque, Iowa: Kendall/ Hunt, 1979.

Porterfield, E. "Black-American Intermarriage in the United States." *Psychology Today,* Jan. 1973, pp. 71–78.

Pouissant, A. "Black-on-Black Homicide: A Psychological-Political Perspective." *Victimology,* 1983, *8,* 161–169.

President's Commission. *Report of the Commission on Obscenity and Pornography.* New York: Random House, 1971.

Rainwater, L. "The Crucible of Identity: The Lower Class Negro Family." *Daedalus,* 1966, *95,* 258–264.

Rainwater, L. *Behind Ghetto Walls: Black Families in a Federal Slum.* Hawthorne, N.Y.: Aldine, 1970.

Rainwater, L., and Yancey, W. *The Moynihan Report and the Politics of Controversy.* Cambridge, Mass.: MIT Press, 1967.

Ramsey, P. G. "Young Children's Thinking About Ethnic Differences." In J. S. Phinney and M. J. Rotheram (eds.), *Children's Ethnic Socialization.* Newbury Park, Calif.: Sage, 1987.

Rank, M. R. "The Formation and Dissolution of Marriages in the Welfare Population." *Journal of Marriage and the Family,* 1987, *49,* 15–20.

Ransford, H. E., and Miller, J. "Race, Sex, and Feminist Outlooks." *American Sociological Review,* 1983, *48,* 46–59.

Rao, V. V., and Rao, V. N. "Sex Role Attitudes: A Comparison of Race and Sex Groups." *Sex Roles,* 1985, *12,* 939–953.

Raspberry, W. "New Interest in an Old Problem." *Chicago Tribune,* Feb. 6, 1984, Sec. 1, p. 11.

Reed, R. J. "Education and Achievement of Young Black Males." In J. T. Gibbs (ed.), *Young, Black, and Male in America: An Endangered Species.* New York: Auburn House, 1988.

Reeder, A. L., and Conger, R. D. "Differential Mother and Father Influences on the Educational Attainment of Black and White Women." *Sociological Quarterly,* 1984, *25,* 239–250.

Reeves, R. "A Look at Unemployment." *San Francisco Chronicle,* June 13, 1986, p. 85.

Rein, M. "Work in Welfare: Past Failures and Future Strategies." *Social Service Review,* 1982, *56,* 211–229.

Reiss, I. L. *Family Systems in America.* (3rd ed.) Troy, Mo.: Holt, Rinehart & Winston, 1980.

Rindfuss, R., and Stephen, E. H. "Marital Noncohabitation: Separation Does Not Make the Heart Grow Fonder." *Journal of Marriage and the Family,* 1990, *52,* 259–270.

Robinson, C. J. *Black Marxism: The Making of the Black Radical Tradition.* London: Zed Press, 1983.

Robinson, I. E., Bailey, W. C., and Smith, J. M. "Self-Perception of the Husband/Father in the Intact Lower Class Black Family." *Phylon,* 1985, *46*(2), 136–147.

Rodgers, W. L., and Thornton, A. "Changing Patterns of First Marriage in the United States." *Demography,* 1985, *22,* 265–279.

Rodgers-Rose, L. F. *The Black Woman.* Newbury Park, Calif.: Sage, 1980.

Ross, C. E. "The Division of Labor at Home." *Social Forces,* 1987, *65,* 816–833.

Rutten, T. "Inner Cities in Need of a Living Wage." *Los Angeles Times,* Aug. 2, 1991, p. E-1.

Saxe, J. "Review of *Black Rage.*" *Black Scholar,* 1970, *1,* 58.

Scanzoni, J. *The Black Family in Modern Society.* Chicago: University of Chicago Press, 1978.

Schulz, D. A. "The Role of the Boyfriend in Lower-Class Negro Life." In R. Staples (ed.), *The Black Family: Essays and Studies.* (3rd ed.) Belmont, Calif.: Wadsworth, 1986.

Sebald, H. "Patterns of Interracial Dating and Sexual Liaison of Black and White College Men." *International Journal of Sociology of the Family,* 1974, *4,* 23–26.

Selik, R. M., Castro, K. G., and Pappaioanou, M. "Distribution of AIDS Cases by Racial Ethnic Group and Exposure Category." *MMWR*, 1988, *37*, 1-10.

Shah, F., and Zelnick, M. "Parent and Peer Influence on Sexual Behavior, Contraceptive Use, and Pregnancy of Young Women." *Journal of Marriage and the Family*, 1981, *43*, 339-348.

Shange, N. *For Colored Girls Who Have Considered Suicide When the Rainbow Is Enuf: A Choreopoem*. New York: Macmillan, 1977.

Shinoff, P. "The Elusive Idea of Full Employment." *San Francisco Examiner*, Apr. 24, 1986, p. C-7.

Simenauer, J., and Carroll, D. *Singles: The New Americans*. New York: Simon & Schuster, 1982.

Simms-Brown, R. J. "The Female in the Black Family: Dominant Mate or Helpmate?" *Journal of Black Psychology*, 1982, *9*(1), 45-55.

Simpson, R. "The Afro-American Female: The Historical Context of the Construction of Sexual Identity." In A. Snitow, C. Stansell, and S. Thompson (eds.), *Powers of Desire: The Politics of Sexuality*. New York: Monthly Review Press, 1983.

Sisters for Black Community Development. *Black Women's Role in the Revolution*. Newark, N.J.: Sisters for Black Community Development, 1971.

Skolnick, A. *Embattled Paradise: The American Family in an Age of Uncertainty*. New York: Basic Books, 1992.

Smerglia, V. L., Deimling, G. T., and Barresi, C. M. "Black/White Family Comparisons in Helping and Decision-Making Networks of Impaired Elderly." *Family Relations*, 1988, *37*, 305-309.

Smith, E. A., and Udry, J. R. "Coital and Non-Coital Sexual Behaviors of White and Black Adolescents." *American Journal of Public Health*, 1985, *75*, 1200-1203.

Smith, E.M.J. "Ethnic Minorities: Life Stress, Social Support, and Mental Health Issues." *Counseling Psychologist*, 1985, *13*(4), 537-579.

Snowden, F. M., Jr. *Blacks in Antiquity*. Cambridge, Mass.: Harvard University Press, 1970.

Spanier, G., and Glick, P. "Mate Selection Differentials Between Whites and Blacks in the United States." *Social Forces,* 1980, *58,* 726–738.

Spickard, P. R. *Mixed Blood: Intermarriage and Ethnic Identity in Twentieth-Century America.* Madison: University of Wisconsin Press, 1989.

Stampp, R. *The Peculiar Institution: Slavery in the Ante-Bellum South.* New York: Knopf, 1956.

Staples, R. *The Black Woman in America: Sex, Marriage, and the Family.* Chicago: Nelson-Hall, 1973.

Staples, R. "Race, Liberalism, Conservatism, and Premarital Sexual Permissiveness: A Biracial Comparison." *Journal of Marriage and the Family,* 1978, *40,* 78–92.

Staples, R. *The World of Black Singles: Changing Patterns of Male-Female Relations.* Westport, Conn.: Greenwood Press, 1981.

Staples, R. *Black Masculinity: The Black Male's Role in American Society.* San Francisco: Black Scholar Press, 1982.

Staples, R. "An Explosive Controversy: The Mother-Son Relationship in the Black Family." *Ebony,* Oct. 1984, pp. 74–78.

Staples, R. "Changes in Black Family Structure: The Conflict Between Family Ideology and Structural Conditions." *Journal of Marriage and the Family,* 1985, *47,* 1005–1114.

Staples, R. *The Urban Plantation: Racism and Colonialism in the Post Civil Rights Era.* San Francisco: Black Scholar Press, 1987.

Staples, R. "Beauty and the Beast: The Importance of Physical Attractiveness in the Black Community." In N. Hare and J. Hare (eds.), *Crisis in Black Sexual Politics.* San Francisco: Black Think Tank, 1989.

Staples, R. "Black Male Genocide: The Final Solution." In B. Bowser (ed.), *Black Male Adolescents: Parenting and Education.* Lanham, Md.: University Presses of America, 1991a.

Staples, R. "Substance Abuse and the Black Family Crisis: An Overview." In R. Staples (ed.), *The Black Family: Essays and Studies.* (4th ed.) Belmont, Calif.: Wadsworth, 1991b.

Staples, R. "Intermarriage." *Encyclopedia of Sociology.* New York: Macmillan, 1992, pp. 968–974.

Staples, R., and Mirande, A. "Racial and Cultural Variations

Among American Families: A Decennial Review of the Family Literature." *Journal of Marriage and the Family,* 1980, *42,* 887–904.

Star, B., Clark, C. G., Goetz, K. M., and O'Malia, L. "Psychosocial Aspects of Wife Battering." *Social Casework: The Journal of Contemporary Social Work,* 1979, *60*(8), 479–486.

Steady, C. *The Black Woman Cross-Culturally.* Rochester, Vt.: Schenkman, 1981.

Steckel, R. H. "Slave Marriage and the Family." *Journal of Family History,* 1980, *5,* 406–421.

Stein, P. *Single.* Englewood Cliffs, N.J.: Prentice-Hall, 1976.

Stember, C. *Sexual Racism.* New York: Elsevier, 1976.

Stephens, J. H. "Black Grandmothers' and Black Adolescent Mothers' Knowledge About Parenting." *Developmental Psychology,* 1984, *20*(6), 1017–1025.

Stephens, W. N. *The Family in Cross-Cultural Perspective.* Troy, Mo.: Holt, Rinehart & Winston, 1963.

Stewart, J., and Hyclak, T. J. "The Effects of Immigrants, Women, and Teenagers on the Relative Earnings of Black Males." *Review of Black Political Economy,* 1986, *15,* 93–101.

Stewart, J., and Scott, J. "The Institutional Decimation of Black Males." *Western Journal of Black Studies,* 1978, *2,* 82–92.

Stewart, P. "Shades of Black." *Oakland Tribune,* May 13, 1979, p. 18.

Strong, B., and DeVault, C. *The Marriage and Family Experience.* (4th ed.) St. Paul, Minn.: West, 1992.

Sudarkasa, N. "Female Employment and Family Organization in West Africa." In F. C. Steady (ed.), *The Black Woman Cross-Culturally.* Rochester, Vt.: Schenkman, 1981.

Sudarkasa, N. "Interpreting the African Heritage in Afro-American Family Organization." In H. P. McAdoo (ed.), *Black Families.* (2nd ed.) Newbury Park, Calif.: Sage, 1988.

"Summer Vacation Travails." *San Francisco Examiner,* June 8, 1986, p. D-1.

Swinton, D. H. "The Economic Status of African Americans: Permanent Poverty and Inequality." In J. Dewart (ed.), *The State of Black America 1991.* New York: National Urban League, 1991.

Swinton, D. H. "The Economic Status of African-Americans:

Limited Ownership and Persistent Inequality." In J. Dewart (ed.), *The State of Black America 1992.* New York: National Urban League, 1992.

Taylor, R. J. "Receipt of Support from Family Among Black Americans: Demographic and Familial Differences." *Journal of Marriage and the Family,* 1986, *43,* 67–77.

Taylor, R. J., and Chatters, L. M. "Family, Friend, and Church Support Networks of Black Americans." In R. L. Jones (ed.), *Black Adult Development.* Berkeley, Calif.: Cobb & Henry, 1989.

Taylor, R. J., Chatters, L. M., Tucker, N. B., and Lewis, E. "Developments in Research on Black Families: A Decade Review." *Journal of Marriage and the Family,* 1990 *52*(4), 993–1014.

Taylor, R. J., Leashore, B., and Toliver, S. "An Assessment of the Provider Role as Perceived by Black Males." *Family Relations,* 1988, *37,* 426–431.

"Ten Things Men Notice About Women." *Jet Magazine,* June 7, 1982, pp. 38–39.

"Ten Things Women Notice About Men." *Jet Magazine,* May 31, 1982, pp. 52–53.

Terborg-Penn, R. "Women and Slavery in the African Diaspora: A Cross-Cultural Approach to Historical Analysis." In R. Staples (ed.), *The Black Family: Essays and Studies.* (4th ed.) Belmont, Calif.: Wadsworth, 1991.

Thibaut, J. W., and Kelley, H. W. *The Social Psychology of Groups.* New York: Wiley, 1959.

Thoits, P. A. "Multiple Identities and Psychological Well-Being: A Reformulation and Test of the Social Isolation Hypothesis." *American Sociological Review,* 1983, *48,* 174–187.

Thomas, Evan. "Crime: A Conspiracy of Silence." *Newsweek,* May 18, 1992, p. 37.

Thorne, B., and Yalom, M. (eds.). *Rethinking the Family: Some Feminist Questions.* White Plains, N.Y.: Longman, 1982.

Timberlake, C. A., and Carpenter, W. D. "Sexuality Attitudes of Black Adults." *Family Relations,* 1990, *39,* 87–91.

Toure, Y. "Elder Statesmen: An Era Is Passing for Five Authors Known for Reclaiming the Role of Blacks in History." *Los Angeles Times,* Mar. 3, 1991, p. E-1.

Tucker, M. B., and Mitchell-Kernan, C. "New Trends in Black American Interracial Marriage: The Social Structure Context." *Journal of Marriage and the Family,* 1990, *52,* 209–218.

Tucker, M. B., and Taylor, R. J. "Demographic Correlates of Relationship Status Among Black Americans." *Journal of Marriage and the Family,* 1989, *51,* 655–665.

Turner, C. B., and Turner, B. F. "Black Families, Social Evaluations, and Future Marital Relationships." In C. E. Obudho (ed.), *Black Marriage and Family Therapy.* Westport, Conn.: Greenwood Press, 1983.

Udry, J. R. "The Importance of Being Beautiful: A Re-Examination and Racial Comparison." *American Journal of Sociology,* 1977, *83,* 154–160.

Udry, J. R., Bauman, K. E., and Chase, C. "Skin Color, Status, and Mate Selection." *American Journal of Sociology,* 1971, *76*(4), 722–733.

Ulbrich, P. M. "The Determinants of Depression in Two-Income Marriages," *Journal of Marriage and the Family,* 1988, *50,* 121–131.

Uzzell, O. "Racial and Gender Perceptions of Marriage Roles at a Predominantly Black University." *Western Journal of Black Studies,* 1986, *10,* 167–171.

Uzzell, O., and Peebles-Wilkins, W. "Black Spouse Abuse: A Focus on Relational Factors and Intervention Strategies." *Western Journal of Black Studies,* 1989, *13,* 131–138.

Valentine, C. A. *Culture and Poverty: Critique and Counterproposals.* Chicago: University of Chicago Press, 1968.

Villa, L. *The Sexuality of a Black American.* Oakland, Calif.: Ashford Press, 1981.

Vontress, C. "The Black Male Personality." *Black Scholar,* 1971, *2,* 10–17.

Wallace, M. *Black Macho and the Myth of the Superwoman.* New York: Dial Press, 1979.

Wallace, M. *Invisibility Blues.* New York: Verso, 1990.

Walters, R. *The New Negro on Campus.* Princeton, N.J.: Princeton University Press, 1975.

Washington, V. "Community Involvement in Recruiting Adoptive Homes for Black Children." *Child Welfare League of America,* 1987, *56*(1), 57–67.

Washington, V. "Child Care Policy, African Americans, and Moral Dilemmas." Paper presented at a conference titled "One Third of a Nation: African American Perspectives," Harvard University, Nov. 1989.

Watson, B. J., Rowe, C. L., and Jones, D. J. "Dispelling Myths About Teenage Pregnancy and Male Responsibility: A Research Agenda." In D. J. Jones and S. E. Battle (eds.), *Teenage Pregnancy: Developing Strategies for Change in the Twenty-First Century.* New Brunswick, N.J.: Transaction, 1990.

Westney, O. E., Jenkins, R. R., Butts, J. D., and Williams, I. "Sexual Development and Behavior in Black Pre-Adolescents." In R. Staples (ed.), *The Black Family: Essays and Studies.* (4th ed.) Belmont, Calif.: Wadsworth, 1991.

Wheeler, W. H. "Socio-Sexual Communication Between Black Men and Black Women." Unpublished manuscript, Florida State University, 1977.

White, D. G. *Ain't I a Woman? Female Slaves in the Plantation South.* New York: Norton, 1985.

White, E. C. "Black Women Find an Oasis of Respect: More and More Turn to Islam for Its Stability and Love of Family." *San Francisco Chronicle,* Nov. 3, 1991, *This World* sec., pp. 9–11.

White, J. E. "The Limits of Black Power." *Time,* May 11, 1992, pp. 38–40.

"Why Skin Color Suddenly Is a Big Issue Again." *Ebony,* Mar. 1992, pp. 120–122.

Whyte, M. K. *Dating, Mating, and Marriage.* New York: Aldine de Gruyter, 1990.

Williams, M. "Polygamy and the Declining Male to Female Ratio in Black Communities: A Social Inquiry." In H. E. Cheatham and J. B. Stewart (eds.), *Black Families: Interdisciplinary Perspectives.* New Brunswick, N.J.: Transaction, 1990.

Willie, C. V. *A New Look at Black Families.* (3rd ed.) Dix Hill, N.Y.: General Hall, 1988.

Willie, C. V. *The Family Life of Black People.* Columbus, Ohio: Merrill, 1970.

Willie, C. V. "The Role of Mothers in the Lives of Outstanding Scholars." *Journal of Family Issues,* 1984, 5(3), 291–306.

Willie, C. V., and Levy, J. D. "On White Campuses, Black Students Retreat into Separatism." *Psychology Today,* Mar. 1972, pp. 50–52, 76, 78, 80.

Wilson, M. "Perceived Parental Activity of Mothers, Fathers, and Grandmothers in Three-Generational Black Families." *Journal of Black Psychology,* 1986, *12*(2), 43–59.

Wilson, M., Tolson, T.F.J., Hinton, I. D., and Kiernan, M. "Flexibility and Sharing of Child Care Duties in Black Families." *Sex Roles,* 1990, *22*(7/8), 409–425.

Wilson, R. "The State of Black Higher Education: Crisis and Promise." In J. Dewart (ed.), *The State of Black America 1989.* New York: National Urban League, 1989.

Wilson, W. J. *The Declining Significance of Race: Blacks and Changing American Institutions.* Chicago: University of Chicago Press, 1980.

Wilson, W. J. *The Truly Disadvantaged: The Inner City, the Underclass, and Public Policy.* Chicago: University of Chicago Press, 1987.

Wolf, N. "The Beauty Myth: How Images of Beauty Are Used Against Women." New York: Morrow, 1991.

Wyatt, G. E. "Identifying Stereotypes of Afro-American Sexuality and Their Impact upon Sexual Behavior." In B. A. Bass, G. E. Wyatt, and G. J. Powell (eds.), *The Afro-American Family: Assessment, Treatment, and Research Issues.* Philadelphia: Grune & Stratton, 1982.

Wyatt, G. E. "The Sexual Abuse of Afro-American and White-American Women in Childhood." *Child Abuse and Neglect,* 1985, *9,* 507–519.

Wyatt, G. E., and Lyons-Rowe, S. "African American Women's Sexual Satisfaction as a Dimension of Their Sex Roles." *Sex Roles,* 1990, *22*(7/8), 509–523.

Wyatt, G. E., Peters, S. D., and Guthrie, D. "Kinsey Revisited, Part IL: Comparisons of the Sexual Socialization and Sexual Behavior of Black Women over 33 Years." *Archives of Sexual Behavior,* 1988, *17,* 289–332.

Yetman, N. R., and Steele, C. H. *Majority and Minority: The Dynamics of Racial and Ethnic Relations.* Boston: Allyn & Bacon, 1975.

" 'You Can't Join Their Clubs': Six Mixed Couples Get Together to Talk About Love, Marriage, and Prejudice." *Newsweek,* June 10, 1991, pp. 48–49.

Zetterberg, H. *Theory and Verification in Sociology.* New York: Bedminster Press, 1965.

Zinn, M. B. "Family, Race, and Poverty in the Eighties." In M. R. Malson, E. Mudimbe-Boyi, J. F. O'Barr, and M. Wyer (eds.), *Black Women in America: Social Science Perspectives.* Chicago: University of Chicago Press, 1990.

Zollar, A. C. "Ideological Perspectives on Black Families: Related Typologies." *Free Inquiry in Creative Sociology,* 1986, *14,* 169–172.

Zollar, A. C., and Williams, J. S. "The Contribution of Marriage to the Life Satisfaction of Black Adults." *Journal of Marriage and the Family,* 1987, *49,* 87–92.

Selected Readings

Aldridge, D. *Black Male-Female Relationships.* Dubuque, Iowa: Kendall/Hunt, 1989.

Anderson, M. J., and Collins, P. H. *Race, Class, and Gender: An Anthology.* Belmont, Calif.: Wadsworth, 1991.

Ball, R. E. "Marital Status, Household Structure, and Life Satisfaction of Black Women." *Social Problems,* 1983, *30,* 399–409.

Ball, R. E., and Robbins, L. R. "Marital Status and Life Satisfaction of Black Men." *Journal of Social and Personal Relationships,* 1984, *1,* 459–470.

Barnes, A. S. *The Black Middle Class Family.* Bristol, Ind.: Wyndham Hall Press, 1985.

Barnes, A. S. *Black Women: Interpersonal Relationships in Profile.* Bristol, Ind.: Wyndham Hall Press, 1986.

Barnes, A. S. *Black Single Parents in America.* Bristol, Ind.: Wyndham Hall Press, 1987.

Bass, B., Wyatt, G., and Powell, G. *The Assessment and Treatment of Afro-American Families: A Book of Readings.* Philadelphia: Grune & Stratton, 1980.

Battle, S. F. *The Black Adolescent Parent.* New York: Haworth Press, 1987.

Beam, J. (ed.). *In the Life: A Black Gay Anthology.* Boston: Alyson, 1986.

Bell-Scott, P., and Taylor, R. J. (eds.). "Black Adolescents." *Journal of Adolescent Research,* 1989, *4*(entire issue 2).

Bennett, D. "Delores Bennett: A Dream Maker." *Ebony*, Aug. 1991, p. 106.

Bennett, L. "The Black Bourgeoisie Revisited." *Ebony*, Aug. 1973, pp. 50–55.

Bennett, N. G. "The Divergence of Black and White Marriage Patterns." *American Journal of Sociology*, 1989, *95*, 692–722.

Bernard, J. "Note on Educational Homogamy in Negro-White and White-Negro Marriages." *Journal of Marriage and the Family*, 1966, *28*, 274–276.

Boykin, W. A., and Toms, F. D. "Black Child Socialization: A Conceptual Framework." In H. P. McAdoo and J. L. McAdoo (eds.), *Black Children: Social, Educational, and Parental Environments*. Newbury Park, Calif.: Sage, 1985.

Bracey, J., Meier, A., and Rudwick, E. *Black Matriarchy: Myth or Reality*. Belmont, Calif.: Wadsworth, 1971.

Broman, C. L. "Satisfaction Among Blacks: The Significance of Marriage and Parenthood." *Journal of Marriage and the Family*, 1988, *50*, 45–51.

Browan, P. J. "Research Perspectives on Black Men: Role Strain and Adaptation Across the Adult Life Cycle." In R. L. Jones (ed.), *Black Adult Development and Aging*. Berkeley, Calif.: Cobb & Henry, 1989.

Bumpass, L. L., and Sweet, J. L. "Differentials in Marital Instability: 1970." *American Sociological Review*, 1972, *37*, 754–766.

Bureau of the Census. *Marital Status and Living Arrangements: March 1988*. Washington, D.C.: U.S. Government Printing Office, 1989.

Bureau of the Census. *Household and Family Characteristics, March 1989 and 1990*. Washington, D.C.: U.S. Government Printing Office, 1991.

Bureau of the Census. *Poverty in the United States: 1990*. Current Population Reports, series P-60, no. 175. Washington, D.C.: U.S. Government Printing Office, 1991.

Chapman, A. B. *Man Sharing: Choice or Dilemma*. New York: Morrow, 1986.

Clark, K. B. *Dark Ghetto*. New York: HarperCollins, 1965.

Coner-Edwards, A., and Spurlock, J. (eds.). *Black Family in Crisis: The Middle Class.* New York: Brunner/Mazel, 1988.

Cooley, C. H. *Human Nature and Social Order.* New York: Scribner's, 1902.

Davidson, B. *The African Slave Trade.* Boston: Little, Brown, 1961.

Dennis, R. "Theories of the Black Family: The Weak Family and Strong Family Schools as Competing Ideologies." *Journal of Afro-American Issues,* 1976, *4,* 315–328.

DeRachewitz, B. *Black Eros.* New York: Lyle-Stuart, 1964.

Edelman, M. W. *Families in Peril: An Agenda for Social Change.* Cambridge, Mass.: Harvard University Press, 1987.

Felder, C. H. *Troubling Biblical Waters: Race, Class, and Family.* Maryknoll, N.Y.: Orbis Books, 1989.

Franklin, N. B. *Black Families in Therapy.* New York: Guilford Press, 1989.

Gary, L. E. (ed.). *Black Men.* Newbury Park, Calif.: Sage, 1981.

Gary, L. E., Beatty, L. A., and Berry, G. L. "Patterns of Well-Being in Strong Black Families: Gender and Household Structure Comparisons." Paper presented at the 46th annual meeting of the National Council on Family Relations, San Francisco, Nov. 1984.

Gibbs, J. T. (ed.). *Young, Black & Male in America: An Endangered Species.* New York: Auburn House, 1988.

Glazer, N., and Moynihan, D. *Beyond the Melting Pot.* Cambridge, Mass.: MIT Press and Harvard University Press, 1968.

Goode, W. "The Theoretical Importance of Love." *American Sociological Review,* 1961, *24,* 39–47.

Gopaul-McNicol, S. "Racial Identification and Racial Preference of Black Preschool Children in New York and Trinidad." *Journal of Black Psychology,* 1988, *14*(2), 63–68.

Gordon, V. V. *Black Women, Feminism, and Black Liberation: Which Way?* Chicago: Third World Press, 1984.

Hare, N., and Hare, J. *Bringing the Black Boy to Manhood: The Passage.* San Francisco: Black Think Tank, 1985.

Hare, N., and Hare, J. (eds.). *The Crisis in Black Sexual Politics*. San Francisco: Black Think Tank, 1989.

Hendricks, L. E. "Unmarried Black Adolescent Fathers' Attitudes Toward Abortion, Contraception, and Sexuality: A Preliminary Report." *Journal of Adolescent Health Care*, 1982, *2*, 199–203.

Henriques, R. *Children of Conflict: A Study of Interracial Sex and Marriage*. New York: Dutton, 1975.

Hooks, B. *Talking Back: Thinking Feminist, Thinking Black*. Boston: South End Press, 1989.

Hooks, B. *Yearning: Race and Gender in the Cultural Marketplace*. Boston: South End Press, 1990.

"Income Gap Widens Among U.S. Blacks, New Report Says." *San Francisco Chronicle*, Aug. 9, 1991, p. A-2.

Jackson, J. J. "Kinship Relations Among Urban Blacks." *Journal of Social and Behavioral Sciences*, 1970, *16*, 1–13.

Jackson, J. J. "Aged Blacks: A Potpourri in the Direction of the Reduction of Inequities." *Phylon*, 1971, *32*, 260–271.

Jahoda, G. "Love, Marriage, and Social Change: Letters to the Advice Column of a West African Newspaper." In P. L. Van Berghe (ed.), *Africa: Social Problems of Change and Conflict*. San Francisco: Chandler, 1965.

James-Myers, L. "Family Stability in Black Families: Values Underlying Three Different Perspectives." *Journal of Comparative Family Studies*, 1987, *18*, 1–24.

Jewell, K. S. "The Changing Character of Black Families: The Effects of Differential Social and Economic Gains." *Journal of Social and Behavioral Sciences*, 1987, *33*, 143–154.

Johnson, L. B. "Sexual Attitudes on SDA Campuses 1978: A Comparative Perspective." *Spectrum*, 1989, *19*, 27–34.

Kennedy, T. R. *You Gotta Deal with It: Black Family Relations in a Southern Community*. New York: Oxford University Press, 1980.

Ladner, J. A. "Black Women Face the 21st Century: Major Issues and Problems." *Black Scholar*, 1986, *17*, 12–20.

Lewis, J. M., and Looney, J. G. *The Long Struggle: Well-Functioning Working Class Black Families*. New York: Brunner/Mazel, 1983.

McAdoo, H. P. (ed.). *Black Families.* (2nd ed.) Newbury Park, Calif.: Sage, 1988.

McAdoo, H. P., and McAdoo, J. L. (eds.). *Black Children: Social, Educational, and Parental Environments.* Newbury Park, Calif.: Sage, 1985.

Mack, D. E. "The Power Relationship in Black Families and White Families." In R. Staples (ed.), *The Black Family: Essays and Studies.* (2nd ed.) Belmont, Calif.: Wadsworth, 1978.

Matthews, B. *The Crisis of the West Indian Family.* Westport, Conn.: Greenwood Press, 1971.

Mead, G. H. *Mind, Self, and Society.* Chicago: University of Chicago Press, 1934.

Noble, J. *The Negro Woman College Graduate.* New York: Columbia University Press, 1956.

Nobles, W. W. "African Root and American Fruit: The Black Family." *Journal of Social and Behavioral Sciences,* 1974, *20,* 52-64.

Nobles, W. W. "Africanity: Its Role in Black Families." *Black Scholar,* 1974, *5,* 10-17.

"Not Your Typical Teen Mother." *Ebony,* Aug. 1986, pp. 67-74.

Peters, M. F. "The Black Family: Perpetuating the Myths: An Analysis of Family Sociology Textbooks' Treatment of Black Families." *Family Coordinator,* 1974, *23,* 349-359.

Philbrick, J. L., Thomas, F. F., and Cretser, G. A. "Sex Differences in Love Attitudes of Black University Students." *Psychological Reports,* 1988, *62,* 414.

"Racial Stereotypes Still Persist Among Whites, Survey Finds." *San Francisco Chronicle,* Jan. 9, 1991, p. A-10.

Rainwater, L. *Family Design: Marital Sexuality, Family Size, Contraception.* Hawthorne, N.Y.: Aldine, 1965.

Sampson, R. J. "Urban Black Violence: The Effect of Male Joblessness and Family Disruption." *American Journal of Sociology,* 1987, *93,* 348-382.

Santiago, R. "Sex, Lust, and Videotapes: How Pornography Affects Black Couples." *Essence,* Nov. 1990, pp. 62-65.

Scott, P. B., and others. *Double Stitch: Black Women Write About Mothers and Daughters.* Boston: Beacon Press, 1991.

Shehan, C. L., Bock, E. W., and Lee, G. R. "Religious Heterogamy, Religiosity, and Marital Happiness Among Catholics." *Journal of Marriage and the Family,* 1990, *52,* 73–85.

Sizemore, B. "Sexism and the Black Male." *Black Scholar,* 1973, *4,* 2–11.

Smith, W. C. *The Church in the Life of the Black Family.* Valley Forge, Pa.: Judson Press, 1985.

Spaights, E. "The Evolving Black Family in the United States, 1950–1974." *Negro Educational Review,* 1976, *27*(2), 113–128.

Spanier, G., and Lewis, R. A. "Marital Quality: A Review of the Seventies." *Journal of Marriage and the Family,* 1980, *42*(4), 825–839.

Stack, C. B. *All Our Kin: Strategies for Survival in a Black Community.* New York: HarperCollins, 1974.

Staples, R. *The Lower Income Negro Family in Saint Paul.* St. Paul, Minn.: Urban League, 1967.

Staples, R. *The Black Family: Essays and Studies.* (1st ed.) Belmont, Calif.: Wadsworth, 1971.

Staples, R. *Introduction to Black Sociology.* New York: McGraw-Hill, 1976.

Staples, R. *The Black Family: Essays and Studies.* (2nd ed.) Belmont, Calif.: Wadsworth, 1978.

Staples, R. *The Black Family: Essays and Studies.* (3rd ed.) Belmont, Calif.: Wadsworth, 1986.

Staples, R. *The Black Family: Essays and Studies.* (4th ed.) Belmont, Calif.: Wadsworth, 1991.

Stokes, J., and Greenstone, J. "Helping Black Grandparents and Older Parents Cope with Child Rearing: A Group Method." *Child Welfare League,* 1981, *60*(10), 691–701.

Taylor, R. J. "Black Youth and Psychosocial Development: A Conceptual Framework." In R. Staples (ed.), *The Black Family: Essays and Studies.* (3rd ed.) Belmont, Calif.: Wadsworth, 1986.

Taylor, R. J., Chatters, L. M., and Tolliver, S. "An Assessment of the Provider Role as Perceived by Black Males." *Family Relations,* 1988, *37,* 426–431.

Thomas, V. G. "Determinants of Global Life Happiness and

Marital Happiness in Dual-Career Black Couples." *Family Relations,* 1990, *39,* 174–178.

Washington, V., and LaPoint, V. *Black Children and American Institutions.* New York: Garland, 1988.

Weinberg, M. S., and Williams, C. J. "Black Sexuality: A Test of Two Theories." *Journal of Sex Research,* 1988, *25,* 197–218.

White, D. G. "Female Slaves: Sex Roles and Status in the Antebellum Plantation South." *Journal of Family History,* 1983, *8,* 248–261.

White, E. C. "Grandmothers Bear a Burden Sired by Drugs." *San Francisco Chronicle,* May 22, 1989, p. A-2.

Willie, C. V. "Dominance in the Family: The Black and White Experience." *Journal of Black Psychology,* 1981, 7(2), 91–97.

Willie, C. V. *Black and White Families: A Study in Complementarity.* Bayside, N.Y.: General Hall, 1985.

Wilson, M. "Mothers' and Grandmothers' Perceptions of Parental Behavior in Three-Generational Black Families." *Child Development,* 1984, *55,* 1333–1339.

Wilson, M. "The Black Extended Family: An Analytical Consideration." *Developmental Psychology,* 1986, *22,* 246–258.

Zollar, A. C. *A Member of the Family: Strategies for Black Family Continuity.* Chicago: Nelson-Hall, 1985.

Index

A

Abuse: physical, 158–163; verbal, 158–163
Accommodation, in singlehood, 101
Acquired immunodeficiency syndrome (AIDS), 92
Adolescents: marriage of, 164–165; sexual behavior of, 77–79
Adoptions: informal, 202–203; post-slavery, 201–206
Affection, importance of, 143–144
Affinity, in African marriages, 140
Africa: marriage formation and function in, 140–141; sexual behavior in, 73–74
African children, circle of, 197–198
African elders, circle of, 196–197
African families, 195–197; affection in, 143–144
African societies: Black history in, 1–3; children's role in, 2–3; fostering children in, 198–200; marriage in, 2; men's role in, 2; women's role in, 2
Africanisms, 12; retention of, 16, 142–143
Afrocentric model, of Black family life, 24–26

Afrocentricity, described, 25
AIDS. *See* Acquired immunodeficiency syndrome
Alcohol abuse, in Black men, 105–106
Ali, S., 124, 132, 159
Allen, W. R., 39, 44
Alternative life-styles, 118

B

Ballard, C., 219
Baraka, I., 131
Beatty, L. A., 234
Beauty, and intelligence, 114–115
Bell, A. P., 78
Bell, N., 221
Bell, R., 156
Bennett, W., 206
Bernard, J., 42–43
Billingsley, A., 37, 43–44, 222
Births, out-of-wedlock, 11
Bisexuality, 89
Black(s): alternative life-styles of, 61–69; cultural traits of, 16–17; educational level of, 59–60; income level of, 59; in Union Army, 50. *See also* Men; Women
Black children. *See* Children
Black church, 211–218

Black community, women's contribution to, 68-69
Black family: alternative life-styles
in, 61-69; best- and worst-case
scenarios of, 235-239; Black
feminist theory of, 26-27; close
relationships in, 177; college
education in, 175-176; conceptual models for, 24-33; culture
of poverty theory of, 28; disorganization of, 34-35; dual
earners among, 61-66; economic
factors in, 224-228; employment
effects on, 65; exchange theory
of, 28-30; extended, 205-211;
free, 9; gender economics in,
57-60; history of, 1-21; ideology
of, 18-19; impact of slavery on,
15-20, 52-53; job crisis situation
in, 56-57; kinship group in,
1-2; kinship of, 194-220; multigenerational households of, 195;
perceptions of, 33-34; poverty
and, 170, 173; problems and
prospects of, 228-235; public
policy and, 221-224; religion in,
211-218; research studies of,
22-46; scholars of, 40-46; sexual
behavior of 72-93; social change
effects on, 221-241; social support system in, 167-168; urbanization effects on, 52-53; violence
in, 158-163; welfare effects on,
56; women's roles in, 66-69, 132;
work and money in, 47-71. See
also Family studies; Historical
background; Sexual behavior
Black female–White male relations,
150-151
Black feminist theory, of Black
family life, 26-28
Black girls, socialization of, 127-128
Black male–White female relations,
148-150
Black men. See Men
Black nationalist family studies,
37-38
Black Panther Party, gender role
views of, 130-131

Black singles: characteristics of, 98;
closed-couple relationships, of
101; committed, 101; free-float-
ing, 100-101; open-couple rela-
tionships of, 101; types of,
98-102
Black teachers, 174
Black women. See Women
Blassingame, J., 17
Blauner, R., 31
Boyle, G., 219
Brown, I. C., 4
Brown v. Board of Education, 179
Bunche, R., 179
Burton, E., 219
Butts, J. D., 78

C

Canady, H., 230
Carroll, D., 85
Carson, B., 179
Catholic Church, slavery safeguards by, 9
Caucasians. See Whites
Centers for Disease Control, 92
Child abuse, 187-189
Child neglect, causes of, 172
Child-rearing: grandmothers' role
in, 205-206, 210-211; and socialization into gender roles, 123-128
Children: African, 2-3, 197-198,
197-200; clothing importance
to, 173-174; college education
for, 175-176; foster care for,
203-204; negative sex education
techniques for, 76; of poverty,
170-171; punishment of, 186;
self-dignity in, 173; self-esteem
in, 189-191; of slaves, 6,
171-175; speech pattern of,
181-182; in today's world,
175-177; of women prisoners,
204-205
Church, in Black family life,
211-218
Civil War, interracial relations during, 147
Clark, K. B., 179, 189, 212, 213

Clark, M., 189, 212, 213
Class values, sexual behavior and, 84–87
Cleaver, E., 130
Closed-couple relationship, 101
Clothing, importance of, 173–174
Cobbs, P. M., 131, 160
College campus, Black men and White women on, 148–149
College education, in Black family, 175–176
Colonial system, described, 31
Colonialism, internal, 31–33
Commission on Civil Rights, 105, 223
Commission on Obscenity and Pornography, 91
Community support, kinship and, 194–220
Compliance, in Black men, 127
Conceptual models, for studying Black family life, 24–33
Consanguinity, in African marriages, 140
Cooley, C. H., 189
Coping styles, of middle-class Blacks, 118
Crime, incidence of, 160
Crown Heights Youth Collective, 219
Cultural deprivation theory, 28
Cultural deviant approach, in Black family studies, 39
Cultural domination, 31
Cultural equivalent perspective, in Black family studies, 39
Cultural variant orientation, in Black family studies, 39
Culture of poverty theory, of Black family life, 28
Cunnilingus, performance of, 88

D

Dating: interracial, 151, 152; process of, 106–110; sexual behavior during, 107–108
Davis, A., 14–15
Deculturization, of African slaves, 4

Depression, effects on Black families, 53
Discrimination, marital effects of, 65–66
Division of labor, in sharecropping, 52
Divorce: among Blacks, 57; rates of, 99, 163–168
Dropout rate, 128
Drug abuse, in Black men, 105–106
Dual earners, in Black families, 61–66
DuBois, W.E.B., 34, 172, 195

E

Economics, gender, 57–60
Education: of Black men, 134, 174–175; of Black women, 134, 174–175; effect on Blacks' marketability, 59–60; effect on unemployment rate, 59, 60; financial assistance for, 208–209; marital effects of, 106; single mothers and, 180–185
Ehrenreich, B., 232
Elderly: African, 196–197; care of, 209–211; health and economic status of, 209–210; role of, 196–197
Elkins, S., 17
Emancipation: Africanisms following, 12; Black family following, 10–12; effect on marriage, 10–12; 142–143; out-of-wedlock birth rates following, 11; sharecropping following, 12; women's role following, 10–11
Employment: for Blacks, 54–55, 104; and effect on family life, 65; effects of imports on, 55–56; men's attitudes about, 64–65; in mom-and-pop stores, 54, 55; types of, 226–227; women's attitudes about, 64
Engels, F., 30
Engerman, S., 17, 54
Engram, E., 24

Exchange theory, of Black family
  life, 28-30
Extramarital affairs, 156-157

F

Family disorganization, 34-35
Family organization, pattern of,
  139-141
Family studies: Black nationalist,
  37-38; conceptual models for,
  24-33; cultural deviant approach
  in, 39; cultural equivalent perspective in, 39; cultural variant
  orientation in, 39; ideological
  perspectives in, 39; neoconservative era in, 38-39; pathologists
  approach to, 35-36; and poverty-acculturation, 34-35; reactive period in, 36-37; scholars
  of, 40-46; stages of, 33-39; theory building in, 22-23
Family substitutes, 118
Farber, B., 109
Father-daughter relationships,
  closeness of, 178-179
Fellatio, performance of, 88
Feminism: in the Black community, 26-28; rise of, 133-137
Fisk University, sexual regulations
  at, 85-86
Fogel, R. S., 17, 54
Foster care, for Blacks, 203-204
Franklin, C. W., 97, 119, 135
Franklin, J. H., 12, 179
Frazier, E. F., 4, 17, 38, 40-41, 52,
  59, 85, 131, 148-149, 162, 172,
  195
Freud, S., 75, 84, 124
Furstenberg, R., 18

G

Garvey, M., 71
Gary, L. E., 234
Gender roles, 121-128; historical
  forces in, 121-123; Muslim view
  of, 129-130; socialization into,
  123-128
Genovese, E. D., 17

Gilliam, D., 132
Glick, P., 165
Glick effect, 165
Goddard, L. L., 8
Goode, W. J., 22
Government service jobs, decline
  in, 225-226
Grandmothers, child-rearing by,
  205-206, 210-211
Grandparents, as agents of sociali-
  zation, 197
Greece, slave system in, 4
Grier, W. H., 131, 160
Gutman, 10, 17-18, 195
Guttentag, M., 232

H

Hampton, R. L., 232
Hansen, D. A., 23-24
Happiness, marital effects on, 71
Heiss, J., 44
Hendricks, L. E., 78
Hernton, C., 146
Hershberg, T., 18
Herskovits, M., 16, 195
Heterogamy, 144; in divorce proba-
  bility, 167
Hill, R., 23-24, 37, 44
Historical background of Black
  family, 1-21; after emancipa-
  tion, 10-12; ideology in, 18-19;
  and North American slavery,
  3-5; objectivity versus ideology
  in, 19; and preslavery period,
  1-3; role of women in, 12-15;
  and slave family, 5-9; by White
  middle-class standards, 20
Historical materialism, 30-31
Hite, S., 86
Homicide, deaths due to, 160
Homogamy, 144
Homosexuality, 88-89
Hooks, B., 133, 137
Housework, by slaves, 49-50

I

Ibo tribe of the Niger Delta region,
  task assignments of, 48

Ideology: in Black family history, 18–19; woman qua property, 79

Imports, job loss due to, 55–56

"In-law" parenting, 199

Indentured servants; defined, 3; history of, 3–5

Infanticide, during slavery, 14

Infants, mortality of, 170, 200–201

Intelligence, beauty and, 114–115

Intercourse. *See* Sexual intercourse

Internal colonialism theory, of Black family life, 31–33

Interracial couples, on college campuses, 148–149

Interracial dating, by location, 151, 152

Interracial marriages, 146–153; during Civil War, 147; percentage of, 146–147

Interracial relations: among slaves, 506; during slavery, 147

J

Jackson, J., 218

Jenkins, R. R., 78

Jewell, K. S., 44–45

Jewell, L. N., 39

Job strain, sources of, 65

Jobs for the Future program, 219

Joe, T., 104, 231

Johnson, L. B., 39

"Jumping the broomstick," 141–142

Juvenile delinquency, causes of, 172

K

King, D. H., 137

King, M., 32

King, M. L., 213, 214, 217

Kinsey, A. W., 89

Kinship: and community support, 194–220; during slavery, 194, 195, 200–206; and upward mobility, 206–211

Kinship group, described, 1–2

L

Labor division, slavery and, 48–51

Labor force, effects on Blacks, 54–55

Ladner, J., 26, 83

Latin America, slave system in, 5

Leashore, B., 223

Lesbianism, 90

Levirate, 199

Lewis, D. K., 126

Liebow, E., 81

Love: defined, 139; importance of, 144; as a prerequisite to marriage, 140

Loving v. Virginia, 146

Lyons-Rowe, S., 88

M

Malcolm X, 130

Male sexism, 128–133

Male virility cult, 80–81

Mannheim, K., 33

Manumission, 9

Marital conflict, 155–158

Marital patterns: heterogamy, 144; homogamy, 144; and interactions, 139–169. *See also* Marriage

Marital sexuality, 154–155

Marriage: adolescent, 164–165; affection in, 143–144; affinity in, 140; after emancipation, 10–12; alternatives to, 115–119; among slaves, 5–6; arranged, 140; Black Panther Party views of, 130–131; Black women's views of, 95; community control of, 2; consanguinity in, 140; discrimination effects on, 65–66; dissolution of, 163–168; education effects on, 106; and effect on happiness, 71; effects of women's economic independence on, 62; emancipation effects on, 142–143; history of, 139–146; influence of sex ratios on, 102–106; instability of, 53–54; of interracial couples,

Marriage *(continued)*
146–153; love as prerequisite to,
140; love in, 144; partner selec-
tion for, 110–115; in rural
Southern regions, 65; and slavery, 96, 141–142; welfare effects
on, 56. *See also* Marital patterns
Married women, prevalence of, 95
Martin, E. P., 203
Martin, J. M., 203
Marx, K., 30
Masculinity: among Blacks, 126;
sexual conquest and, 81
Masturbation, in White men versus
Black men, 77–78
Matriarchy, defined, 15
McAdoo, H., 117
Men: alcohol abuse in, 105–106;
and attitudes about women,
63–64, 129; and attitudes about
working, 64–65; drug abuse in,
105–106; education of, 134;
employment rate of, 104; job-
related stress of, 65; masturbation in, 77–78; in mental institutions, 105–106; in precolonial
Africa, 2; in prisons, 103, 218;
and role during slavery, 122;
role of, 121–128; sexism of,
128–133; sexual behavior of,
77–82; skin color preferences of,
113–114; supportiveness of, 81;
traits in women preferred by,
113–114; unemployment rate of,
105; in U.S. Military, 104–105; as
wage earners, 57–60; White
women and, 146–153
Mental institutions, Black men in,
105–106
Migration North, 52
Miller, K., 214
Mitchell-Kernan, C., 152
Modell, J., 18
Mom-and-pop stores, job opportunities in, 54, 55
Money: marital conflict about,
157–158; work and, 47–71
Monogamous marriage, alternatives to, 115–119

Mother-daughter relationship, 127
Mother-son relationship, 126–127
Mothers: single, 180–185; teenage,
183–184
Moynihan, D. P., 28, 35, 38, 41–42,
181, 228
Muslim society, gender role views
of, 129–130

N

Nambikwara, task assignments of,
48
Nation of Islam, women's role in,
129–139
National Association of Black
Social Workers, 204
National Institute of Fatherhood
and Family Development, 219
Native Americans, as slaves, 3–4
Neoconservative era, in Black fam-
ily studies, 38–39
Nobles, W. W., 8

O

Obedience of Black sons, 127
Open-couple relationship, 101
Oral-genital relations, 88
Out-of-wedlock births, after eman-
cipation, 11

P

Parent-child relationships, cross-
gender, 177–180
Parenting, 170–193; child abuse
and, 188–189; encouragement in,
207–208; "in-law," 199; in
lower-income families, 185–187;
racism and, 176–177; by single
mothers, 180–185; during slavery
and emancipation, 171–175
Partner selection, 106–120; and
physique, 111–112; and socioeconomic status, 112; standards
for, 110–115
Pathologist's approach to Black
family life, 35–36

Peer group, sex education through, 76–77
Permanent availability, in partner selection, 109–110
Peters, M., 192, 225
Petting, 88
Physical abuse, 158–163
Physique, importance of, 111–112
Pietropinto, A., 76, 82, 87–89
Political system, Black family and, 222–224
Polygamy: historical relevance of, 141; retention of, 142–143
Pornography, Black involvement in, 90–91
Pouissant, A., 160
Poverty: Black children and, 170–171; culture of, 28; effects of on families, 170, 173
Povery-acculturation, 34–35
Premarital sex, Black women and, 83–84
Price, M., 234
Prison(s): Black population in, 103; Black men in, 218; Black women in, 204–205, 218
Punishment, of Black children, 186

R

Racial privilege, 31
Racism, and parenting, 176–177
Rainwater, L., 28, 38, 42
Rape, of Black women, 90
Raspberry, W., 124
Reactive period, in Black family studies, 36–37
Reeves, R., 228
Reinforcement patterns, of Black family life, 28–29
Religion: Black family life and, 211–218; as divorce deterrant, 168; sexual behavior and, 74–75
Remarriages, among Blacks, 57
Research studies, of Black families, 22–46
Rewards and costs theory, 28–29
Robinson, W. H., 8

S

Scanzoni, J., 44, 70, 124, 176, 180, 214
Scholars, of Black families, 40–46
Schulz, D. A., 81
Secord, P., 232
Self-dignity, 173
Self-esteem: of Black women, 68–69; in children, 188–191
Sex: anal, 87–88; information sources about, 76–77; oral, 87–88; premarital, 83–84
Sex ratios, singlehood and, 102–106
Sexual assault, of Black women, 90
Sexual behavior: in adolescents, 77–78; and age of onset, 77–78; Black religion's role in, 74–75; books on, 90–91; class values in, 84–87; dating and, 107–108; and double standard, 84; education about, 76–77; exposure to, 77; factors influencing, 72–93; at Fisk University, 85–86; gender differences in, 80–84; historical background of, 73–75; human breeding aspect of, 74; image of, 72–73; of men, 77–82; negative sex education techniques in, 76; permissive, 74–75; sexual revolution effects on, 86–87; slavery and, 73–74, 147; socialization into, 75–79; violent, 79; of women, 82–83
Sexual intercourse, first experience with, 85
Sexual intimacy, patterns of, 72–93. *See also* Sexual behavior
Sexual practices, 87–91
Sexuality, marital, 154–155
Sharecroppers, 50–52; division of labor in, 51; after emancipation, 12; wages of, 51–52
Simenauer, J., 76, 82, 85, 87–89
Single mothers, and educational achievement, 180–185
Singlehood, 94–106; accommodation in, 101; Black's views on, 97; education effects on, 106;

Singlehood *(continued)*
    influence of sex ratios on,
    102–106; prevalence of, 94, 95;
    prolonged, 86; reasons for, 97;
    social forces causing, 97; types
    of, 98–102. *See also* Black singles
Skin color, preferences of, 113–114,
    145–146
Slave children: lessons taught to, 8;
    socialization of, 7–8
Slave era, free Black families dur-
    ing, 9
Slave family, 5–9; affection in, 8–9;
    after emancipation, 10–12; chil-
    dren in, 6; functioning of, 7–8;
    interracial relationships in, 5;
    legal marriage in, 9; life-style of,
    15–20; men's role in, 7–8; sepa-
    ration in, 6–7; as survival mech-
    anism, 7; wedlock in, 10;
    women as center of, 15
Slave marriages, 5–6
Slave women: as center of the fam-
    ily, 15; functions of, 14; sexual
    subjugation of, 14–15
Slavemasters: and role in slave
    marriages, 6; sexual abuse by, 8;
    sexual attitudes of, 74
Slavery: Black family during,
    17–18; Black men's role during,
    122; Catholic church in, 9;
    causes and nature of, 3–5; decul-
    turization in, 4; division of
    labor in, 48–51; and effect on
    marriage formation and func-
    tion, 141–142; and effect on sex-
    ual attitudes, 73–74; in Greece,
    4; housework during, 49–50; and
    impact on Black family, 15–20;
    infanticide during, 14; interra-
    cial relationships in, 5; kinship
    bonds during, 194, 195, 200–206;
    in Latin America, 5; manumis-
    sion from, 9; marriage during,
    96; namesakes of, 200; in North
    America, 5; parenting during,
    171–175; in South America, 9
Slaves: infant mortality rate of,
    200–201; marriage between,

141–142; sexual relations of, 147
Smith, E. A., 84
"Social looking-glass" theory,
    189–190
Social support system, of Black
    family, 167–168
Socioeconomic status, in partner
    selection, 112
Soronate, 199
South America, slavery in, 9
Spanish Slave Code, 9
Speech pattern, of Black children,
    181–182
Staples, R., 78
Stein, P., 100
Stress, job-related, 65, 67

T

Technical virgin, 88
Teen mothers, 183–184
Theory: definitions of, 23–24; test-
    ing of, 23
Tribal societies, women's role in,
    13
Turner, N., 217

U

Udry, J. R., 84
Unemployment: rates of, 59, 60,
    105; trends in, 225–226, 228
Union Army, Blacks in, 50
Unmarried people, 94–106. *See also*
    Singlehood
Upward mobility, 206–211
Urbanization, effects on Black fam-
    ilies, 52–53
U.S. military, Blacks in, 104–105,
    165–166

V

Verbal abuse, 158–163
Vessey, D., 217
Villa, L., 113
Violence: family, 158–163; retalia-
    tion from, 163; in sexual behav-
    ior, 79; social class and, 159–162

Virgins, technical, 88
Vogel, E., 221

W

Wage earners, men's role as, 57–60
Wages, of sharecroppers, 51–52
Welfare, and effect on marriage, 56
Westney, O. E., 78
White women, and Black men, 146–153
Whites: income levels of, 59; sexual behavior of, 77–78; sexual permissiveness of, 75; as slaves, 3–4
Widowed Blacks, 99–100
William, I., 78
Williams, C., 19
Willie, C. V., 44, 179
Wilson, W. J., 39, 45
Women: African versus Afro-American, 13; after emancipation, 10–11; and age of first intercourse, 85; and attitudes about working, 64; Black feminist theory of, 26–27; child-rearing by, 123–128; clothing importance for, 59; as consumers, 58–59; and contribution to Black community, 68–69; criticisms of, 131–132; earnership of, 61–66; economic independence of, 62; education of, 134; historical role of, 12–15; independence of, 127; job-related stress of, 67; in labor force following emancipation, 11; laboring in the fields by, 13–14; marriage views of, 95; multiple roles of, 66–69; Muslim, 129–130; in political organization of tribal societies in Africa, 13; in precolonial Africa, 2; in prisons, 204–205, 218; prolonged singlehood of, 86; rape of, 90; self-esteem of, 68–69; sexuality of, 82–83; sharecropping role of, 51–52; skin color preferences of, 113–114; social roles of, 68; task assignments of, 47–48; traits preferred by, 112–113. *See also* Slave women
Wyatt, G. E., 85, 88

Y

Yu, P., 104, 231